T0222167

Digital Library Technologies

Complex Objects, Annotation, Ontologies,
Classification, Extraction, and Security

Synthesis Lectures on Information Concepts, Retrieval, and Services

Editor
Gary Marchionini, *University of North Carolina, Chapel Hill*

Digital Library Technologies: Complex Objects, Annotation, Ontologies, Classification, Extraction, and Security

Edward A. Fox and Ricardo da Silva Torres

ISBN: 978-3-031-01157-3   print
ISBN: 978-3-031-02285-2   ebook

DOI: 10.1007/978-3-031-02285-2

A Publication in the Springer series
SYNTHESIS LECTURES ON INFORMATION CONCEPTS, RETRIEVAL, AND SERVICES
Series ISSN: 1947-945X print   1947-9468 ebook

Lecture #33
Series Editor: Gary Marchionini, University of North Carolina, Chapel Hill

First Edition
10 9 8 7 6 5 4 3 2 1

Digital Library Technologies

Complex Objects, Annotation, Ontologies,
Classification, Extraction, and Security

Edward A. Fox
Virginia Tech, Dept. of Computer Science, Blacksburg, VA 24061, USA

Ricardo da Silva Torres
Institute of Computing, University of Campinas, Campinas, SP, Brazil

Chapter Authors:
Pranav Angara, Lois M. Delcambre, Noha Elsherbiny, Nádia P. Kozievitch, Mohamed Magdy Gharib Farag, Uma Murthy, Sung Hee Park, Venkat Srinivasan, Ricardo da Silva Torres, and Seungwon Yang

SYNTHESIS LECTURES ON INFORMATION CONCEPTS, RETRIEVAL,
AND SERVICES #33

ABSTRACT

Digital libraries (DLs) have introduced new technologies, as well as leveraging, enhancing, and integrating related technologies, since the early 1990s. These efforts have been enriched through a formal approach, e.g., the 5S (Societies, Scenarios, Spaces, Structures, Streams) framework, which is discussed in two earlier volumes in this series. This volume should help advance work not only in DLs, but also in the WWW and other information systems.

Drawing upon four (Kozievitch, Murthy, Park, Yang) completed and three (Elsherbiny, Farag, Srinivasan) in-process dissertations, as well as the efforts of collaborating researchers and scores of related publications, presentations, tutorials, and reports, this book should advance the DL field with regard to at least six key technologies. By integrating surveys of the state-of-the-art, new research, connections with formalization, case studies, and exercises/projects, this book can serve as a computing or information science textbook. It can support studies in cyber-security, document management, hypertext/hypermedia, IR, knowledge management, LIS, multimedia, and machine learning.

Chapter 1, with a case study on fingerprint collections, focuses on complex (composite, compound) objects, connecting DL and related work on buckets, DCC, and OAI-ORE. Chapter 2, discussing annotations, as in hypertext/hypermedia, emphasizes parts of documents, including images as well as text, managing superimposed information. The SuperIDR system, and prototype efforts with Flickr, should motivate further development and standardization related to annotation, which would benefit all DL and WWW users. Chapter 3, on ontologies, explains how they help with browsing, query expansion, focused crawling, and classification. This chapter connects DLs with the Semantic Web, and uses CTRnet as an example. Chapter 4, on (hierarchical) classification, leverages LIS theory, as well as machine learning, and is important for DLs as well as the WWW. Chapter 5, on extraction from text, covers document segmentation, as well as how to construct a database from heterogeneous collections of references (from ETDs); i.e., converting strings to canonical forms. Chapter 6 surveys the security approaches used in information systems, and explains how those approaches can apply to digital libraries which are not fully open.

Given this rich content, those interested in DLs will be able to find solutions to key problems, using the right technologies and methods. We hope this book will help show how formal approaches can enhance the development of suitable technologies and how they can be better integrated with DLs and other information systems.

KEYWORDS

5S, annotation, CINET, classification, complex objects, Crisis/Tragedy/ Recovery network (CTRnet), digital libraries (DLs), ETDs, fingerprints, Flickr, formalization, network science, OAI-ORE, ontologies, security, subdocuments, SuperIDR, superimposed information, text extraction

This book is dedicated to all those who have worked in, or collaborated with,
Virginia Tech's Digital Library Research Laboratory.

Contents

List of Figures

List of Tables

Preface

Because of the importance of digital libraries, we integrated, organized, and condensed our related findings and publications into a single volume version of this book series, ultimately over 600 pages in length, that was successfully used in a semester-long class in 2011, as well as field tested at different universities. To make it easier for others to address their need for a digital library textbook, we have re-organized the original book into four parts, to cover: introduction and theoretical foundations, key issues, technologies/extensions, and applications. We are confident that this third book, and the others in the series, address digital library-related needs in many computer science, information science, and library science (e.g., LIS) courses, as well as the requirements of researchers, developers, and practitioners.

The main reason for our confidence is that our *5S* (Societies, Scenarios, Spaces, Structures, Streams) framework has broad descriptive power. This is proved in part by the recent expansion of interest related to each of the five Ss, e.g., Social networks, Scenario-based design, geoSpatial databases, Structure-based approaches (e.g., databases, metadata, ontologies, XML), and data Stream management systems.

The first book, *Theoretical Foundations for Digital Libraries,* the essential opening to the four book series, has three main parts. Chapter 1 is the key to 5S, providing a theoretical foundation for the field of digital libraries in a gentle, intuitive, and easy-to-apply manner. Chapter 2 explains how 5S can be applied to digital libraries in two ways. First, it covers the most important services of digital libraries: browsing, searching, discovery, and visualization. Second, it demonstrates how 5S helps with the design, implementation, and evaluation of an integrated digital library (ETANA-DL, for archaeology). The third part of book 1, made up of five appendices, demonstrates how 5S enables a formal treatment of digital libraries. It is freely accessible online, at https://sites.google .com/a/morganclaypool.com/dlibrary/.

Book 1 Appendix A gives a small set of definitions that cover the mathematical preliminaries underlying our work. Appendix B builds on that set to define each of the five Ss, and then uses them to define what we consider a minimal digital library. Thus, we allow people asking "Is X a digital library?" to answer that question definitively. Appendix C moves from a minimalist perspective to show how 5S can be used in a real, interesting, and complex application domain: archaeology. Appendix D builds upon all the definitions in Appendices A-C, to describe some key results of using 5S. This includes lemmas, proofs, and 5SSuite (software based on 5S). Finally, Appendix E, the Glossary, explains key terminology. Concluding book 1 is an extensive bibliography and a helpful Index.

The second book in the series, *Key Issues Regarding Digital Libraries: Evaluation and Integration,* discusses key issues in the digital library field: evaluation and integration. It covers the Information Life Cycle, metrics, and software to help evaluate digital libraries. It uses both archaeology and electronic theses and dissertations to provide additional context, since addressing quality in highly distributed digital libraries is particularly challenging.

The following two books of this series are further elaborations of the 5S framework, as well as a comprehensive overview of related work on digital libraries.

This book, third in the series, describes six case studies of extensions beyond a minimal digital library. Its chapters cover: Complex Objects, Annotation, Ontologies, Classification, Text Extraction, and Security. *Regarding Complex Objects:* While many digital libraries focus on digital objects and/or metadata objects, with support for complex objects, they could easily be extended to handle aggregation and packaging. Fingerprint matching provides a useful context, since there are complex inter-relationships among crime scenes, latent fingerprints, individuals, hands, fingers, fingerprints, and images. *Regarding Annotation:* This builds upon work on superimposed information, closely related to hypertext, hypermedia, and subdocuments. A case study covers the management of fish images. *Regarding Ontologies:* We address this key area of knowledge management, also integral to the Semantic Web. As a context, we consider our Crisis, Tragedy, and Recovery Network. That is quite broad, and involves interesting ontology development problems. *Regarding Classification:* We cover this core area of information retrieval and machine learning, as well as Library and Information Science (LIS). The context is electronic theses and dissertations (ETDs), since many of these works have no categories that can be found in their catalog or metadata records, and since none are categorized at the level of chapters. *Regarding Text Extraction:* Our coverage also is in the context of ETDs, where the high-level structure should be identified, and where the valuable and voluminous sets of references can be isolated and shifted to canonical representations. *Regarding Security:* While many digital libraries support open access, it has been clear since the early 1990s that industrial acceptance of digital library systems and technologies depends on their being trusted, requiring an integrated approach to security.

The final book, *Digital Library Applications: CBIR, Education, Social Networks, eScience/ Simulation, and GIS,* fourth in the series, focuses on digital library applications from a 5S perspective. *Regarding CBIR:* We move into the multimedia field, focusing on Content-based Image Retrieval (CBIR)—making use, for context, of the previously discussed work on fish images and CTRnet. *Regarding Education:* We describe systems for collecting, sharing, and providing access to educational resources, namely the AlgoViz and Ensemble systems. This is important since there has been considerable investment in digital libraries to help in education, all based on the fact that devising high-quality educational resources is expensive, making sharing and reuse highly beneficial. *Regarding Social Networks:* We address very popular current issues, on the Societies side, namely Social Networks and Personalization. *Regarding e-Science/Simulation:* There has only been a limited adaptation and extension of digital libraries to this important domain. Simulation aids many disciplines to test models and predictions on computers, addressing questions not feasible through other approaches to experimentation. More broadly, in keeping with progress toward e-Science, where data sets and shared information support much broader theories and investigations, we cover (using the SimDL and CINET projects as context) storing and archiving, as well as access and visualization, dealing not only with metadata, but also with specifications of experiments, experimental results, and derivative versions: summaries, findings, reports, and publications. *Regarding Geospatial Information (GIS):* Many GIS-related technologies are now readily available in cell phones, cameras, and GPS systems. Our coverage (that uses the CTRnet project as context) connects that with metadata, images, and maps.

How can computer scientists connect with all this? Although some of the early curricular guidelines for computing advocated coverage of information, and current guidelines refer to the area of Information Management, generally, courses in this area have focused instead either on data or knowledge. Fortunately, Virginia Tech has had graduate courses on information retrieval since the early 1970s and a senior course on "Multimedia, Hypertext, and Information Access" since the early 1990s. Now, there are offerings at many universities on multimedia, or with titles including keywords like "Web" or "search". Perhaps parts of this book series will provide a way for computing programs to address all areas of information management, building on a firm, formal, integrated approach. Further, computing professionals should feel comfortable with particular Ss, especially Structures (as in data structures) and Spaces (as in vector spaces), and to lesser extents Streams (related to multimedia) and Scenarios (related to human-computer interaction). Today, especially, there is growing interest in Societies (as in social networks).

How can information scientists connect with all this? Clearly, they are at home with "information" as a key construct. Streams (e.g., sequences of characters or bitstreams) provide a first basis for all types of information. Coupled with Structures, they lead to all types of structured streams, as in documents and multimedia. Spaces may be less clear, but GIS systems are becoming ubiquitous, connecting with GPS, cell phone, Twitter, and other technologies. Scenarios, especially in the form of Services, are at the heart of most information systems. Societies, including users, groups, organizations, and a wide variety of social networks, are central, especially with human-centered design. Thus, information science can easily connect with 5S, and digital libraries are among the most important types of information systems. Accordingly, this book series may fit nicely into capstone courses in information science or information systems. Further, our handling of "information" goes well beyond the narrow view associated with electrical engineering or even computer science; we connect content representations with context and application, across a range of human endeavors, and with semantics, pragmatics, and knowledge.

How can library scientists connect with all this? One might argue that many of the librarians of the future must be trained as digital librarians. Thus, all four books should fit nicely into library science programs. While they could fit into theory or capstone courses, they also might serve well in introductory courses, if the more formal parts are skipped. On the other hand, they could be distributed across the program. Thus, the first book might work well early in a library school program, the second book could fit midway in the program, and the last two books might be covered in specialized courses that connect with technologies or applications. Further, those studying archival science might find the entire series to be of interest, though some topics like preservation are not covered in detail.

How can researchers connect with all this? We hope that those interested in formal approaches will help us expand the coverage of concepts reported herein. A wonderful goal would be to have an elegant formal basis and useful framework for all types of information systems. We also hope that the theses and dissertations related to this volume, all online (thanks to Virginia Tech's ETD initiative), will provide an even more in-depth coverage of the key topics covered herein. We hope you can build on this foundation to aid in your own research, as you advance the field further.

How can developers connect with all this? We hope that concepts, ideas, methods, techniques, systems, and approaches described herein will guide you to develop, implement, and deploy even better digital libraries. There should be less time "reinventing the wheel." Perhaps this will stimulate the emergence of a vibrant software and services industry as more and more digital libraries emerge. Further, if there is agreement on key concepts, then there should be improvements in: interoperability, integration, and understanding. Accordingly, we hope you can leverage this work to advance practices as well as provide better systems and services.

Even if you, the reader, do not fit clearly into the groups discussed above, we hope you nevertheless will find this book series interesting. Given the rich content, we trust that those interested in digital libraries, or in related systems, will find this book to be intellectually satisfying, illuminating, and helpful. We hope the full series will help move digital libraries forward into a science as well as a practice. We hope too that this four book series will broadly address the needs of the next generation of digital librarians. Please share with us and others what ways you found these books to be useful and helpful!

Edward A. Fox, Editor
Blacksburg, Virginia
February 2014

Acknowledgments

As lead in this effort, my belief is that our greatest thanks go to our families. Accordingly, I thank my wife, Carol, and our sons, Jeffrey, Gregory, Michael, and Paul, along with their families, as well as my father and many other relatives. Similarly, on behalf of my co-editor and each of the chapter co-authors, I thank all of their families.

Since this book is the third in a series of four books, and draws some definitions and other elements from content that either was presented in the first or second book, or will appear in the fourth book, it is important to acknowledge the contributions of all of the other co-authors from the full series: Monika Akbar, Pranav Angara, Yinlin Chen, Lois M. Delcambre, Noha Elsherbiny, Alexandre X. Falcão, Eric Fouh, Nádia P. Kozievitch, Spencer Lee, Jonathan Leidig, Lin Tzy Li, Mohamed Magdy Gharib Farag, Uma Murthy, Sung Hee Park, Venkat Srinivasan, Ricardo da Silva Torres, and Seungwon Yang. Special thanks go to Uma Murthy for helping with the bibliography and to Monika Akbar, Pranav Angara, and Shashwat Dave for assistance with technical aspects of book production. Further, Shashwat Dave assisted with the glossary, found in the first book of the series as well as online; it is useful in this book, too.

Teachers and mentors deserve a special note of thanks. My interest in research was stimulated and guided by J.C.R. Licklider, my undergraduate advisor, author of *Libraries of the Future*,[1] who, when at ARPA, funded the start of the Internet. Michael Kessler, who introduced the concept of bibliographic coupling, was my B.S. thesis advisor; he also directed MIT's Project TIP (technical information project). Gerard Salton was my graduate advisor (1978–1983); he is sometimes called the "Father of Information Retrieval."

Likewise, we thank our many students, friends, collaborators, co-authors, and colleagues. In particular, we thank students who have collaborated in these matters, including: Scott Britell, Pavel Calado, Yuxin Chen, Kiran Chitturi, Fernando Das Neves, Shahrooz Feizabadi, Robert France, S.M.Shamimul Hasan, Nithiwat Kampanya, Rohit Kelapure, S.H. Kim, Neill Kipp, Aaron Krowne, Sunshin Lee, Bing Liu, Ming Luo, Paul Mather, Sai Tulasi Neppali, Unni. Ravindranathan, W. Ryan Richardson, Nathan Short, Ohm Sornil, Hussein Suleman, Wensi Xi, Baoping Zhang, and Qinwei Zhu.

---

1. In this 1965 work, Licklider called for an integrative theory to support future automated libraries, one of the inspirations for this book.

Further, we thank faculty and staff, at a variety of universities and other institutions, who have collaborated, including: A. Lynn Abbott, Felipe Andrade, Robert Beck, Keith Bisset, Paul Bogen II, Peter Brusilovsky, Lillian Cassel, Donatella Castelli, Vinod Chachra, Hsinchun Chen, Debra Dudley, Roger Ehrich, Hicham Elmongui, Joanne Eustis, Tiago Falcão, Weiguo Fan, James Flanagan, James French, Richard Furuta, Dan Garcia, C. Lee Giles, Martin Halbert, Kevin Hall, Eric Hallerman, Riham Hassan, Eberhard Hilf, Gregory Hislop, Michael Hsiao, Haowei Hsieh, John Impagliazzo, Filip Jagodzinski, Andrea Kavanaugh, Douglas Knight, Deborah Knox, Alberto Laender, Carl Lagoze, Madhav Marathe, Gary Marchionini, Susan Marion, Gail McMillan, Claudia Medeiros, Barbara Moreira, Henning Mortveit, Sanghee Oh, Donald Orth, Jeffrey Pomerantz, Manuel Perez Quinones, Naren Ramakrishnan, Evandro Ramos, Mohammed Samaka, Steven Sheetz, Frank Shipman, Donald Shoemaker, Layne Watson, and Barbara Wildemuth.

Clearly, with regard to this volume, my special thanks go to my co-author, Ricardo da Silva Torres. He played a key role in the unfolding of the theory, practice, systems, and usability of what is described herein. Regarding earlier work on 5S, Marcos André Gonçalves helped launch our formal framework, and Rao Shen extended that effort, as can be seen in the first two books of the series.

At Virginia Tech, there are many in the Department of Computer Science and in Information Systems that have assisted, providing very nice facilities and a creative and supportive environment. The College of Engineering, and before that, of Arts and Sciences, provided an administrative home and intellectual context.

In addition, we acknowledge the support of the many sponsors of the research described in this volume. Our fingerprint work was supported by Award No. 2009-DN-BX-K229 from the National Institute of Justice, Office of Justice Programs, U.S. Department of Justice. The opinions, findings, and conclusions or recommendations expressed in this publication are those of the authors and do not necessarily reflect those of the Department of Justice.

Some of this material is based upon work supported by the National Science Foundation (NSF) under Grant Nos. CCF-0722259, DUE-9752190, DUE-9752408, DUE-0121679, DUE-0121741, DUE-0136690, DUE-0333531, DUE-0333601, DUE-0435059, DUE-0532825, DUE-0840719, DUE-1141209, IIS-9905026, IIS-9986089, IIS-0002935, IIS-0080748, IIS-0086227, IIS-0090153, IIS-0122201, IIS-0307867, IIS-0325579, IIS-0535057, IIS-0736055, IIS-0910183, IIS-0916733, IIS-1319578, ITR-0325579, OCI-0904844, OCI-1032677, and SES-0729441. Any opinions, findings, and conclusions or recommendations expressed in this material are those of the authors and do not necessarily reflect the views of the National Science Foundation.

This work has been partially supported by NIH MIDAS project 2U01GM070694-7, DTRA CNIMS Grant HDTRA1-07-C-0113, and R&D Grant HDTRA1-0901-0017. Students in our VT-MENA program in Egypt have been supported through that program.

We thank corporate and institutional sponsors, including Adobe, AOL, CNI, Google, IBM, Microsoft, NASA, NCR, OCLC, SOLINET, SUN, SURA, UNESCO, U.S. Department of Education (FIPSE), and VTLS. A variety of institutions have supported tutorials or courses, including AUGM, CETREDE, CLEI, IFLA-LAC, and UFC.

Visitors and collaborators from Brazil, including from FUA, UFMG, and UNICAMP, have been supported by CAPES (4479-09-2), FAPESP, and CNPq. Our collaboration in Mexico had support from CONACyT, while that in Germany was supported by DFG.

Finally, we acknowledge the support of the Qatar National Research Fund for Project No. NPRP 4-029-1-007, running 2012-2015.

CHAPTER 1

Complex Objects

Nádia P. Kozievitch and Ricardo da Silva Torres

Abstract: In order to reuse, integrate, and unify different resources from a common perspective, Complex Objects (COs) have emerged to support digital library (DL) initiatives from both theoretical and practical perspectives. From the theoretical perspective, the use of COs facilitates aggregation abstraction. From the implementation point of view, the use of COs helps developers to manage heterogeneous resources and their components. On the other hand, DL applications still lack support for mechanisms to process and manage COs in services such as reference creation, annotation, content-based searches, harvesting, and component organization. This chapter extends the discussions in the previous books of this series regarding: (i) the formalization of complex objects based on the 5S framework; (ii) the study of three widely used technologies for managing COs; and (iii) a case study discussion on how to handle complex image objects in DL applications. The concepts addressed in this chapter can be used to classify, compare, and highlight the differences among CO-related components, technologies, and applications, impacting DL researchers, designers, and developers.

1.1 INTRODUCTION

Advances in data compression, data storage, and data transmission have facilitated the creation, storage, and distribution of digital resources. These advances led to an exponential increase in the volume and assortment of data deployed and used in many applications. In order to deal with those data, it is necessary to develop appropriate information systems to efficiently manage data collections.

Users involved in the creation and management of, and access to, heterogeneous resources are often concerned with improving productivity. For this, it is important to provide developers with effective tools to reuse and aggregate content. This has been the goal of a quickly evolving research area, namely Digital Libraries (DLs).

In order to reuse and aggregate different resources, Complex Objects (COs) have been created, motivating solutions for integration and interoperability. Such objects are aggregations of different information elements combined together into a unique logical object [114, 154 155]. Among the several advantages of structuring together individual components, we can cite their reuse in

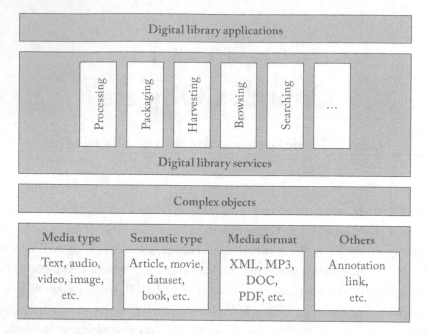

FIGURE 1.1: Architecture for a CO-based digital library. (Adapted from [105])

multiple representations with flexibility, or the exploration of complex inter-object relationships (e.g., semantic linkages) [65].

Figure 1.1 shows the architecture of a CO-based digital library. The bottom layer has the data sources, accommodating different media types with different semantic types and formats. The data sources are aggregated in COs, which are later accessed through different services, such as processing, packaging, harvesting, browsing, and searching. These services are later used by DL applications. Yet, these applications have faced some challenging issues [11, 187]: (i) inadequate support by available DL software for working with COs; (ii) complicated management of COs arising from specific component particularities (such as documents' legal rights); and (iii) inadequate support for multimodal search of complex objects and all their components.

Most of the existing solutions dealing with these issues have focused only on textual data. With the creation of large image and video collections motivated by novel technologies for data acquisition and sharing, new challenges have emerged. In particular, if we consider image and video data, significant research efforts have been spent in the development of appropriate systems to efficiently manage multimedia collections [219]. In many cases, however, those initiatives are not enough to deal with COs that integrate both textual and visual components.

In fact, in spite of all the advances, there is a lack of consensus on the precise formalization involved in reusing, integrating, unifying, managing, and supporting CO-related tasks in diverse application domains. To tackle this issue, we can take advantage of formal concepts to understand clearly and unambiguously the characteristics, structure, and behavior of complex information systems. The benefits of adopting a formal model include the abstraction of general characteristics and common features, and the definition of structures for organizing components (e.g., aggregations, collections). A precise specification of requirements also strengthens the correctness of an implementation [72]. On the other hand, formalized concepts can be used to classify, compare, and highlight the differences among components, technologies, and applications, thus aiding DL researchers, designers, and developers.

In this chapter, we address the formal definitions and descriptions for COs by exploiting concepts of the 5S framework. Later these definitions are explored in a practical case study, illustrating how CO technologies and the 5S framework can fit together to support the description and management of COs in digital libraries.

1.2 COMPLEX OBJECTS

This section introduces the definition of a CO and compares widely used technologies for implementing CO-related services.

1.2.1 DEFINITIONS

Some authors name the integration of resources into a single digital object as *Aggregation* [226], a *Component-Based Object* [195, 196], a *Complex Object* [154], or a *Compound Object* [10]. We adopt the same definition of structuring digital objects present in [10]: atomistic, compound, and complex. The atomistic approach is when the user has a single file (whether made up from a single or multiple text files) in a preferred format. The compound approach is made up from multiple content files, which may have different formats. A complex object is described using a network of digital objects within the repository.

According to Krafft et al. [108], COs are single entities that are composed of multiple digital objects, each of which is an entity in and of itself. Cheung et al. [31] defined CO in the scientific context as the encapsulation of various datasets and resources, generated or utilized during a scientific experiment or discovery process, within a single unit, for publishing and exchange. In other words, a complex object is an aggregation of objects that can be grouped together and manipulated as a single object.

COs also were defined as aggregations of distinct information units that, when combined, form a logical whole [114]. Santanchè, on the other hand, used the idea of COs in the field of software reuse and exchange [195, 196]. Like the script concept [198] or the frame concept [135], the components in a CO are supposed to have the same behavior, respect the same rules, or represent the same concept.

1.2.2 TECHNOLOGIES FOR HANDLING COMPLEX OBJECTS

Several complex object (CO) formats arise from different communities [107, 124, 154, 155] and can be used under different domains [99]. In scientific computing, standards arise, such as Network Common Data Form (NetCDF) [160], Hierarchical Data Format (HDF) [82], and Extensible File System (ELFS) [92]. HDF and NetCDF, for example, are used in multi-dimensional storage and retrieval, while ELFS is an approach to address the issue of high-performance I/O by treating files as typed objects.

COs often are found in persistent database stores. They may be represented using standards from the Moving Picture Experts Group (MPEG) [22] or Metadata Encoding and Transmission Standard (METS) [45]. One example for including digital object formats is the Moving Picture Experts Group—21 Digital Item Declaration Language (MPEG-21 DIDL) [15].

Even though there are a number of standards aiding in the management of COs, there is still incompatibility, motivating solutions for integration and interoperability. As each standard is specialized for a particular domain, it is hard to interoperate across contexts. Yet, it is possible to match some of them, as proposed in [49]; see their comparative study of the IMS Content Package (IMS CP) [205] and Reusable Asset Specification (RAS) [204].

Newer standards have emerged, like SQL Multimedia and Application Packages (SQL/MM) [132]. These were defined to describe storage and manipulation support for complex objects. A number of candidate multimedia domains were suggested, including full-text data, spatial data, and image data.

The Open Archival Information System (OAIS) [29] is an International Organization for Standardization (ISO) reference model, with a particular focus on digital information, both as the primary form of information held and as supporting information for both digitally and physically archived materials. The objects are categorized by their content and function in the operation of an OAIS, into Content Information objects, Preservation Description Information objects, Packaging Information objects, and Descriptive Information objects.

The Open Archives Initiative (OAI) [111] is a framework for archives (e.g., institutional repositories) containing digital content (i.e., a type of DL). The OAI technical infrastructure, specified in the Open Archives Initiative Protocol for Metadata Harvesting (OAI-PMH) [167, 212], defines a mechanism for data providers to expose their metadata. This protocol mandates that individual archives map their metadata to the Dublin Core, a simple and common metadata set for this purpose.

METS [119] addresses packaging to collect digital resource metadata for submission to the repository. It is a Digital Library Federation initiative. A METS document consists of the following sections: header, descriptive metadata, administrative metadata, file section, structural map, structural links, and behavior. METS uses a structural map to outline a hierarchical structure for the DL object, where file elements may be grouped within fileGrp elements, to provide for subdividing the files by object version. A $\langle fileGrp \rangle$ structure is used to comprise a single electronic version of the DL object. $\langle FContent \rangle$ was created to embed the actual contents of the file within the METS document, but it is rarely used. METS provides an XML Schema designed for the purpose of:

- creating XML document instances that express the hierarchical structure of DL objects,
- recording the names and locations of the files that comprise those objects, and
- recording associated metadata.

METS can, therefore, be used as a tool for modeling real world objects, such as particular document types.

SCORM [2] is a compilation of technical specifications to enable interoperability, accessibility and reusability of Web-based learning content. With a Content Aggregation Model, resources described in a manifest (*imsmanifest.xml* file), organized in schema/definition (.xsd and .dtd) files, and placed in a zip file, are used as a content package. SCORM defines a Web-based learning Content Aggregation Model and Run-Time Environment for learning objects. In SCORM, a content object is a Web-deliverable learning unit. Often, a content object is just an HTML page or document that can be viewed with a web browser. A content object is the lowest level of granularity of learning resources and can use all the same technologies a webpage can use (e.g., Flash, JavaScript, frames, and images).

MPEG-21 [22] aims to define an open framework for multimedia applications, to support, for example, declaration (and identification), digital rights management, and adaptation. MPEG-21 is based on two essential concepts: the definition of a fundamental unit of distribution and transaction, which is the digital item; and the concept of users interacting with them. Within an item, an anchor binds descriptors to a fragment, which corresponds to a specific location or range within a resource. Items are grouped in a structured container using an XML-based Digital Item Declaration Language (DIDL). In addition, a W3C XML Schema definition of DIDL is provided.

Table 1.1 summarizes METS, SCORM, and MPEG-21 regarding basic principles available in complex objects: what is the data basic unit, how to relate a part of a document, how to identify it, and how to structure the components.

1.2.3 COMPARISON OF CO-RELATED TECHNOLOGIES (DCC, BUCKETS, OAI-ORE)

Each of the CO technologies were created to address different problems, so DL developers will have to judge which technology best addresses existing requirements. From the several CO technologies available, three different approaches were chosen for a comparison. DCC was chosen for comparison

TABLE 1.1: How standards handle basic CO concepts

Name	Unit	Internal Component	Identifier	Structure
METS	Simple object	FContent structure	OBJID	Structural Map
SCORM	Asset	Sequence rules	——	Schema/definition files
MPEG-21	Resource	Anchors and fragments	URI	XML-DIDL

because it can be implemented in several languages, it supports the encapsulation of software, and it allows the reuse/composition of components. OAI-ORE is a widely used protocol for representing and describing aggregations for future reuse and exchange (metadata harvesting). Several applications have been developed lately taking advantage of the OAI-ORE standard. Finally, Buckets are used in the DL community, as an aggregation construct (allowing links to remote packages, networks, or databases) which can be archived and manipulated as a single object. For instance, OAI-ORE is a metadata harvesting approach and focuses on data integration, while Buckets and DCC have an operational orientation focusing on the repository level.

Digital Content Component (DCC)

Digital Content Component (DCC) [49, 175, 194, 195, 196] was proposed in 2006, as a generalization format for representing complex objects. The approach derives from an analysis and comparison of content packages, and Open Complex Digital Object (OCDO) and reuse standards [194].

A DCC is composed of four distinct subdivisions (see Figure 1.2):

content. the content itself (data in its original format such as a PDF, Word, or HTML file);

structure. the declaration of a management structure that defines how components within a DCC relate to each other, in XML;

interface. a specification of the DCC interfaces using open standards for interface description—a WSDL and OWL-S (semantics); and

metadata. metadata to describe version, functionality, applicability, and use restrictions—using OWL.

Buckets

Buckets [156, 157, 158] provide an archive-independent container construct in which all related semantic and syntactic data types and objects can be logically grouped together, archived, and manipulated as a single object. Buckets are active archival objects and can communicate with each other or with arbitrary network services. Buckets are based on standard World Wide Web (WWW)

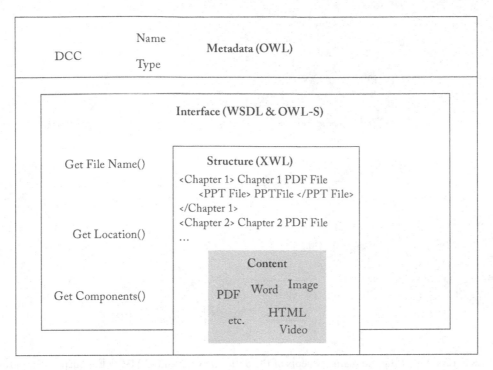

FIGURE 1.2: Digital Content Component (DCC) representation.

capabilities to function, managed by two tools. One is the author tool, which allows the author to construct a bucket with no programming knowledge. The second one is the management tool, which provides an interface to allow site managers to configure the default settings for all authors at that site.

Open Archives Initiative Protocol—Object Reuse and Exchange (OAI-ORE)

OAI-ORE [114, 124] aims to develop, identify, and profile extensible standards and protocols to allow repositories, agents, and services to interoperate in the context of use and reuse of COs. OAI-ORE makes it possible to reconstruct the logical boundaries of compound objects, the relationships among their internal components, and their relationships to other resources. Figure 1.3 highlights some concepts from the 5S framework and OAI-ORE. Note that concepts such as resource—digital object and complex object—can be mutually mapped.

A named graph can be described by a resource map. OAI-ORE defines an abstract data model [112] conformant with the architecture of the Web, essentially consisting of:

URIs. (Uniform Resource Identifiers) for identifying objects;

resources. which are items of interest;

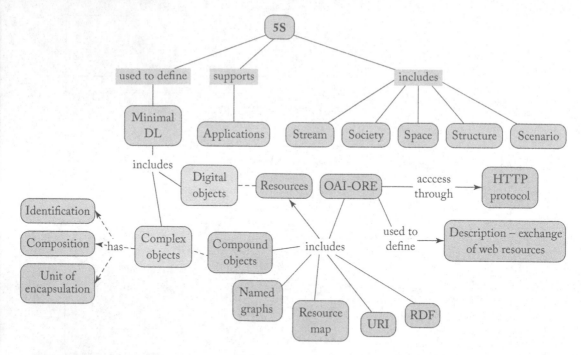

FIGURE 1.3: Matching the main concepts of the 5S framework and OAI-ORE. (Adapted from [102])

standard protocols. such as HTTP, that enable access to the data;

named graphs. for encapsulating information into a CO. The encoded description (serialization) of the named graph is called a resource map; and

proxy. a virtual resource acting as a proxy for an aggregated resource in the context of a certain aggregation. Its use is optional.

DCC, Buckets, and OAI-ORE have been used with different purposes, but their focus is still on the aggregation of resources. For example, different advantages arise: from the space perspective, DCC works with ontologies, while from the structure perspective, the HTML-based organization in OAI-ORE facilitates data integration across applications. Their operations and restrictions are different, since they deal with different perspectives of the CO. The information aggregation can use several abstractions to differentiate internal parts, such as named graphs, XML files, and file system hierarchical structures such as Unix directories. Different perspectives of the same entity can be explored in interfaces, methods, or named graphs.

For highlighting their differences even more, we selected other parameters related to the identification, component organization, structure, boundary, and manipulation of COs (see Table 1.2):

TABLE 1.2: Basic CO concepts from DCC, buckets, and OAI-ORE perspectives			
Description	DCC	Buckets	OAI-ORE
Unique identifier	URI	Handle	URI
Component Division	Process and passive DCCs	Unix directories	Resource map, aggregations
What is encapsulated?	Metadata, content, processes	Metadata, content	Aggregation description
Format	Content, structure, interface and metadata	Buckets, packages, and elements	Map resources, URIs, aggregation
Implementation	JAR file, extensible to other languages	Access through Author and Management Tool	Mapping resources to resource map
CO Organization	Parts accessed through relative URI, other DCCs	Packages and nested Buckets	Resource map and aggregations
Advantages	Ontology, interface, encapsulate executable	Pointer to remote package, network or database, log	Move repository, used as standard between content different systems
How to manage software?	Can encapsulate content with respective SW	As a normal file	As a normal file
Preservation	Encapsulate executable and non-executable content, structure and description allows reuse	Directories can be easily compressed for archival or transport	Description allows easy transport and reuse

(i) unique identifier; (ii) component division; (iii) how the components are composed; (iv) what is encapsulated; (v) usage; (vi) internal format and structure; (vii) implementation or access tools; (viii) advantages; (ix) how they manage software; and (x) how they handle preservation issues.

All DCCs and each component of a CO in OAI-ORE have a URI associated, thereby making them web URI-identified resources. Each bucket has its own unique identifier (handle). The component division is implemented by process and passive DCCs, Unix directories in Buckets, and resource maps in OAI-ORE. Each of these components can encapsulate metadata, content, and processes in DCCs; metadata and content in Buckets; and descriptions of aggregations in OAI-ORE.

In DCC, the internal CO format is divided into content, structure, interface, and metadata. In Buckets, the internal CO format is divided into elements, packages, and the final bucket. In OAI-ORE the resource map describes the aggregation of resources identified by URIs.

The three technologies have different implementations, but all of them allow component reuse. They present different advantages, but all include characteristics of digital preservation (e.g., encapsulate content and software, allow directories to be compressed for archiving, and include description facilities for exchange and reuse).

1.3   RELATED WORK

In different portions of the literature, a variety of perspectives and parameters have been presented for exploring COs and aggregations:

Ontologies.   Gerber et al. in [68] specified, for example, an ontology for the encapsulation of digital resources and bibliographic records;

Granularity.   Fonseca et al. in [60] cited vertical navigation, where accessing a class immediately above or below implies a change of level of detail;

Standards for aggregations.   In the context of the DELOS project, a DL Manifesto [26] has been proposed, in which Candela et al. explored the completeness of the CO (measuring whether a minimal required set of elements is available). If we consider standards for aggregations, other parameters could still be included, like the number of components, types of accepted compositions, or the minimum/maximum elements that the composition should have;

Priority among components.   In the context of the DELOS project [26], also the priority explored was of one component compared to the complete set, so, if this component is copied or deleted, the other parts are copied or deleted along with it;

Portability for the CO structure.   Park et al. in [174] explored the adaptation of the CO structure to different domains, such as portable devices, where some components (such as videos) might not be necessary;

Access to components.   Manghi et al. in [126] suggested different access roles for the different parts, as suggested in the authentication and authorization service;

Reuse and preservation.   Rehberger et al. in [185] examined the role that secondary repositories can play in the preservation and access of digital historical and cultural heritage materials;

Others.   Tracking of provenance [138], timelines [77], etc.

COs also have been used in preservation and harvesting [131, 189], to combine current objects to create new ones [194], to combine services [105], or even for grouping information with respect to the same permissions or operations. Depending on the aggregation, different layers can be exposed, using different information granularity, or type of media, for example. Within applications for CO, we can mention LORE [68] and Escape [215].

1.4   FORMALIZATION

Formalizing complex objects facilitates the development, comparison, and evaluation of solutions based on distinct information resources; makes clear to users what a solution means; indicates how components are related; and helps users to evaluate the applicability of a solution. Furthermore, it allows us to leverage special-purpose techniques for combining, aggregating, and understanding the integration process. In this section, we introduce, having the 5S formal framework as foundation, concepts related to the minimum CO and a novel type of CO, named CIO (CIO), defined to encapsulate images.

Notation: Let DL_1 be a DL; let $\{do_1, do_2, \ldots, do_n\}$ be the set of digital objects *do* present in DL_1; let H be a set of universally unique handles (unique identifiers); let SM be a set of streams; and let set ST be a set of structural metadata specifications.

1.4.1   COMPLEX OBJECT

Recall the 5S definition of a digital object (Def. MI B.18 of Appendix B, first book of this series). A *digital object* is defined as a tuple $do = (h, SM, ST, StructuredStreams)$, where:

1. $h \in H$, where H is a set of universally unique handles (unique identifiers);

2. $SM = \{sm_1, sm_2, \ldots, sm_n\}$ is a set of streams;

3. $ST = \{st_1, st_2, \ldots, st_m\}$ is a set of structural metadata specifications;

4. *StructuredStreams* $= \{stsm_1, stsm_2, \ldots, stsm_p\}$ is a set of StructuredStream functions defined from the streams in the SM set (the second component) of the digital object and from the structures in the ST set (the third component).

Streams are sequences of elements of an arbitrary type (e.g., bits, characters, images, etc.). *Structural Metadata Specifications* correspond to the relations between the object and its parts (as chapters in a book). *StructuredStreams* define the mapping of a structure to streams (for example, how chapters, sections, etc. are organized in a book).

Definition 1.1   We define a **complex object** as a tuple $cdo = (h, SCDO, S)$ where:

1. $h \in H$, where H is a set of universally unique handles (labels);

2. $SCDO = \{DO \cup SM\}$, where $DO = \{do_1, do_2, \ldots, do_n\}$, and do_i is a digital object or another complex object; and $SM = \{sm_a, sm_b, \ldots, sm_z\}$ is a set of streams;

3. S is a structure that composes the complex object cdo into its parts in $SCDO$.

Note that the 5S definitions consider the object's metadata in a separate catalog. The DO and SM components are finite sets, therefore the S structure is also finite, defining what belongs to the CO or not (concept referred to as a boundary).

The S structure in the CO is not specified. It can be seen as any structure that represents parts of a whole, such as a list, a tree, or even a graph. As a practical example, we can mention the Fedora Commons approach [10], where lists represent multiple single files that were packed together, and graphs represent files that are related, creating networks of digital objects. If we consider files arranged in HTML5 [174], the S structure encodes a cyclic graph. Our focus is not to explore these fine-grained concepts, but to consider a high-level approach: aggregate logically, and perhaps physically, distinct objects, so they can be represented as a single unit.

Another type of structuring resource comprises the concept of a collection. The main difference is that a collection is a simple set of objects (Def. MI B.19 in Book 1), while the elements in a CO represent parts of a single concept and might have specific relations connecting them. In particular, consider the issue of Compound Scholarly Publications, explored through several organizations and projects (Europeana [48], SURF Foundation [214], and Eco4r [52]).

The definitions presented in this section can be used to formally describe aggregations and their several aspects available in the 5S framework. These definitions also could be used to construct and initialize applications, similar to initiatives presented in [197, 202, 233], or to devise novel concepts when looking for interoperability and compatibility among different technologies.

Definition 1.2 We consider the minimum CO as a tuple $cdo = (h, SCDO, S)$, where:

1. $h \in H$, where H is a set of universally unique handles (labels);

2. $SCDO = \{DO \cup SM\}$, where $DO = \{do_1\}$, where do_1 is a digital object; and $SM = \{sm_a, sm_b, \ldots, sm_z\}$ is a set of streams;

3. S is a structure that indicates $\{do_1\}$ as a component of cdo.

Our definition considers that a CO should comprise at least one digital object. If a lower granularity is necessary, the atomistic definition (Def. MI B.18 in Book 1) can be applied.

Definition 1.3 In particular, the *complex image object* (CIO) [101] is a CO with the following components: the digital image object, feature vector, and similarity scores (presented in Figure 1.4). If we consider the CO definition, the CIO has the structure $ico = (h, SCDO, S)$, where:

- h is a unique handle that identifies ico;

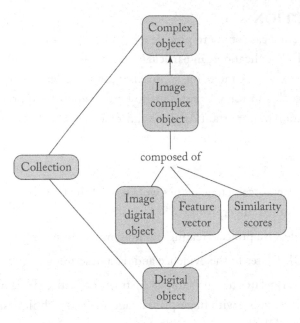

FIGURE 1.4: The CIO. (Adapted from [101])

- $SCDO = \{DO \cup SM\}$, where $DO = \{do_1, do_{21}, \ldots, do_{2k}, do_{31}, \ldots, do_{3k}\}$, where do_1 is an *image*, k is the number of descriptors, $do_{21}, \ldots, do_{2k}$ is a set of *feature vector digital objects*, and $do_{31}, \ldots, do_{3k}$ is a set of *StructuredFeatureVectors* (with the similarity measures, according to a specific descriptor k); and $SM = \{sm_a, sm_b, \ldots, sm_z\}$ is a set of streams;

- S is a structure that identifies how $do_1, do_{21}, \ldots, do_{2k}$, and $do_{31}, \ldots, do_{3k}$ are composed.

Note that each CIO component is a *digital object*, therefore having its own handle. This allows users to explore the collection not only by the COs, but also by the individual components (digital objects).

A *complex image object collection* $ImgCO$ is a tuple $(C, S_{imgdesc})$, where C is a collection (Def. MI B.19 in Book 1), and $S_{imgdesc}$ is a set of image descriptors. Function FV_{desc} defines how a feature vector was obtained, given a CIO $ico \in C$ and a image descriptor $\hat{D} \in S_{imgdesc}$.

1.5   CASE STUDY: FINGERPRINT DIGITAL LIBRARY

This section briefly describes a case study concerning the use of COs in the construction of a fingerprint digital library. For further details on other examples and services, the reader is referred to [98, 100, 101, 105]. A detailed description on concepts related to fingerprint analysis can be found in [19].

1.5.1   INTRODUCTION

In this section, we present a case study to provide a better understanding of how the CO concepts can fit together in real DL applications, in particular, in a fingerprint digital library [104]. We offer this as an example of how database modeling approaches can be enriched with a theoretical handling of CO concepts. The goal is to use CO concepts to better support requirements analysis and the design and implementation of important database and/or DL applications.

Consider a fingerprint digital library which unifies four different digital libraries, from a complex object (CO) perspective.

- Those aware of law enforcement activities will know of the first type of DL (DL1), associated with databases of stored fingerprints.

- Another type relates to a project creating training materials for fingerprint examiners (DL2).

- A third type of DL relates to the evidence and data describing a crime scene (DL3).

- A fourth type of DL relates to our National Institute of Justice (NIJ) funded research studies supporting experimentation with fingerprint image analysis techniques, quality measures, and matching methods (DL4).

The integration of these DLs faces several challenges: syntactic and semantic mismatches, service interoperability, transparency, etc.

In DL1, digital objects are used to identify a person. It manages large law enforcement databases that may have millions of individuals' sets of prints, where each one can come with 10 fingers, 10 toes, palm, pads of feet, etc. One of the biggest biometric database and fingerprint identification systems is from the Federal Bureau of Investigation [56]. It has at least 66 million subjects in the criminal master file, along with more than 25 million civilian print images.

DL2 has a different purpose: to educate and train users. Ideally, for testing fingerprint examiners, the combination of examples identified could be used for assessment, so each case in an exam is distinct, reducing opportunities for cheating. The training modules will have examples for instruction, and yet others for exercises and examinations, taken from all of the other DLs.

In DL3, images are used for matching or excluding individuals. The evidence from a crime scene can come from thousands of people who visited a popular place, or touched an object, creating data which later can be compared with a criminal history record. Each person has ten fingers, and each finger can produce different images depending on the type of distortion, e.g., from a finger sliding. In addition, there are overlays of different prints, i.e., combinations of images from the fingers under the same substrate.

In DL4, the focus is on fingerprint algorithms and used parameter values. Examples include parameters that encode skin distortion and blurring effects. Distorted or synthetic images are created by algorithms that simulate motion and/or skin distortion. The combination of a single recorded print with the 10 different parameter values, for example, can synthetically generate about 10,000 images.

Through the integration, the DL unifies four different communities, allowing each one to see different perspectives, explore the system as a whole, or focus on a determined DL collection. In addition, users can take advantage of DL services (e.g., browsing and searching) to have a unified view of all collections.

1.5.2 INTEGRATION OF DIGITAL LIBRARIES

According to [191], the integration process is divided into four steps: (i) discovery: systems learn about the existence of each other; (ii) identification: systems unambiguously identify their individual items; (iii) access: systems access their items; and (iv) utilization: systems synthesize their items. Our case study presents the first two steps. We used COs to facilitate the aggregation abstraction (as shown in Fig. 1.5), embracing components from different domains and unifying them with a single concept.

Figure 1.6 presents the concept map of the main classes as a summary of the entity-relationship diagram [103]. Class Individual, for example, aggregates all the information from the 10 fingers,

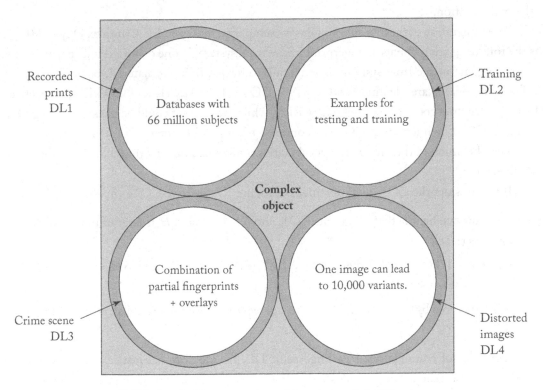

FIGURE 1.5: The integration of fingerprint digital libraries.

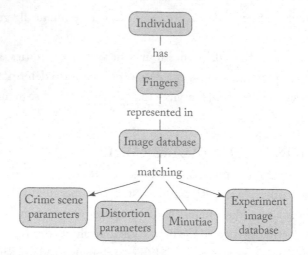

FIGURE 1.6: The main classes representing the fingerprint DL.

along with images, minutiae, and other metadata for a single person. Later the user can explore if the same person has images distorted by algorithms, extracted from a crime scene, or manipulated at the police station.

The integration of the four sub-systems is exemplified in Figure 1.7. Complex Object 1 (CO1) has the following components: a fingerprint image from system A, one distorted image from system B, a crime scene image from system C, and a link to related training material, taken from system D. The components are identified by CO1.A.1, CO1.B.1, CO1.C.1, and CO1.D.1, respectively. The CO1 structure could be represented by RDF, while the content could be packaged using OAI-ORE or DCC. The interface of CO1 can comprise the union information of its four components, along with the union of their respective vocabularies (individual, fingers, thumb, quality, distortion, parameters, etc.).

If we consider the CO formal treatment of Figure 1.7, we have CO1= $(h, SCDO, S)$ where:

1. h is a unique handle that represents CO1, and $h \in H$, where H is a set of universally unique handles (labels);

2. $SCDO = \{DO \cup SM\}$, where $DO = \{A.1, B.1, C.1, D.1\}$; and $SM = \{sm_a, sm_b, \ldots, sm_z\}$ is a set of streams;

3. S is structured by means of an XML file, aggregating the complex object cdo into its parts in $SCDO$.

Examples of communities in a fingerprint DL include criminal justice agencies, scholars, students, and researchers. Specific rules and different roles also can be used to map restrictions, such as the public non-availability of recorded prints from the police station.

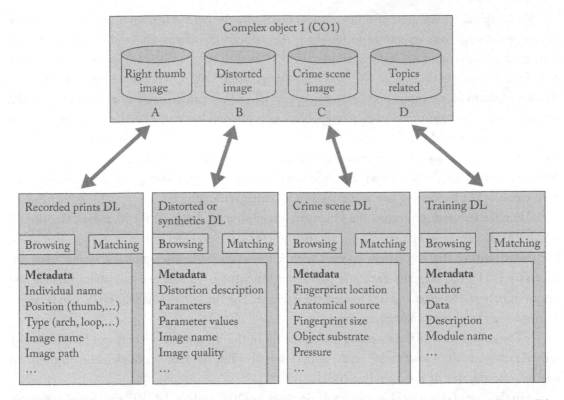

FIGURE 1.7: An example of complex object using four digital libraries [104]: (A) Recorded Prints, (B) Distorted Images, (C) Crime Scene Images, and (D) Training Material.

Different scenarios can be defined to describe each of the four DLs and their interactions as a CO. Processes such as matching, creating distortions, and training also can be described in scenarios. Software used for creating fingerprint distortions and matching include detailed information about parameters (such as angles, flows, plasticity, displacement, number of matches, etc.) and can take advantage of scenarios for their description.

Examples of structures in a fingerprint DL include the information organization (such as Figure 1.6). Each person has 10 fingers, and each finger can produce different images depending on whether it is from a police station, a distortion, or from a crime scene. If they belong to the same finger, structures are used to represent this hierarchy.

Streams refer to the different types of images and files managed. Users can explore not only the individual components, but also the CO as a unique digital object. As services, we can list browsing, matching, textual search, and multimodal search.

The vocabulary used for the description of the content, structure, metadata, versions, functionality, applicability, and use restrictions relates to the conceptual space.

The initial exploration of CO concepts under the 5S perspective on a project in an early development stage was important to highlight the amount of information and details needed to manage and aggregate. DCCs, for example, could be used to encapsulate each image, the details of each DL, the aggregation of the CO, and the software used. OAI-ORE could be used to describe the aggregations in an integrated DL service, providing the match between latent and recorded fingerprints, or a chain of evidence to convince a jury of confidence of match, for example. Since both technologies use URIs to identify resources, they could be integrated for further exchange and reuse of resources among the different communities. Other integrated DL services could consider the *object versions* (with the composition of distortions, for example), *correspondence of versions with provenance,* or the harvesting and matching in a DL integration process.

For the harvesting process, the Open Archives Initiative Protocol for Metadata Harvesting (OAI-PMH) can be used, defining a mechanism for data providers to expose their metadata. For disseminating the content in concert with a metadata harvesting protocol, some steps are necessary [131]: (i) wrap the data in a packaging format; (ii) include the metadata; (iii) encode the references to the files; and (iv) harvest the package. For this, OAI-ORE or DCC can be used, representing the objects and aggregations.

The complexity of the mapping and updating in the integration process can be affected by several factors, such as knowledge of the application domain, the number of elements in the local schema, and the size of the collection [202].

In the case of complex object technologies, such as DCC and OAI-ORE, the mapping process also depends on other factors, such as how the components are aggregated, what is their granularity, which vocabulary each technology is using, how the components are identified and structured, or how they are organized in a schema.

In summary, our case study explored two steps of the integration process: the discovery of each system, and the identification of individual items for possible aggregation. For this, we used the 5S framework along with the CO technologies to analyze the integrated fingerprint DL, from the identity, components, structure, and boundary perspectives. Finally, we discussed how the components can be accessed later, along with their individual metadata.

1.5.3 IMPLEMENTATION

This section presents issues regarding the implementation of a fingerprint DL prototype that integrates the four digital libraries discussed in the previous section.

Considering the large size and types of variance of the fingerprint images, as well as the computational costs of fingerprint verification algorithms, for the prototype we used a pre-processing phase, using Content-Based Image Retrieval (CBIR) techniques (see Chapter 1 of Book 4 of this series). This phase is responsible for ranking similar images based on a texture descriptor. The objective is to reduce the number of one-to-one comparisons, seeking improvements both in terms of effectiveness and retrieval speed. In this sense, we study the characterization of textural patterns that can be found in fingerprints.

This solution requires the definition of appropriate image descriptors, which are characterized by (i) an extraction algorithm (such as about texture, shape, or color) to encode image features into feature vectors; and (ii) a similarity measure to compare two images based on the distance between their feature vectors. The similarity measure is a matching function (e.g., using Euclidean distance), which gives the degree of similarity for a given pair of images represented by their feature vectors. The larger the distance value, the less similar the images.

The prototype had the following phases: (i) the definition of the fingerprint CO under the 5S perspective; (ii) the identification of the compound parts; (iii) the CBIR process; (iv) the encapsulation of the image and related metadata; and (v) the CO publishing.

Phase 1

The definition of the fingerprint CO under the 5S perspective played a key role in understanding the data types and different DLs of the fingerprint integration. The objective of the prototype was to aggregate data including the images and metadata. Only two fingerprint digital libraries were selected for the prototype: the recorded prints from the police and the crime scene fingerprints.

Phase 2

In phase 2, we defined that the aggregation would comprise the individual concept (as shown in Figure 1.6). The identification and relation of the compound parts were stored in a DBMS, matching images to respective fingerprint DL, metadata, image content descriptors, and similarity distances.

Phase 3

In phase 3, the integration of the CBIR process allowed a pre-categorization of the image, using comparisons based on texture features. For this, the Statistical Analysis of Structural Information (SASI) [28] descriptor was used. The CBIR processing of Figure 1.8 (fingerprint 11), for example, generates a feature vector, and the similarity distances to the other images in the collection. Figure 1.10 shows the ranking for Figure 1.8 (fingerprint 11) according to the texture comparison. The 10 top-down images are the most similar images compared to Figure 1.8 (fingerprint 11).

The CBIR processing of a second image (Figure 1.9—fingerprint 3) generates a second feature vector, and another set of similarity distances. Figure 1.11 presents the search results for Figure 1.9 (fingeprint 3) regarding the employed texture-based comparison.

Phase 4

In phase 4, a DCC was used for the encapsulation of resources. DCC allows the recursive construction of components using composition of other components, based on a model which generalizes reuse content practices of composition and decomposition of components. The main characteristics

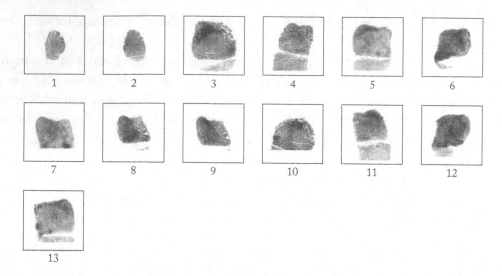

FIGURE 1.8: Samples of images from a recorded print DL from the police.

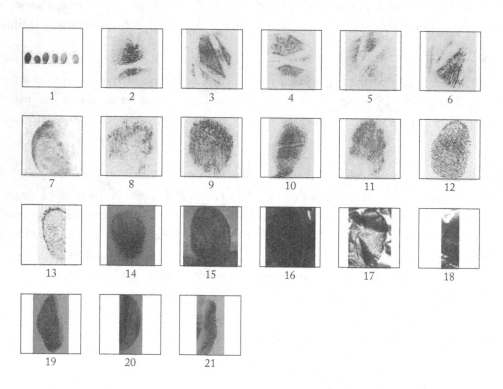

FIGURE 1.9: Samples of fingerprints from a DL which simulates a crime scene.

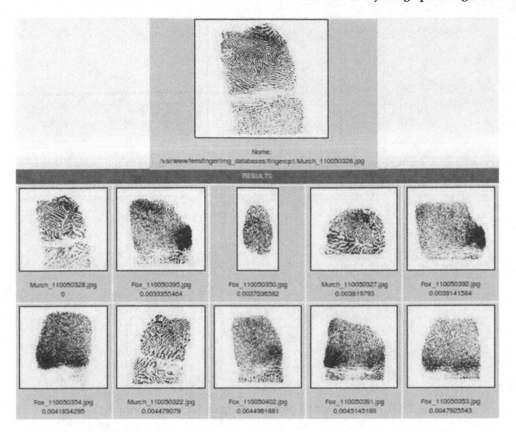

FIGURE 1.10: CBIR process for Figure 1.8—fingerprint 11.

of DCC are: (i) it can uniformly encapsulate both executable (programs, processes, etc.) and non-executable (data sets) content; (ii) it provides a context description for its content, using references to ontologies; (iii) it provides descriptions of interfaces to operations, also with references to ontologies; and (iv) it is independent of platform or programming environment.

The encapsulation of resources was built in a three-layer model (as shown in Figure 1.12): (i) the CIO aggregating the CBIR and image information (encapsulated in the DCC entitled ImageCODCC); (ii) the individual fingerprint DL, represented by the police fingerprint DL (encapsulated in the DCC entitled PoliceCODCC) and the crime scene DL (encapsulated in the DCC entitled CrimeCODCC); and (iii) the individual complex object, aggregating all the images and metadata for a same person (encapsulated in the DCC entitled IndividualDCC).

In the mentioned example, Figure 1.8 (fingerprint 11) and Figure 1.9 (fingerprint 3) were aggregated into two ICOs. They are represented by the ImageCODCC, which centralizes the

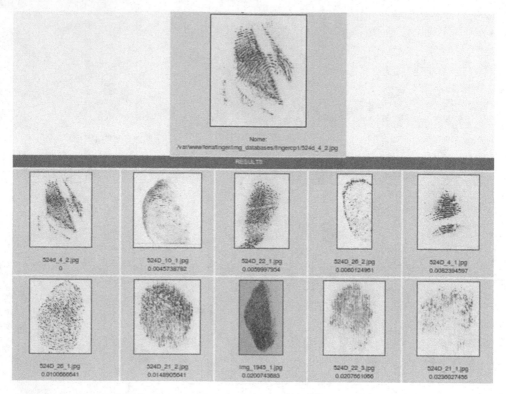

FIGURE 1.11: CBIR process for Figure 1.9—fingerprint 3.

encapsulation of the CO, concerning the JPEG images, an XML file (with metadata and similarity distance), and feature vectors for each respective image. In this case, the feature vectors are binary files. Operations available include the generation of the image CO compressed file and image CO XML. DCC metadata includes the image CO name and file location.

The second layer contains the information aggregation relative to the respective fingerprint library. In this case, Figure 1.8 (fingerprint 11) belongs to an individual from the police fingerprint DL and is encapsulated in PoliceCODCC. Figure 1.9 (fingerprint 3) belongs to the same individual, but now in the crime scene DL, which is encapsulated in CrimeCODCC. Operations available include the generation of the CO compressed file for the respective fingerprint DL. DCC metadata includes the individual name, the finger position, and the object substrate of the crime scene fingerprint.

The third layer corresponds to the Complex Object 1 presented in Figure 1.7, aggregating information from one individual using different fingerprint DLs. In the mentioned example, this represents the aggregation of all images from Figures 1.8 and 1.9 (since they represent the same

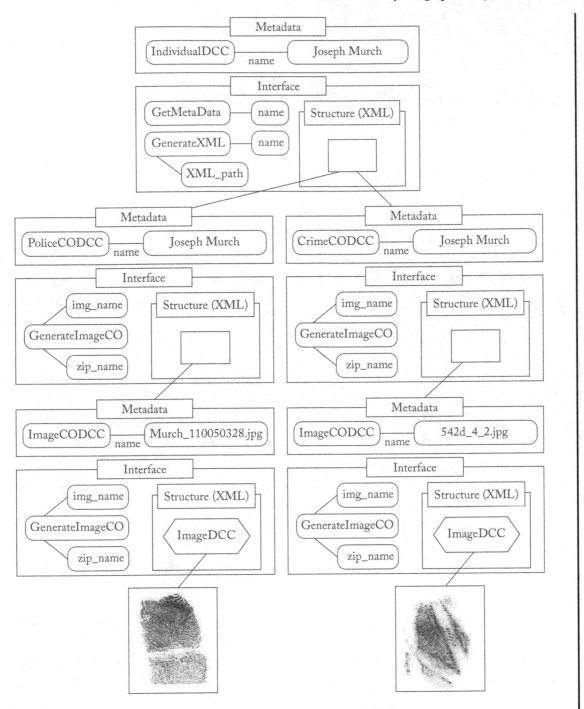

FIGURE 1.12: Structure for IndividualDCC.

```
<?xml version="1.0" encoding="UTF8"?>
<individual>Joseph Murch
 <individual_name>Joseph Murch</individual_name>
 <individual_age>22</individual_age>
 <individual_sex> M</individual_sex>
 <image_DL_indiv>Joseph Murch
  <image_DL>Police Prints Digital Library</image_DL>
  <image> Murch_110050328.jpg
     <image_name>Murch_110050328.jpg</image_name>
     <image_feature_vector_name>/home/nadiapk/data/fv/Murch_110050328.jpg.txt
        </image_feature_vector_name>
     <image_descriptor>SASI
     <image_name> Murch_110050328.jpg <image_dist_value>0</image_dist_value></image_name>
     <image_name>Fox_110050395.jpg<image_dist_value>0.0033</image_dist_value></image_name>
     <image_name>Fox_110050350.jpg<image_dist_value>0.0037</image_dist_value></image_name>
     <image_name>Murch_110050327.jpg<image_dist_value>0.0038</image_dist_value></image_name>
     <image_name>Fox_110050392.jpg<image_dist_value>0.0039</image_dist_value></image_name>
     </image_descriptor><\image></image_DL_indiv>
 <image_DL_indiv>Joseph Murch
  <image_DL>Crime Scene Digital Library</image_DL>
  <image> 524d_4_2.jpg
     <image_name>524d_4_2.jpg</image_name>
     <image_feature_vector_name>/home/nadiapk/data/fv/524d_4_2 .txt
        </image_feature_vector_name>
     <image_descriptor>SASI
        <image_name> 524d_4_2.jpg <image_dist_value>0</image_dist_value></image_name>
        <image_name>524D_10_1.jpg<image_dist_value>0.0045</image_dist_value></image_name>
        <image_name>524D_22_1.jpg<image_dist_value>0.0059</image_dist_value></image_name>
        <image_name>524D_25_2.jpg<image_dist_value>0.0060</image_dist_value></image_name>
        <image_name>524D_4_1.jpg<image_dist_value>0.0082</image_dist_value></image_name>
     </image_descriptor>
  </image>
 </image_DL_indiv><individual>
```

FIGURE 1.13: XML for the individual aggregation.

individual), along with their respective feature vectors, similarity distances, and metadata. In the mentioned example, this is represented by the IndividualDCC having the name Joseph Murch. Figure 1.13 presents the XML for the individual aggregation: the initial block presents the individual metadata (name, age, sex); the second block presents the XML for the police fingerprint DL CO, and the last block presents the XML for the crime scene DL CO. Note that the second and third block have the image CO, starting with the tag <image>. Operations for the IndividualDCC include the generation of the CO with all the information from an individual. DCC metadata includes the number of components from each DL, and the individual name (in case there is a difference between the DLs).

Phase 5

In phase 5, the OAI-PMH protocol was used for the publishing of the individual CO metadata. It also can be used to understand which complex objects and fingerprint digital libraries are correlated to a specific individual CO. The objective is to facilitate the interchange and integration of the different fingerprint digital libraries.

Our prototype enables the installation of different image descriptors, but for the tests presented, the Statistical Analysis of Structural Information (SASI) [28] descriptor was used. The library was implemented in C, the DCCs in Java [104]. The functions and parameters available for each DCC are described in the PostgreSQL database. The image COs are published using the jOAI software [222]. The jOAI data provider allows XML files from a file system to be exposed as items in an OAI data repository and made available for harvesting by others using the OAI-PMH.

1.6   SUMMARY

Many DL implementations and applications demand additional and advanced services to effectively reuse and aggregate different resources. Examples of commonly required services include those related to the support of newer, more complex media types such as images, multimedia objects, and related information.

In this chapter, we introduce formal definitions and descriptions of Complex Objects. The proposed constructs take advantage of formalism to help one to understand clearly and unambiguously the characteristics, structure, and behavior of the main concepts related to CO components, technologies, and applications. Later, these definitions are used in a case study, to exemplify how CO concepts can be explored to define the CIO. Our contribution relies on (i) the formalization of complex objects; (ii) the initial analysis of three CO technologies; and (iii) a case study discussion on how to handle CIOs in applications.

The set of definitions may impact future development efforts of a wide range of DL experts since it can guide the design and implementation of new DL services based on COs. Another straightforward benefit of this work is the use of these formal definitions to construct applications (as with image collections), including requirement gathering, conceptual modeling, prototyping, and code generation, similar to initiatives presented in [71, 232, 110]. As an example, consider the use of 5S formal theory to integrate an archaeological DL (Appendix C in Book 1), using applications such as 5SGraph [232]. From the implementation perspective, COs also can be used for service reuse and combination [98].

There are several research efforts that can be explored to further extend our current work. These include the study of the impact of COs on other 5S constructs, the comparison and interaction with other technologies (such as the use of metadata in METS and Dublin Core), and the use of COs in other domains and specific services (such as content-based and multimodal search, and annotation).

1.7   EXERCISES AND PROJECTS

1.1 Pick your favorite DL. Identify three different types of complex objects that are important in that DL.

1.2 For each type of complex object mentioned previously, identify possible services and users. Why can COs help different users to have different views/layers of information?

1.3 How could one extend the 5S framework to define other CO-related concepts, such as CO packaging and content-based search services?

1.4 Besides data aggregation, the concept of complex object could be used for service integration. Identify two services that could be combined in the DL mentioned previously (in question 1).

1.5 Please give a 5S-oriented description for the fingerprint case study presented in this chapter. Be sure to cover each of the Ss separately, first. Then, consider combinations of pairs or triples of Ss too, as seems appropriate.

1.6 Using the CO definition, how can we formally describe DCC, OAI-ORE, and Buckets?

1.7 Please list and explain another example of CO technology that could be easily integrated with DCC.

1.8 Consider the DCC illustrated in Figure 1.12. How can we formally describe this CO? What would be the formal description, if we consider CIOs instead of images?

1.9 Consider the XML illustrated in Figure 1.13. How can we formally describe the CIOs presented in the aggregation? How many digital objects are present in this figure? How could we modify the CO for supporting image annotations?

1.10 Still considering Figure 1.13, list the advantages of publishing/integrating individual digital objects and COs. Please write another scenario where aggregations are useful for publishing.

In this case, what are the advantages of using XML? What other kind of structure would you suggest?

1.11 Consider a software Soft_SO that is composed of individual components DO1 and DO2. Can we apply the complex object definition under Soft_SO? What are the main differences compared to other objects, such as documents and images?

1.12 This chapter discussed three CO technologies. Pick some other technology used to aggregate objects, and formalize it by taking into account 5S aspects. Discuss the key limitations of this technology compared to DCC, OAI-ORE, and Buckets.

1.13 Chapter 2 of Book 2 discusses the DL integration problem. Can we extend the same problem under the complex object management perspective? What are the similarities?

1.14 Three students are working together in a group to solve an assignment from a DL class, and then one of them will send the group solution to the professor on behalf of every-one in the group. Discuss different scenarios of how the assignment was divided. Can we apply complex object definition in order to describe these scenarios? Are there limita-tions?

1.15 Pick some aspect of CO that has not been formally described in this chapter. Building upon the discussion in this chapter and in the prior books in the series, add to the formalisms given, to characterize the aspect of concern. Explain how the 5S framework has helped, or made more difficult, this formal approach.

CHAPTER 2

Annotation

Uma Murthy, Lois M. Delcambre, Ricardo da Silva Torres, and Nádia P. Kozievitch

Abstract

Many scholarly tasks involve annotation and related types of working with contextualized fine-grain information, such as subdocuments. Current approaches to working with subdocuments involve a mix of paper-based and digital techniques, such as superimposed information (SI). SI refers to new information that is created to reference subdocuments in existing information resources. We combine this idea of SI with traditional Digital Library (DL) services to define and develop a DL with SI (an SI-DL). This chapter extends the discussions in the previous books of this series regarding: (i) the review of select definitions; (ii) the extension of the formalization of a DL with superimposed information based on the 5S framework; and (iii) one case study discussion on how to explore the metamodel for SI-DLs.

2.1   INTRODUCTION

Many scholarly tasks involve working with fine-grain information or information that is part of some larger unit. Consider the following examples.

- A student reviews his notes, which might refer to highlighted portions in textbooks and papers, while studying for an exam.

- A doctor carefully examines her medical notes, along with marked-up X-rays of a patient's shoulder, to check for a fracture.

- A microbiologist analyzes and compares a newly found strain of bacteria, with marked-up images and descriptions of similar strains, in order to make deductions about it.

- A music professor develops a multimedia lecture on a musical style, combining snippets of compositions of the said style.

The student, the doctor, the microbiologist, and the musician are all working with *subdocuments*, or fine-grain information, *in situ*, or in their original information context. For the student, the subdocuments are highlighted portions of the textbooks and papers and the student views those subdocuments in the context of the full text of the books and papers. For the doctor, the subdocument is the portion of the X-ray indicated by markings on the shoulder and the doctor views that subdocument in the context of the entire X-ray. For the microbiologist, the subdocuments are parts of images of the new bacteria strain as well as parts of images of previously known strains in the context of the entire organism. For the music professor, the subdocuments are the snippets of musical compositions (in the context of entire compositions) that the professor chooses to include in his presentation.

Working with subdocuments is an important part of such scholarly tasks, and sometimes a necessary one. For example, while comparing bacterial strains, the microbiologist might need to look at the similar/different distinguishing features among the strains. The prevalence of such use of subdocuments has been noted in past studies of use of scholarly materials. For example, in a study of annotations in 150 college textbooks [130], Marshall found that notes, symbols, etc. are often found near highlighted portions of text. In another study on the use of National Science Digital Library (NSDL) educational resources in creating instructional materials [184], Recker and Palmer found that teachers preferred to use resources at a smaller granularity level than what was catalogued for NSDL.

Subdocument information might be of varying content types and formats and might be distributed across locations, media, and devices. Current approaches to working with subdocuments include a combination of paper-based and digital techniques. For example, a student might have class notes, images, audio lectures, etc. in digital form and refer to textbooks, personal notes, and drawings in paper form. The student might be able to manage this fragmentation of information across various sources if the volume of information is not too large. However, the combination of large volumes of heterogeneous data in varied formats (marked-up images, notes, websites, etc.) coupled with manual information organization and retrieval, can lead to ineffective and inefficient task execution (verified by the findings in various user studies [146, 148, 149]). Two key problems are:

- subdocuments and whole documents are dispersed across several places (paper and digital), making information management, searching, browsing, and access tedious, and
- capabilities to work with subdocuments (*in situ*) and whole documents also are dispersed across tools (storing in one place, taking notes in another, searching for information in a third place, etc.), leading to ineffective and inefficient task execution.

A DL is an information system, with collections of documents/digital objects[1] and their metadata, and services including those to manage, organize, access, browse, index, and search

---

1. Information in a DL might be manifested in the form of digital objects of various content types.

FIGURE 2.1: Searching on subimages and associated information. (Source: [85])

through those collections in order to support one or more user communities.[2] However, most DLs provide limited support to work with subdocuments. We use the following scenario to illustrate such a need in scholarly tasks. Consider a fisheries student who is trying to identify the species of a fish using an image (Figure 2.1). She looks at the fish in the image and identifies the family of the fish.[3] Then, to help with identifying the species of the fish, she might use this image to frame a query, such as:

Find species that are darters that have a dorsal fin that looks like Figure 2.1-A *that is connected to another dorsal fin that looks like* Figure 2.1-B, *and that have an orange hue on the species' belly like* Figure 2.1-C.

Typically, support for such searches (as that mentioned above) is not present in DLs and, to the best of our knowledge, there is no facility for identifying or distinguishing subdocuments of interest from their enclosing documents. Furthermore there is no provision for a subdocument to have its own metadata. As a result, subdocuments are not separately accessible, searchable, or manageable in most DLs. This motivated us to define and develop a *Digital Library with Superimposed Information* (henceforth referred to as SI-DL), which combines the idea of SI with traditional DL services that operate in context in domains such as education.

SI refers to new information laid over subdocuments, which are part of existing information [9, 44, 125, 143]. Examples include new content such as annotations, labels, and tags; new structures/organizations such as citations, indexes, and concordances; and combinations of new content and structure such as in concept maps, multimedia presentations composed from existing information, etc. A core property of an SI system is to enable working with subdocuments, while

---

2. This is an informal description of a DL. There are other definitions; see Book 1 of this series.

3. Fishes might follow a taxonomical classification, consisting of families, where each family consists of genera, and where each genus consists of species.

retaining its original information context, also referred to as working with information *in situ*. Thus, in an SI system, a user can select or work with information elements at the subdocument level while retaining the original context.

By combining the architecture and concepts of an SI system with those in a DL, we can introduce subdocuments into a DL. This combination enables us to treat subdocuments as first-class objects in a DL, allowing DL services that apply to regular digital objects to now apply to subdocuments. Thus, subdocuments might be managed, organized, accessed, indexed, searched for, browsed for, and used in a way similar to digital objects. This opens numerous possibilities for working with subdocuments to support various tasks, some of which we explore in [146].

The focus of this chapter is the description and definition of an SI-DL. We abstract and model the data and services in an SI-DL by using and building upon existing abstractions and models in digital libraries and SI systems. This enables us to extend the notion of digital libraries in a systematic manner. We build upon DL formalization work, including that presented in Book 1 of this series, to extend a minimal DL to include SI.

The rest of the chapter is organized as follows. In Section 2.2, we discuss related work in SI, hypertext, annotations, and subdocuments in digital libraries. Following that, we review select definitions from both Book 1 of this series and Chapter 1, which we reuse and/or build upon in this chapter. In Section 2.4, we abstract the components of an SI-DL to develop an SI-DL metamodel. We formally define these components, leading to the definition of an SI-DL. Finally, in Section 2.5, we present case studies to verify the descriptive power of the SI-DL metamodel.

2.2   RELATED WORK

This section presents related work and basic concepts.

2.2.1   SUPERIMPOSED INFORMATION

The notion of SI is the foundation of this chapter. SI refers to new information created to reference subdocuments, or elements in existing information resources [44, 125]. SI might be created for various reasons, such as to select, highlight, reference, extend, supplement, connect, or organize subdocuments. SI can be in the form of new content (annotations or tags over a few lines in a text or an object in a photograph), new structure or organization (table of contents in a book, a trailer of a movie), or new content and organization (a report, which cites information from multiple sources, or a multimedia presentation developed using audio/video clips and personal notes).

Figure 2.2 shows the conceptual model of an SI system. The *base layer* consists of existing information resources and might include content in various formats and media types. A *mark* is an abstraction that specifies an addressable/reference-able region, or subdocument, in the base layer. Note that a mark is created after the creation of a base document and need not pertain to

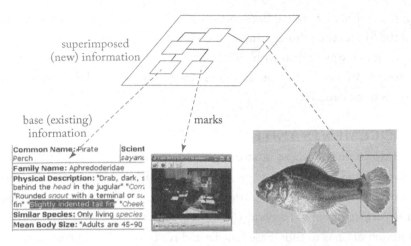

FIGURE 2.2: Working with information selections *in situ*.

an information element as specified by the structure of the base document. New information resides in the *superimposed layer*, which consists of one or more marks, and might include new content and/or organization. A mark is created in the base layer and used in the superimposed layer, and thus links both these layers. An important characteristic of SI systems is that they enable users to work with subdocuments *in situ*, or while keeping the original information context intact. Thus, using the notion of SI enables us to select or work with information elements at the subdocument level while retaining the original context (by referencing, not replicating, information).

Superimposed applications (SAs) allow users to lay new information over existing or base information. SAs employ marks to work with subdocuments. Prior SI work has included the development and demonstration of infrastructure for creation, resolution, and use of SI (through SAs) [41, 42, 44, 125, 141, 142, 143, 144, 145]. Notable among this work is the Superimposed Pluggable Architecture for Contexts and Excerpts (SPARCE) [143], a middleware approach for managing SI. SPARCE was used in various SAs, such as Sidepad [143], which may be used to manage and visualize marks, and SIMPEL [147], a multimedia presentation editor and player.

More recently, Archer et al. [9] defined and demonstrated an architecture for representing marks (i.e., subdocuments) as first-class objects in a DL. Their work leveraged the DSpace DL system[4] and the Fab4 browser[5] [35], a derivative of the Multivalent browser [179, 180] with annotation capability. They demonstrated the same capability in the Fedora DL system.[6]

---

4. http://www.dspace.org

5. http://bodoni.lib.liv.ac.uk/fab4/

6. http://fedora-commons.org/

Most of the earlier SI work has been on development of infrastructure and systems. In [146], we augmented the SI literature through multiple contributions. In general, combining the notion of SI with DLs provides a way to deal with collections of subdocuments and associated information. The SI-DL metamodel provides a formal representation of SI in a DL environment, including precise definitions of SI concepts.

2.2.2   SUBDOCUMENTS AND HYPERTEXT

In the hypertext world, the notion of subdocuments is included. Typically, these are author-created parts of documents. In HTML, the #-tag is used to point to a specific part of a document [174].

Hypertext reference models such as the Dexter model [78] make explicit the concepts (such as linking) in hypertext systems. Hypermedia models such as the Amsterdam model [80] extend the hypertext notion of links to time-based media and compositions of different media. Obviously, SI is rooted in these ideas. The main additional capability it brings is being able to work with subdocument information *in situ*. There is limited support in hypertext models and systems to work with information *in situ*. In standards such as XLink and XPath, subdocuments may typically be referenced as long as they have been predefined by the author, or if they are encompassed within XML tags [216, 217]. SI enables linking information at varying document granularities after a document has been created, thus supporting reader-created subdocuments along with author-created subdocuments.

Ted Nelson's Xanadu system presented two ideas—deep content links and transclusion. Both of these, he felt, describe his vision of hypertext (connected, networked documents), more than what the Web implemented [159]. Marks being viewed in their context are very similar to the idea of transclusion, where quotations and annotations may be connected to subdocuments in their original context.

Work by Kerne et al. [93, 94, 95], on recombinant information and hypersigns, focuses on developing compositions for visual semiotics (to construct and to understand new meanings) supporting personal expression to promote the creative process and information discovery. This can be considered an application or type of SI. In the SI-DL metamodel, we developed a representation for such SI in a DL environment.

2.2.3   SUBDOCUMENTS AND SI IN DIGITAL LIBRARIES

Many DL systems have annotation capabilities, usually focusing on annotations of complete documents. DiLAS is a DL annotation service that brings together multiple DL annotation systems to create a framework for a decentralized annotation service [4]. Agosti and Ferro worked on various annotation projects, including conducting a comprehensive review of digital libraries and other information systems with annotation capabilities [5], and integrating annotation and search capabilities into digital libraries to annotate images of historical manuscripts [8]. They developed a formal model for annotations in a DL, which provides precise specifications for such annotations [6]. The focus of our work is to incorporate subdocuments and SI in a digital library. Our SI-DL metamodel does not explicitly include an annotation as a component. However, an annotation might be represented as SI in the metamodel.

SI also relates to the idea of secondary repositories, where users may compose structured collections of complex digital objects [185]. These objects point back to the primary digital objects (similar to base information) from which they are produced. The focus of one project [185] is to examine the role of secondary repositories in access and preservation. Secondary repositories are similar to the idea of collections of aggregate works [21]; Buchanan et al. discuss challenges of representing aggregate works in a DL, such as an encyclopedia, an anthology of poems, etc. In both works [21, 185], a unit of information is a document, as structured and specified by the document's author. The aggregate work is a new complex object composed of documents. Our work might be considered an extension in the opposite direction, where a user might create and use a subdocument, a unit of information that is smaller than a document. Our goal is to represent such fine-grain information inside a DL. Once we are able to treat these subdocuments as digital objects, they might be combined in the same ways as other digital objects, to form complex digital objects, or secondary works, or aggregates.

2.2.4   SUBDOCUMENTS AND ANNOTATIONS

There has been considerable work done on annotation standards [90] and frameworks [14, 179, 180]. The Open Annotation Collaboration (OAC) project [81, 166], launched in 2009, is working on an annotation model to enable interoperability and communication across annotations on Web-based content. The OAC annotation model focuses on enabling various annotation use cases dealing with multimedia content in heterogeneous formats.

2.3   REVIEW OF SELECT DEFINITIONS

Next we review select definitions in the 5S framework and build upon these and other DL and set theory concepts to yield SI-DL concept definitions. First, we review the definitions of a stream, structure, system state, event, and scenario. These definitions are used in subsequent definitions in the 5S framework and in the definition of SI-DL concepts. Next, we review the definitions of a digital object, descriptive metadata specification, metadata format, hypertext, and minimal DL. For further details of these definitions and for other definitions, readers are referred to Appendix B of Book 1 of this series.

The first important definition is the concept of **stream** (Def. MI B.3 of Appendix B, Book 1 of this series), which is a *sequence* whose codomain is a nonempty set. Examples of a stream might be sequences of bits, characters, and numbers.

A **structure** (Def. MI B.4 of Appendix B), in turn, refers to a graph, with the vertices and edges labeled.

A **transition event** (or simply **event**) on a state set encodes the transition from one state to another (Def. MI B.8 of Appendix B). For example, consider two system states. In the first one, s_i, there is an image collection with k images. An event, e, might be the uploading of a new image to the collection, yielding a new system state, s_j. The condition function, $c(s_i)$, might be a test for the adequate availability of space in the collection for the new image. The action function, p, is to upload the new image in the collection. A variable (or logical *location*), X, such as the size of the collection, might be different in the two states. It might be represented as $s_i(X)$ and $s_j(X)$ in the two states, with values k and $k + 1$, respectively.

A **scenario** (Def. MI B.9 of Appendix B) is a sequence of related transition events on a state set. Considering the aforementioned example of uploading an image to a collection, a scenario might involve uploading an image, adding metadata about the image, and publishing the image to a blog or a website.

The **structural metadata** (Def. MI B.13 of Appendix B) specifies the internal structure of a digital object and its component parts. This usually refers to author-defined parts of the digital object. For example, the author of a paper specifies the components of the paper, including paper title, sections, section titles, figures, tables, and references. The structure in this case is linear, for the most part, with elements of hypertext linking via cross-referencing.

A **descriptive metadata specification** (Def. MI B.16 of Appendix B) is a structure used to describe digital objects. It might be considered as a labeled graph, specifying the relationships between resources and between a resource and its properties. The aforementioned definition of a specification is related to Resource Description Framework (RDF) [25] statements in the Semantic Web [16]. It makes use of triples to describe properties of resources, where each property of a resource is associated with a value. For example, the descriptive metadata about a journal paper might include statements such as (Journal1, 'editor', 'Edward A. Fox'), (Journal1, 'format', 'PDF'), (Paper1, 'journal', 'Journal1'), and (Paper1, 'creation-date', '18 February 2011').

A **metadata format** (Def. MI B.15 of Appendix B) uses the property definition function, def, to constrain the types of resources that might be associated together in statements. For example, $def(\mathcal{R}, 'creation - date') = Date$ and $def(\mathcal{R}, 'format') = AllowedTextFormats$. In a digital library, a descriptive metadata specification conforms to a metadata format.

A **digital object** (Def. MI B.18 of Appendix B) is a tuple composed of a handle, a set of streams, a set of structural metadata specifications, and a set of functions, named StructuredStream, that defines a mapping from nodes of a structure to segments of a stream. Consider the example of a journal paper as a digital object. In this case, the streams in the journal paper digital object are the text stream and the image streams. The set of structural metadata specifications represents the organizational structure of the journal paper. For example, it might contain the specifications for the title, each section, figures and captions, tables and captions, and specifications for the bibliography. The structured streams set specifies how the text and image components of the paper map to each item in the organizational structure of the paper. For example, it might specify the text stream that constitutes the title and the text and image streams that constitute a particular section.

A **hypertext** (Def. MI B.24 of Appendix B) is a triple composed of a structure; a set of contents that can include digital objects of a collection, all of their streams (and substreams) and all possible *restrictions* of the *Structured Stream* functions of digital objects; and a function that associates a node of the hypertext with the node content. Consider a hypertext generated by a set of digital articles on the Web, which are linked together via references and citations. The nodes of this hypertext would be all the articles, and all the SubStreams and the SubStructuredStreams within each of the articles, as defined by the author of an article. For example, a SubStream could be the stream of bits in an image or the sequence of characters in a paragraph or a word. Examples of StructuredStreams are sections, title, tables, etc. A hyperlink is a directed edge in the hypertext graph from one node to another. An example of an anchor (source node of a hyperlink) is a phrase, which is linked to a citation or an article elaborating on that phrase.

Finally, a DL (Def. MI B.2 of Appendix B) is a 4-tuple containing a repository; a set of metadata catalogs for all collections in the repository; a set of services containing at least services for indexing, searching, and browsing; and a society. Considering the Flickr[7] photo sharing Web application as an example of a DL, the components of this definition might be described as follows. The collections in Flickr's repository include the collection of images (different for each user or group), collection of user profiles, and the collection of group profiles. A metadata catalog associated with the image collection has a metadata record for each image, which includes information such as image title, description, tags, comments, and image notes (subimages and associated annotations). Services within Flickr include image management (adding, deleting, and other functions to manage and organize images in a user account), user management, indexing (image information), browsing, text-based search, image annotation, and tagging. Societies within Flickr include image owners, image commenters, group administrators, and group moderators. Thus, Flickr includes all the required components and can be considered a digital library.

---

7. http://flickr.com

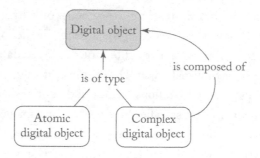

FIGURE 2.3: A concept map for complex object composition. (Source: [107])

2.3.1 COMPLEX OBJECTS

The notion of a complex object, defined by Kozievitch et al. [99, 107] (see also Chapter 1), can be considered as an addition to the original set of 5S definitions. Complex objects are single entities that are composed of multiple digital objects, each of which is an entity in and of itself [108, 113]. A complex digital object is a (simple) digital object or a recursive composition of other complex objects, as shown in Figure 2.3.

A complex digital object can be a digital object or an organization of other complex objects, therefore needing a structure to organize its components (see Def. 1.1 in Chapter 1). An example of a complex object is a dissertation, which is composed of chapters, figures, and tables, where each chapter, figure, and table is a digital object. A complex object is a simple digital object or a composition of other complex objects. The composition of its sub-parts (as seen in Figure 2.3) is represented by the component S.

2.4 FORMALIZATION AND APPROACH TO A DL WITH SUPERIMPOSED INFORMATION (SI-DL)

We extend the 5S minimal DL framework to include support for subdocuments, superimposed documents, and relevant services. In terms of content, we distinguish among three types of digital objects: 1) base document—information existing as whole documents for which subdocuments have been defined; 2) subdocument—part of a base document referenced by an address, which indicates a range or span in the base document; and 3) superimposed document—a document that consists of one or more subdocuments and other associated information. It is important to highlight the temporal ordering that exists among the aforementioned types of digital objects, as depicted in Figure 2.4. The ordering relationship is similar to the temporal dimension of digital objects described by Agosti and Ferro in their formal model of annotations [6]. The temporal ordering states that a base document exists before a subdocument might be (marked and) created in it. Furthermore, a

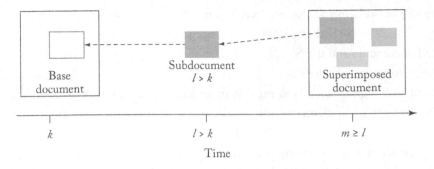

FIGURE 2.4: Temporal relationship among digital objects in an SI-DL.

subdocument exists before the creation of a superimposed document that uses this subdocument. This might be expressed by the following ordering:

$$t_{BD} < t_{sd} \leq t_{sidoc}, \quad \text{where:}$$

- t_{BD} represents the time of creation of a base document, BD;
- t_{sd} represents the time of creation of a subdocument, sd, in the base document BD;
- t_{sidoc} represents the time of creation of a superimposed document $sidoc$, which contains the subdocument, sd.

Base documents, subdocuments, and superimposed documents have all of the ordinary properties of a digital object as well, such as having metadata associated and being part of one or more collections. The content of each of these digital objects and their associated metadata can be browsed, indexed, and searched, as with any other digital object. In addition to existing services, we need a new service to deal with the referencing and presentation of a subdocument *in situ*. We refer to this browsing service as *view in context*. The view-in-context service enables a subdocument to be viewed in the original context of its containing base document.

We assume that subdocuments and all kinds of SI exist in the DL along with ordinary digital objects.[8] The activity of creation/composition is outside the scope of these definitions, just as the authoring of digital objects is generally supported by tools that are outside of the DL. Thus, creating a subdocument, annotating a subdocument or another digital object, and creating/composing a superimposed document, such as a concept map or a strand map, are all outside of the scope of our model. We are only concerned with how this information is represented in a DL and what

---

8. Ordinary digital objects need not be any of: a base document, a subdocument, or a superimposed document.

new services will be added to access, retrieve, and facilitate the viewing of information once it has been added to the DL. Note that specific superimposed applications are responsible for viewing superimposed documents and the SI-DL formalization is not concerned with those applications.[9]

We need to make a comment about *annotation* here. In the SI-DL metamodel, we treat a subdocument as a digital object and provide its definition. An annotation is an important part of an SI-DL, since it is supplemental information associated with a subdocument. However, an annotation might be associated with any kind of digital object and is not restricted to subdocuments. In the formal model of annotation, Agosti and Ferro [6] extensively explore and define the idea of annotation on digital content, of which the basic unit is a digital object. Thus, we do not also formally define annotation in our metamodel. Note that in an SI-DL, an annotation might be represented as a superimposed document consisting of text or other content comprising the annotation (or link to a digital object comprising the annotation) that references a subdocument or other document, i.e., the original material in a base document that is being annotated.

Table 2.1 provides examples of the 5 S's in a DL and in an SI-DL. The new concepts added to a DL are as shown in Figure 2.5. The figure also shows the connection between a superimposed document and a complex object. In the remaining part of this section, we formally define the components of an SI-DL.

2.4.1 5S EXTENSIONS

In this section, we define new concepts, which, along with the set of concepts in the 5S framework for minimal digital libraries and complex objects, are used to define and describe a DL with SI.

Base Document

A *base document* (BD) is a digital object for which a subdocument exists. Any digital object thus can become a BD, upon creation of the first subdocument. In Section 2.4, we described the temporal relationship among base documents, subdocuments, and superimposed documents. In the temporal relation, we represent the time of creation of a BD as t_{BD}. However, it is important to point out that a digital object becomes a BD only at t_{sd}. Before that time, it is considered as a regular digital object (as defined in the 5S framework).

Presentation Specification, Address, and Subdocument

In this section, we define all concepts associated with a subdocument. We build upon the definition of a substream in the 5S framework and the definition of a segment in the formal annotation model [6], to define a subdocument. According to Gonçalves et al., a substream is associated with a pair

---

9. In a similar way, we are not concerned about display of base documents.

TABLE 2.1: Examples of the 5Ss in a DL and in an SI-DL.

Ss	Examples	Objectives	Examples in an SI-DL
Streams	Text, video, audio, and image	Describes properties of the DL content such as encoding and language for textual material or particular forms of multimedia data	(Multimedia) base document, superimposed document, subdocument, metadata about each of the aforementioned documents
Structures	Collection, catalog, hypertext, document, and metadata	Specifies organizational aspects of the DL content	Structure of a superimposed document, structure of metadata formats, extended hypertext defined by links between a superimposed document and the subdocuments that it contains, and between a subdocument and the base document of which it is a part
Spaces	Measurable, topological, vector, and probabilistic	Defines logical and presentational views of several DL components	Span of a subdocument in a base document, view (display) of a subdocument in the context of its containing base document
Scenarios	Creating, searching, browsing, indexing, annotating, and recommending	Details the behavior of DL services	Traditional DL services acting upon base documents, subdocuments, and superimposed documents. Also, view in context
Societies	Service managers, learners, and teachers	Defines managers, responsible for running DL services; actors, that use those services; and relationships among them	Creator of subdocuments and superimposed documents, annotator, user of subdocuments, and a DL administrator

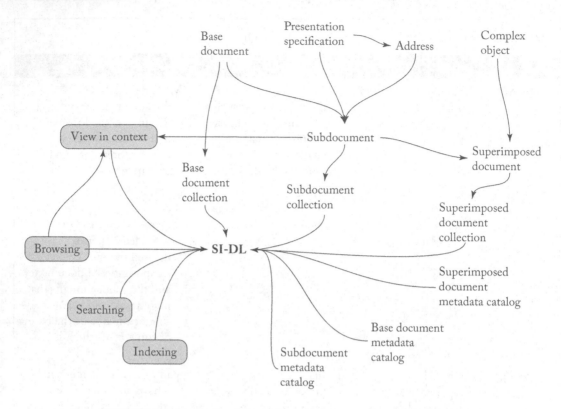

FIGURE 2.5: Definitional dependencies among concepts in an SI-DL.

of natural numbers (a, b), $a < b$, corresponding to a contiguous subsequence $[S_a, S_b]$ of stream S. Or, we can say $sm_t[i, j] = \langle a_0, a_1, \ldots, a_n \rangle$, $0 \le i \le j \le n$ is a substream or segment of stream S. According to Agosti and Ferro, given a stream sm: $I = \{1, 2, \ldots, n\} \to \Sigma$, where Σ is the alphabet of symbols and $n \in N$, $sm \in SM$, a segment is a pair: $st_{sm} = (a, b)$ such that $1 \le a \le b \le n$, where $a, b \in N$.

In addition to getting the content of the BD that comprises the subdocument, we need to retain the BD context of the subdocument (to allow tools to view or present it *in situ*). We do so by extending the aforementioned definitions of substream and segment to include *presentation specification* and *address*. Also, we store other associated information with a subdocument including properties (such as its creator and a timestamp of its creation) and semantic attributes (such as annotations and tags) as part of promoting the subdocument to be a first-class concept within a DL.

A presentation specification provides information about how a subdocument was defined in a BD. This notion is borrowed from the hypertext/hypermedia world, where it refers to the runtime behavior of information units presented to the user [78, 80]. In the hypertext/hypermedia literature, presentation specification refers to the encoding information and the mechanism that is used to present a component (or network of components) to the user. A software application/tool uses the presentation specification to display the contents of a digital object. A presentation specification is a descriptive metadata specification conforming to a presentation-based metadata format. A presentation specification is used to specify how the content in a digital object translates into a particular view/presentation. A presentation specification includes information such as the content type of the BD (text, image, audio, video, etc.), the format of the BD (.PDF, .DOC, .JPEG, .AVI, etc.), and the specific software tool used to view/present the BD (Adobe Acrobat™, Microsoft Word™, Microsoft Image Viewer™, etc.), used when the subdocument was created.

Definition 2.1 A **presentation specification**, $PS = (G_{PS}, \mathcal{R}_{PS} \cup \mathcal{L}_{PS} \cup \mathcal{P}_{PS}, \mathcal{F}_{PS})$ *conforms with* a presentation-based metadata format $MF_{PS} = (V_{MF_{PS}}, \text{def}_{MF_{PS}})$ with the following constraints:

1. $V_{MF_{PS}} = \{\mathcal{R}_{PS1}, \mathcal{R}_{PS2}, \ldots, \mathcal{R}_{PSk}\} \subset 2^{\mathcal{R}_{PS}}_{MF}$ is a family of subsets of the resource labels $\mathcal{R}_{MF_{PS}}$

2. $\text{def}_{MF_{PS}} : V_{MF_{PS}} \times \mathcal{P}_{MF_{PS}} \to V_{MF_{PS}} \cup D_{\mathcal{L}_{MF_{PS}}}$ is a property definition function, where:
    - $\mathcal{P}_{MF_{PS}}$ represents sets of labels for properties;
    - $V_{MF_{PS}}$ represents the nodes of a graph structure;
    - $D_{\mathcal{L}_{MF_{PS}}}$ is the set of domains that make up the set of literals $\mathcal{L}_{MF_{PS}}$.

3. $\mathcal{R}_{PS} \subseteq \mathcal{R}_{MF_{PS}}$,

4. $\mathcal{L}_{PS} \subseteq \mathcal{L}_{MF_{PS}}$,

5. $\mathcal{P}_{PS} \subseteq \mathcal{P}_{MF_{PS}}$, and

6. for every statement $st = (r, p, l)$ derived from PS, $r \in \mathcal{R}_k$ for some $\mathcal{R}_k \in V_{MF_{PS}}$ and $p \in \mathcal{P}_{PS}$ implies

$$l \in \text{def}_{MF_{PS}}(\mathcal{R}_k, p).$$

Examples of resources could be academic papers, images, software applications, etc. Examples of properties include format, content type, software application to view, etc. Consider the example shown in Figure 2.6. Here the object "Shield Darter" is an "image" of "JPEG" format and makes use of the "Java image viewer" software application. Another example is from the Dublin Core metadata format. For any set of labels $\mathcal{R}$ for resources, the Dublin Core metadata format defines that $\text{def}_{DC}(\mathcal{R}, \text{'format'}) = String$ and $\text{def}_{DC}(\mathcal{R}, \text{'format.mimetype'}) = MIME$ where $MIME$ is a finite set of labels for Resources corresponding to MIME types.

A presentation specification of a subdocument consists of all information required to interpret the address of the span/region of the subdocument within the BD. The address is used by an appropriate software application to navigate to and view the subdocument in the context of its

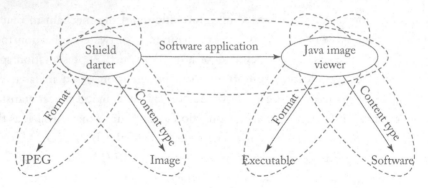

FIGURE 2.6: Example of a presentation specification.

originating BD. Consider the example of an academic paper, which might have mixed content including text and images. It could be a PDF document presented/viewed using Adobe Acrobat. The address of a segment or substream in this case might be different than if the same content were in a .DOC document presented/viewed using Microsoft Word, since the navigation/addressing schemes within each of these tools is different. Adobe Acrobat uses a word-based scheme whereas Microsoft Word uses a character-based scheme. Another example is the address of a subdocument within an image document (or a subimage), which might vary depending on the format, resolution, and software used to view/present the image. Archer et al. expanded upon previous SI work to include subdocuments in the DSpace[10] DL software [9]. They implemented a feature for Microsoft Word (and OpenOffice) that allows for creation of subdocuments, which have been stored in an instance of the Fedora DL.[11] Also, it accepts an address for a subdocument with a Microsoft Word (and OpenOffice) base document and displays it highlighted.

Definition 2.2   Given BD, a *subdocument sd* is a digital object with the following extensions and constraints:

- sd is a *digital object* $= (h, SM, ST, StrStreams, PS, addr)$, where;
    1. $h \in H$, where H is a set of universally unique handles (labels);
    2. $SM_{sd} = \{sm_{sd}[i, j]\} \in SM$, where $sm_{sd}[i, j] = \langle a_i, \ldots, a_j \rangle, 0 \leq i \leq j \leq n$. $sm_{sd}[i, j]$ refers to substreams of a BD.
    3. $ST = \{st_1, st_2, \ldots, st_m\}$ is a set of structural metadata specifications associated with the BD;

---

10. http://www.dspace.org/
11. http://fedora-commons.org/

4. $StrStreams = \{st D_1, st D_2, \ldots, st D_m\}$ is a set of StructuredStream functions defined from the BD substreams in the SM_{sd} set (the second component) of the subdocument and from the structures in the ST set (the third component).

5. PS is a *presentation specification*.

6. $addr$ is the function from the SM_{sd} set (the second component) of the subdocument and from the presentation specification PS of the BD.

Note that the subdocument contains the structures and the contiguous streams of its parent BD that exist within the span defined by the address of the subdocument. It inherits all the descriptive and structural metadata specifications associated with the span defined by the address. Figure 2.7 shows an example of a subdocument with its components, including the substreams and substructures associated with it, as inherited from the containing base document. The left part of the figure shows the BD, with a handle (h_{BD}), a title (`enhance_cmaps.pdf`), and a highlighted subdocument, which is associated with a presentation specification (PS). PS might contain presentation information, such as content-type, format, and software application. The right part of the figure shows details of components of a subdocument (sd), including a handle (h_{sd}), a substream ($sm_{sd}[i,j]$), a substructure (st_{sd}), and an address ($addr$). $sm_{sd}[i,j]$ is the sequence of characters in the sd, where i and j indicate the character numbers of the first and the last character of that substream within BD. In some cases,

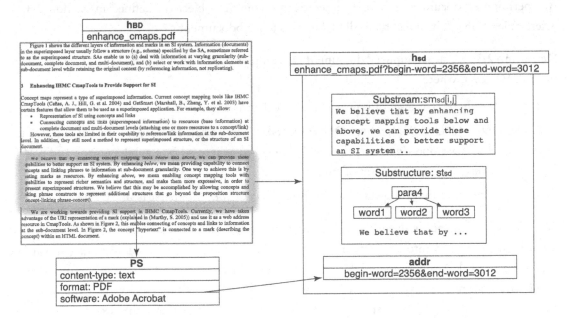

FIGURE 2.7: Example of a subdocument and its components.

there might be multiple substreams, such as in a subdocument that includes text and images. st_{sd} shows the mapping between the structural metadata specification of BD and the streams within sd. $addr$ indicates pointers to the beginning and ending of sd, considering the PS of BD.

Since a subdocument is a digital object, it has its own metadata. This could include properties of subdocument creation such as information about the subdocument creator, the timestamp of creation, etc. Also, as with an ordinary digital object, a subdocument could be associated with semantic information such as annotations and tags. Like other digital objects, a subdocument may have many manifestations. For example, consider a subdocument within a text-based PDF document. One manifestation of the subdocument might be the textual excerpt of the subdocument. Another might be an image transformation of a portion of the base PDF document with the highlighted subdocument.

At this point, it is important to describe the relationship between a mark, as defined in the SI literature (Section 2.2.1), and a subdocument. A mark is a reference to a subdocument. Considering the aforementioned definition, a mark necessarily consists of h, PS, and $addr$. In the SI literature, text-based marks have been known to store the *excerpt*, which is the content of the marked region (or subdocument). However, an excerpt is not necessary to render a mark or reference the marked region (subdocument), and need not be stored.

Superimposed Document

A superimposed document can be represented as a complex object (as defined in Section 2.3.1), where at least one of its constituent digital objects is a subdocument.

Definition 2.3   A **superimposed document** is a complex digital object, defined as a tuple $sidoc = (h, SCDO, ST)$, where

1. $h \in H$, where H is a set of universally unique handles (labels);

2. $SCDO = \{DO \cup SM\}$, where $DO = \{do_1, do_2, \ldots, do_n\}$, and do_i is a digital object, such that $\exists$ at least one $do_i = sd$, for $i = 1, 2, \cdots, n$, where sd is a subdocument and $SM = \{sm_a, sm_b, \ldots, sm_z\}$ is a set of streams;

3. S is a structure that composes the complex object $sidoc$ into its parts in $SCDO$.

This is consistent with earlier work in SI, where the references to subdocuments (i.e., marks) could be incorporated into a variety of superimposed documents structured according to various data models [141]. A superimposed document can be of different types. For example, it may consist of subdocument references (i.e., marks) interspersed with other digital content, such as in a textual document that has citations to specific portions of other documents. Another example is a time-ordered arrangement of audio/video clips merged with textual content from webpages [147]. A concept map [150] and a strandmap [43], where the resources point to subdocuments, are other examples.

2.4.2 COLLECTIONS AND CATALOGS

An important component of a DL with SI support is the ability to deal with various (BD, subdocument, and superimposed document) collections and corresponding metadata catalogs. Here, we define collections and catalogs for the three types of digital objects that we have introduced.

Definition 2.4   A **base document collection** $C_{BD} = \{bd_1, bd_2, \ldots, bd_l\}$ is a set of base documents.

Definition 2.5   A **subdocument collection** $C_{sd} = \{sd_1, sd_2, \ldots, sd_m\}$ is a set of subdocuments.

Definition 2.6   A **superimposed document collection** $C_{sidoc} = \{sidoc_1, sidoc_2, \ldots, sidoc_n\}$ is a set of superimposed documents.

Definition 2.7   Let C_{BD} be a collection of l base documents, with l handles in H, such that there is a unique handle for each BD in C_{BD}. A **base document metadata catalog** $DM_{C_{BD}}$ for C_{BD} is a set of pairs $\{(h, \{dm_{BD_1}, \ldots, dm_{BD_{l_h}}\})\}$, where $h \in H$ and the dm_{BD_i} are descriptive metadata specifications for BD.

Definition 2.8   Let C_{sd} be a collection of m subdocuments, with m handles in H, such that there is a unique handle for each subdocument in C_{sd}. A **subdocument metadata catalog** $DM_{C_{sd}}$ for C_{sd} is a set of pairs $\{(h, \{dm_{sd_1}, \ldots, dm_{sd_{m_{h_{sd}}}}\})\}$, where $h_{sd} \in H_{sd}$ and the dm_{sd_i} are descriptive metadata specifications for the subdocument, sd.

Definition 2.9   Let C_{sidoc} be a collection of n superimposed documents, with n handles in H, such that there is a unique handle for each superimposed document in C_{sidoc}. A **superimposed document metadata catalog** $DM_{C_{sidoc}}$ for C_{sidoc} is a set of pairs $\{(h, \{dm_{sidoc_1}, \ldots, dm_{sidoc_{n_h}}\})\}$, where $h \in H$ and the dm_{sidoc_i} are descriptive metadata specifications for the superimposed document, $sidoc$.

2.4.3 SERVICES

In an SI-DL, traditional services such as browsing, indexing, and searching now act upon different types of digital objects including BDs, subdocuments, and superimposed documents, as well as metadata associated with each of these. For example, using the search service on subdocuments, the query specification can contain subdocument-related information and the results can include subdocuments. In addition, advanced searches on components of superimposed documents and BDs might be possible. For example, one could retrieve all subdocuments within a particular base document. Another example is to retrieve all BDs that contain subdocuments, which are referenced in a particular superimposed document.

In addition to traditional DL services, we add a new service, *view in context*, to the DL to support access for viewing/presentation of subdocuments in the context of their parent BD. This can be considered an extension of the browsing services as defined in the 5S framework, which acts upon the extended hypertext that now includes subdocuments and links between BDs and subdocuments as well as those between superimposed documents and subdocuments. This creates new referential hyperlinks between a subdocument and its parent BD as well as those between a superimposed document and its constituent subdocuments. In addition, we now need to make use of services, for example plugins, that can be invoked by the DL, based on the presentation specification of the BD which contains a subdocument.

Definition 2.10   A *view-in-context service* is a set of scenarios $\{sc_1, \ldots, sc_n\}$ over an extended hypertext where events are defined by edges of the hypertext graph (V_{H_E}, E_{H_E}), where V_{H_E} includes the union of BDs, subdocuments, and superimposed documents and E_{H_E} includes the links between a subdocument and BD, such that the subdocument–BD link events e_i are associated with a function $ViewInContext : V_{H_E} \times E_{H_E} \rightarrow Contents$, which, given a subdocument, instantiates the service that is required to present/view the BD (facilitated through information in the presentation specification, PS), retrieves the content of the base document, and uses the aforementioned service for the base document's presentation with the subdocument highlighted within the BD, i.e.,

$$ViewInContext(v_{k_{sd}}, e_{k_i}) = \mathcal{P}(v_{t_{sd}}) \quad \text{for } e_{k_l} = (v_{k_{sd}}, v_{t_{sd}}) \in E_{H_E}.$$

Here, $v_{k_{sd}}$ is a reference to the subdocument in a superimposed document and $v_{t_{sd}}$ is a reference to the subdocument in its original context, or in its parent BD.

An example of the view-in-context service is shown in Figure 2.8. Here, the subdocument, which is used in a superimposed document (e.g., a concept map), is created in a base document (i.e., a Microsoft Word document), with a plugin that allows subdocument creation and viewing. On instantiating the view-in-context service from this subdocument, an instance of Microsoft Word (an application to work with the BD) is launched, the base document containing the subdocument is opened and presented in the Microsoft Word application, and the subdocument is highlighted in this BD.

When subdocuments are part of a DL, we might consider extracting collections of subdocuments, generated from search results, browse criteria, etc. In such cases, it might be useful to have a view-in-context service, where a subdocument might be viewed in context of a superimposed document, of which it is a part. For example, consider the subdocument presented in Figure 2.8. When this subdocument is presented as part of a search result set, a user might want to view the superimposed documents, where this subdocument is used. Upon activating the view in context of

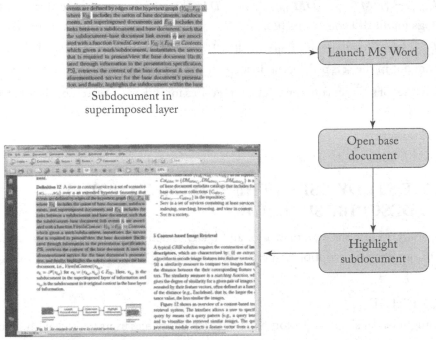

FIGURE 2.8: An example of the view-in-context service.

superimposed document, the DL might display a concept map, highlighting a resource (pointing to the subdocument) attached to a concept.

2.4.4 SI-DL

A DL with SI, or an SI-DL, is a DL that manages a repository of collections of base documents, subdocuments, and superimposed documents; and is associated with services, including indexing, searching, browsing, and view in context.

Definition 2.11 A *SI supported DL* is a 4-tuple $(\mathcal{R}, DM, Serv, Soc)$, where

- $\mathcal{R}$ is a repository;

- $DM = DM_{BD} \cup DM_{sd} \cup DM_{sidoc} \cup DM_{do}$;

- $DM_{BD} = \{DM_{BD_{C_1}}, DM_{BD_{C_2}}, \ldots, DM_{BD_{C_L}}\}$ is a set of BD metadata catalogs for all BD collections $\{C_{BD_1}, C_{BD_2}, \ldots, C_{BD_L}\}$ in the repository;

- $DM_{sd} = \{DM_{sd_{C_1}}, DM_{sd_{C_2}}, \ldots, DM_{sd_{C_M}}\}$ is a set of subdocument metadata catalogs for all subdocument collections $\{C_{sd_1}, C_{sd_2}, \ldots, C_{sd_M}\}$ in the repository;

- $DM_{sidoc} = \{DM_{sidoc_{C_1}}, DM_{sidoc_{C_2}}, \ldots, DM_{sidoc_{C_N}}\}$ is a set of base document metadata catalogs for all BD collections $\{C_{sidoc_1}, C_{sidoc_2}, \ldots, C_{sidoc_N}\}$ in the repository;

- DM_{do} is a set of metadata catalogs for all collections $\{C_{do_1}, C_{do_2}, \ldots, C_{do_K}\}$ in the repository, that are not in the sets of BD, subdocument, and superimposed document collections;

- $Serv$ is a set of services containing at least services for indexing, searching, browsing, and view in context;

- Soc is a society.

2.5 CASE STUDY: USING THE SI-DL METAMODEL TO DESCRIBE SUPERIDR

In this case study, we use the metamodel for an SI-DL to define and analyze content and behavior of SuperIDR, an image description and retrieval application [146, 148, 149].

2.5.1 SUPERIDR

SuperIDR might be considered a prototype SI-DL, which enables users to work with subimages and associated information. It was designed and developed with the aim of supporting scholarly tasks that involve working with subimages. In fisheries sciences people work with subimages to identify species of fish [146, 148]. The SuperIDR version described in this section was customized to include images, descriptions, and taxonomical information for species of freshwater fish of Virginia [85]. The use of subimages might apply to other domains as well, which have tasks that involve working with images with a significant number of details, such as analyzing paintings in art history, reviewing plans in architecture, or studying X-rays of the human body in medicine. In another customization of SuperIDR, it was seeded with parasite images and information to evaluate its applicability in the Zooparasitology domain [106].

SuperIDR brings together SI and *content-based image retrieval* (CBIR) in a personal image-based DL environment. It incorporates the idea of SI and working with parts of images *in situ*, to enable users to select, annotate, explore, retrieve, and compare parts of images in the context of the original image and other associated data. SuperIDR uses CBIR to index and retrieve the visual content of images and subimages. In addition to providing traditional DL services, such as browsing, searching, and indexing, the DL environment is also responsible for managing images, subimages, and all other associated data (such as descriptions, metadata about images, subimages, etc.).

Figure 2.9 outlines the software architecture of SuperIDR. Data collections consist of images, subimages (derived from images), textual descriptions, annotations, taxonomical classification data that might be used for browsing only (such as family- or genera-level images and information), log

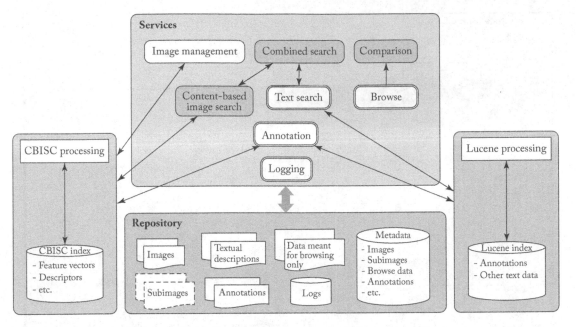

FIGURE 2.9: Software architecture of SuperIDR shows a repository with collections and services. The CBISC and Lucene components are used to index and retrieve image and text data, respectively.

data, and metadata related to all of the aforementioned data. There are three kinds of services in SuperIDR:

- Traditional DL services that have not changed with the addition of subimages—image management.

- Traditional DL services that now work with subimages and related data—browse, text search, annotation, and logging.

- New DL services that work with subimages and related data—browsing subimages and associated annotations, content-based image search, combined search, and comparison.

SuperIDR uses the Content-Based Image Search Component, CBISC, for indexing and retrieving the visual content of images and subimages. CBISC is an Open Archives Initiative (OAI)-compliant component that provides an easy-to-install search engine to query images by content [219]. Lucene,[12] an open-source text retrieval package, is responsible for full-text and field-wise

---

12. http://lucene.apache.org/

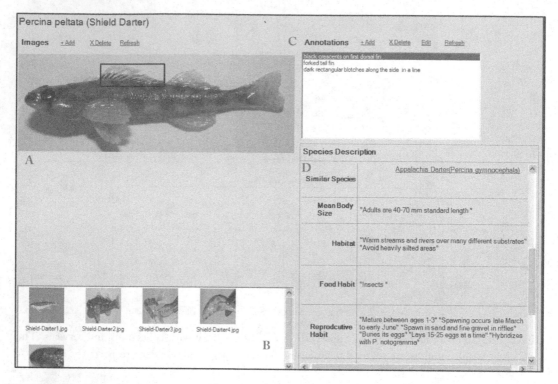

FIGURE 2.10: Species description interface in SuperIDR: A) focus image, showing marked region associated with a selected annotation; B) list of images in the species; C) annotation menu and list of annotations on the focus image; and D) physical description, habitat, and other information about the species.

indexing and search of all text data in the SuperIDR collections, including textual description (of images) and annotations.

We now briefly describe the services of SuperIDR. For further details on these services and on SuperIDR, the reader is referred to Chapter 5 of Uma Murthy's Ph.D. dissertation [146].

Annotation. The annotation service enables a user to select subimages within images and associate them with text annotations. Also, a user can edit and delete annotations.

Image management. A user can add images to and delete (user-added) images from a species using the image management service.

Text search. SuperIDR uses the full-text and/or field-wise search in the Lucene component to match keywords entered by the user against one of the following: 1) annotations; 2) species descriptions; or 3) both—annotations and species descriptions. Depending on the user's selection, a separate, ranked list of results is processed and displayed for species descriptions (Figure 2.11-B) and for annotations (Figure 2.11-A).

Content-based image search. The content-based image search service takes as input a query, which is either an image or a subimage. It then sends this query to CBISC, which in turn matches the visual content of this query image or subimage against the visual content of all images and subimages in the CBISC index. A ranked list of results is produced, which could contain images and/or subimages. Search results are displayed separately for images and subimages.

Combined search. The purpose of including a combined search service is to give the user an idea of how image and text content might be combined in search, especially focusing on how subimages might be combined with text content. As input the combined search service takes a query, which is a combination of an image or subimage and keywords. In addition, the user can specify an image-weight and a text-weight, which indicate the relative importance given by the user to each component (image and text) of the query. The text and image search results are combined[13] to produce a single list for each of species/images and of annotations/subimages. The combined search results are displayed similar to text search results, as shown in Figure 2.11-A,B.

Browse. The browse service enables multiple ways of browsing through species images, descriptions, subimages, and annotations, including:

- browsing through images and description of a species;
- browsing through annotations, and for each image, viewing the associated subimage in the context of its base image;
- browsing through the taxonomical classification, including families, genera, and species of fish using: 1) column-wise organization or 2) tree-based organization; and
- browsing through a digital version of the identification key guide of freshwater fish of Virginia [85].

Comparison. The comparison service is a special case of the browsing service. It enables a user to view two images side-by-side. A user is able to choose from images of the same or different species. While viewing the images side-by-side, a user can browse through annotations and view the associated subimages in the context of their base images. The goal of the comparison service is to enable the user to manually analyze two images side by side.

Logging. The logging service is used to log all user interactions with the tool.

---

13. The combination method is explained in [146].

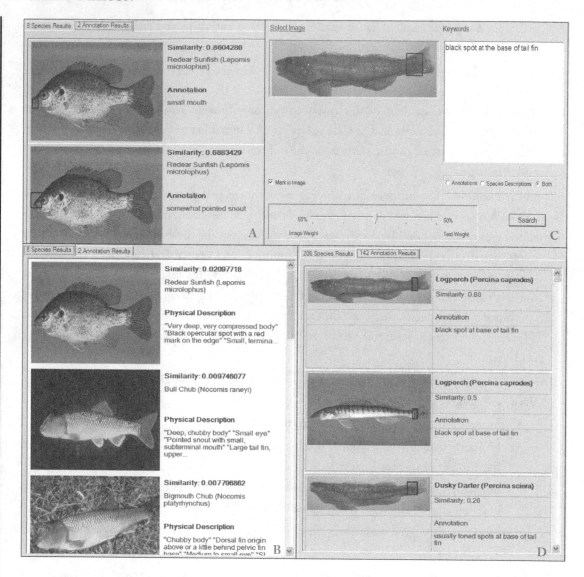

FIGURE 2.11: Search in SuperIDR: A) annotation search results for the text query—"red mark" "small mouth" "pointed snout" "no spots"; B) species description results for the same query; C) combined search query interface; and D) annotation/subimage combined search results.

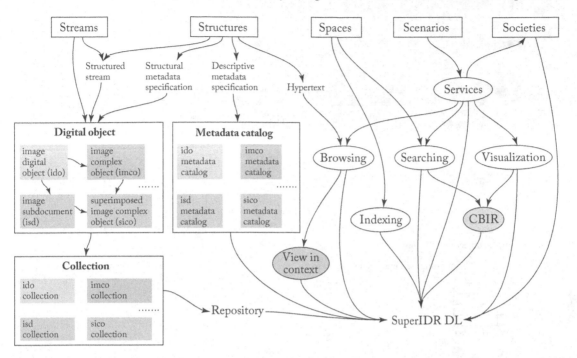

FIGURE 2.12: Definitional dependencies among concepts in an SuperIDR DL, showing connections among concepts in the 5S framework and the extensions defined.

2.5.2   ANALYZING AND DESCRIBING SUPERIDR

SuperIDR might be considered to be an extension of the minimal digital library as defined in the 5S framework. Figure 2.12 shows the components of SuperIDR. We extended the definition of a digital object to include an image digital object, a subimage (or image subdocument), an image complex object, and a superimposed image complex object. In addition, SuperIDR has other digital objects, such as annotation and image complex object description. These conform to the digital object definition as mentioned in the 5S framework. Each of the aforementioned digital objects belongs to respective collections and is associated with a metadata catalog. In addition, SuperIDR has the view-in-context and CBIR services. The rest of this section describes and analyzes the components of SuperIDR.[14]

Figure 2.13 shows the information components within SuperIDR and relationships among them. Here, an image complex object consists of (at least) a description and a collection of image

---

14. Images and CBIR services are important components of SuperIDR. Definitions of these concepts are presented in Chapter 1 of the fourth book of this series.

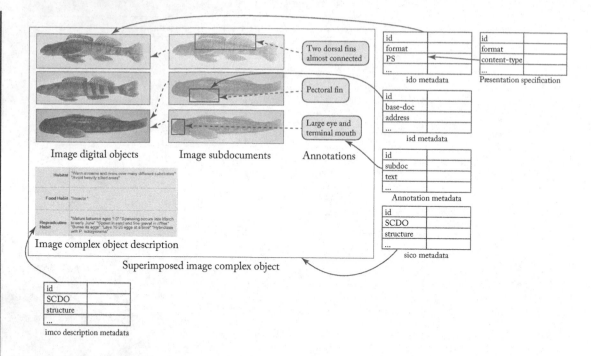

FIGURE 2.13: A superimposed image complex object, its components, associated metadata, and relationships among all of the above.

digital objects (or, images). When at least one of the image digital obejcts is marked up and annotated, an image subdocument (or a subimage) is created and added to the image complex object. Also, the associated annotation object is added to the image complex object. The addition of an image subdocument changes the image complex object into a superimposed image complex object. Each of the aforementioned digital objects—image digital object, image subdocument, annotation, image complex object description, and image complex object—has an associated metadata record. Each type of digital object is also part of a collection of the same type. For the remainder of this section, we use the notation mentioned in Table 2.2 to refer to each of these digital objects. In the case of SuperIDR customized for fish data (as discussed in [146]), the aforementioned digital objects and associated metadata correspond to fish-related data, as mentioned in Table 2.2. An image complex object in this case is a species. When SuperIDR is customized to other, similar, image-based domains, such as species of trees with accompanying images and descriptions and genres of paintings that include images and descriptions, an image complex object might take other forms.

Note that an image digital object and an image complex object are candidate BDs. When an image subdocument is created on an image digital object, the image digital object becomes a

TABLE 2.2: Digital objects in SuperIDR, notations used in the case study, and examples from SuperIDR customized for fish-related data

Digital object	Notation	Example from SuperIDR customized for fish-related data
Image complex object	*imco*	A fish species, consisting of a description and a set of images
Image complex object description	*desc*	Description of a fish species, including details, such as physical description, mean size, and habitat
Image digital object	*ido*	Fish image, such as an image of a trout
Image subdocument	*isd*	Part of a fish image, such as a fin, mouth, or tail
Annotation	*ann*	Textual description of a part, such as large mouth or orange dorsal fin
Superimposed image complex object	*sico*	A fish species, consisting of a description, a set of images, with one or more marked-up images, and annotations associated with marked-up regions in images
BD	*bd*	An image digital object before it has been marked up or a species before it contains a marked-up image and associated annotations

BD. Similarly, at first, an image complex object consists of a description and a set of images. When an image subdocument is created (and hence, an associated annotation) in at least one of the image digital objects of an image complex object, this image complex object becomes a superimposed image complex object. Thus, a single digital object (in this case, an image or an image complex object) might play multiple roles and, as a result, might be part of multiple digital object collections.

We can define a SuperIDR DL as a 4-tuple,

$$SuperIDR\_DL = (SuperIDR\_\mathcal{R}, SuperIDR\_DM, SuperIDR\_Serv, SuperIDR\_Soc),$$

where:

- $SuperIDR\_\mathcal{R}$ is a repository, having collections C_{ido}, C_{isd}, C_{ann}, C_{desc}, C_{imco}, C_{sico}, and C_{bd}, where:
  - C_{ido} is a collection of image digital objects,
  - C_{isd} is a collection of image subdocuments,
  - C_{ann} is a collection of annotations,
  - C_{desc} is a collection of image complex object descriptions,

- C_{imco} is a collection of image complex objects,
- C_{sico} is a collection of superimposed image complex objects, and
- C_{bd} is a collection of BDs.

- $SuperIDR\_DM = \{DM_{ido}, DM_{isd}, DM_{ann}, DM_{desc}, DM_{imco}, DM_{sico}, DM_{bd}\}$ is a set of descriptive metadata specifications, where:
    - DM_{ido} is a metadata catalog for the collection of image digital objects,
    - DM_{isd} is a metadata catalog for the collection of image subdocuments,
    - DM_{ann} is a metadata catalog for the collection of annotations,
    - DM_{desc} is a metadata catalog for the collection of image complex object descriptions,
    - DM_{imco} is a metadata catalog for the collection of image complex objects,
    - DM_{sico} is metadata catalog for the a collection of superimposed image complex objects, and
    - DM_{bd} is a metadata catalog for the collection of BDs.

- $SuperIDR\_Serv$ is a set of services containing services for indexing, searching, browsing, CBIR, and view in context;

- $SuperIDR\_Soc$ of $SuperIDR\_DL$ is a society including {Patron, Student, Faculty, Researchers, Practitioner, Amateur, SuperIDR_Admin, . . . }.

We now describe the contents of some of these components further. The set of streams in $SuperIDR\_DL$ consists of image and text streams. The union set of handles of various digital objects in collections C_{ido}, C_{isd}, C_{ann}, C_{desc}, C_{imco}, C_{sico}, and C_{bd} will compose $SuperIDR\_DL_{IDs}$, the set of handles in $SuperIDR\_DL$. Examples of content of each metadata specification are described here.

1. $DM_{ido} = \{\text{'id'}, \text{'image name'}, \text{'format'}, \text{'size'}, \text{'location'}, . . . \}$;
2. $DM_{desc} = \{\text{'id'}, \text{'author'}, \text{'source'}, ...\}$;
3. $DM_{imco} = \{\text{'id'}, \text{'author'}, \text{'structure'}, . . . \}$;
4. $DM_{bd} = \{\text{'id'}, \text{'name'}, \text{'format'}, \text{'size'}, . . . \}$;
5. $DM_{isd} = \{\text{'id'}, \text{'base document'}, \text{'address'}, \text{'presentation\_specification'}, . . . \}$;
6. $DM_{ann} = \{\text{'id'}, \text{'subdocument'}, \text{'text'}, . . . \}$;
7. $DM_{sico} = \{\text{'id'}, \text{'author'}, \text{'structure'}, . . . \}$.

Items 4, 5, and 6 are added to $SuperIDR\_DL$, when at least one of the images within the image complex object is marked and annotated. Then, the image complex object is modified into a superimposed image complex object as it now contains subdocuments.

Using $SuperIDR\_DL$, we will formally describe two scenarios, each of which involves one or more services of the extensions mentioned in this paper.

1. *AddImageSubdocumentAndAnnotation*

   Informal description: This scenario is part of creating and adding an annotation into DL-SuperIDR. We focus on what happens in a DLSuperIDR before, during, and after a subdocument is created. Given an image, which is associated with an image complex object, an address referencing a part of the image, and an associated text annotation, a subdocument and an annotation object are created. In addition, the newly created subdocument and annotation are added to the species complex object. If this is the first subdocument added to a species, it changes from being an image complex object to a superimposed image complex object.

   Goal: Given an image, which is part of an image complex object, an address of a part of that image, and an associated text annotation, create a subdocument and annotation object and add those to the aforementioned image complex object. This adds a new subdocument to the $DLSuperIDR$ and makes the image complex object a superimposed image complex object.

   Scenario:

   $$\langle e_1 : p = AddImageSubdocumentAndAnnotation(ido_j, imco_i, ps_k, addr_l, ann_m),$$

   $$e_2 : p = response(sico_i, isd_o)\rangle,$$

   where the following constraints apply:

   (a) ido_j is an image digital object, such that $ido_j \in imco_i$ and $ido_j \in C_{ido}$ and $imco_i \in C_{imco}$, where $imco_i$ is an image complex object that consists of images and species descriptions, C_{ido} is a collection of image digital objects in $SuperIDR\_DL$, and C_{imco} is a collection of image complex objects in $SuperIDR\_DL$;

   (b) $addr_l$ is an address, specifying a region/span within the image digital object ido_j, and is associated with a presentation specification ps_k.

   (c) ann_m is an annotation digital object, such that $ann_m \in sico'_i$ and $ann_m \in C_{ann}$, where C_{ann} is a collection of annotations in $SuperIDR\_DL$;

   (d) isd_o is a newly created subdocument, such that $isd_o \in sico'_i$ and $isd_o \in C_{isd}$, where C_{isd} is a collection of image subdocuments in $SuperIDR\_DL$;

   (e) $imco_i$ is modified into $sico'_i$, a superimposed image complex object, such that ido_j and other digital objects in $imco_i$ are now in $sico'_i$, and $sico'_i \in C_s ico$, where $C_s ico$ is a collection of superimposed image complex objects in $SuperIDR\_DL$;

(f) $C'_{imco} = C_{imco} - imco_i$, where C'_{imco} is the modified collection of image complex objects in $SuperIDR\_DL$, which does not contain the image complex object, $imco_i$.

2. *DisplayImageSubdocumentList*

Informal description: This scenario might take place in cases of browsing search results that include image subdocuments and associated information as result items (see Figure 2.11), or in cases of browsing through annotations associated with image subdocuments within an image complex object (see Figure 2.10). Given a list of image subdocuments and associated information, clicking on an image subdocument in that list will cause the system to display the image subdocument in its original context or the context of its containing BD. In a sense, a hyperlink is being traversed from the subdocument in the list (superimposed layer) to the subdocument in its original context (base layer).

Goal: Given a list of image subdocuments, display them in the context of the original BD.

Scenario:

$$\langle e_1 : p = DisplayImageSubdocumentList(isd_1, isd_2, \dots, isd_n),$$

$$e_2 : p = response(\mathcal{P}(v_{t_{isd_1}}), \mathcal{P}(v_{t_{isd_2}}), \dots, \mathcal{P}(v_{t_{isd_n}}))\rangle,$$

such that $\mathcal{P}(v_{t_{isd_i}})$, $1 \leq i \leq n$ is the response to the service $ViewInContext(v_{k_{isd_i}}, e_{k_i})$, with the following constraints:

(a) isd_i, $1 \leq i \leq n$ are image subdocuments;

(b) $e_{k_i} = (v_{k_{isd_i}}, v_{t_{isd_i}}) \in E_{H_E}$, where E_{H_E} is the extended hypertext formed by the network of image BDs, image subdocuments, and superimposed image complex objects;

(c) $v_{k_{isd_i}}$ is a reference of the image subdocument in the superimposed image complex object; and

(d) $v_{t_{isd_i}}$ is the image subdocument in its original context of its containing parent image digital object.

2.6 SUMMARY

We developed the metamodel presented in this chapter to abstract and model the data and services in an SI-DL and to formally define the components of an SI-DL. The SI-DL metamodel builds upon the 5S framework for minimal digital libraries to provide support for working with subdocuments. The main additions to a minimal DL are the notions of a subdocument, a BD, a superimposed document, and a view-in-context service. In essence, by treating a subdocument as a first-class object in a DL, we are now able to organize, index, search, browse, view, and use subdocuments.

We verified the descriptive power of an SI-DL through a case study, where we used the SI-DL metamodel to describe SuperIDR, an image description and retrieval application.

2.7 EXERCISES AND PROJECTS

2.1 Pick your favorite SI-related DL. Identify 3 different types of objects that contain subdocuments that are important in that DL.

2.2 For each type of object mentioned previously, identify possible services and users. How can subdocuments help different users to have different views/layers of information?

2.3 What is an example of the use of subdocuments that is distinct from annotation?

2.4 Describe the components of a subdocument on a video in YouTube, considering the definition of a subdocument presented in this chapter. Note that there are at least three streams involved in this subdocument—a space-based image stream, a time-based audio stream, and a time-based video frame. List/describe associated metadata and other digital objects associated with this subdocument.

2.5 Map subdocuments and associated information between two similar DLs that you believe could fit in with the discussion in this chapter.

2.6 Pick the fingerprint DL mentioned in Chapter 1. How could the metamodel be explored in order to map annotations between the four integrated DLs?

2.7 Consider a student who reviews his notes referring to highlighted portions in textbooks and papers while studying for an exam. Describe the components of subdocuments considering the definition of a subdocument presented in this chapter. List/describe associated metadata. What are the main challenges of (re)-using the same textbooks, papers, and annotations in another semester?

CHAPTER 3

Ontologies

Seungwon Yang and Mohamed Magdy Gharib Farag

Abstract

While many digital libraries (DLs) support taxonomic and/or category systems, few support ontologies in the most general sense. To incorporate the benefits of using ontologies in DLs, it is necessary to understand clearly what ontologies are, how they are developed, current practices of ontology use in DLs, and potential applications in various aspects of DLs. We start from the basics of ontologies, such as how humans perceive and develop concepts, various definitions, and their components. Then, the three types of ontologies, namely upper ontologies, linguistic ontologies, and domain ontologies, are presented with several examples. We next present a spectrum of ontology examples based on their formality and expressiveness. The ontology engineering section includes methodologies for development and tools to support the development process. In the ontology applications section, three application areas—DLs, Semantic Web, and focused crawling—are described. This is followed by a brief discussion of ontology evaluation methodologies. A case study of developing a Crisis, Tragedy, and Recovery (CTR) ontology is presented in the last section.

3.1 INTRODUCTION

In this chapter, we provide an overview of what an ontology is and related topics, such as ontology components, kinds of ontologies, development tools and approaches, applications, and methodologies to evaluate ontologies. We present upper ontologies, which attempt to capture general world knowledge, as well as domain ontologies, which represent knowledge in a specific domain. We use the term "ontology" in its broadest sense. Therefore, we include taxonomies, thesauri, classification systems, and lexical databases—concepts at the boundaries of ontology.

This section presents various definitions, types, and languages of ontologies. Related studies are introduced in Section 3.2. Section 3.3 describes ontology engineering, emphasizing methods and tools to develop ontologies, as well as inference engines to extend ontologies through automatic reasoning. Section 3.4 is about applications of ontologies, including the Semantic Web and focused crawling. A case study of initial ontology development in the field of disaster management is introduced in Section 3.5.

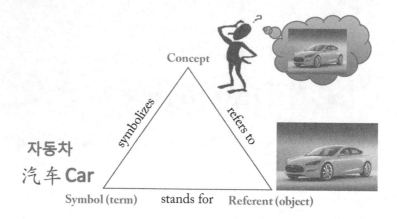

FIGURE 3.1: The meaning triangle.

3.1.1 WHAT IS AN ONTOLOGY

We perceive objects in their surrounding environments and map them into certain concepts in our mind. These intrinsic concepts are expressed as symbols (i.e., terms). Ogden et al. [170] explain these relationships, among objects, concepts, and corresponding terms, as the *meaning triangle* (see Figure 3.1). For example, we see cars on the street. They have various designs, colors, materials, and so on. They also have different performance ratings, such as top speed and horsepower. The object that we call a *car* is mapped as a concept in our minds. When we think of a car, we have general knowledge about what it looks like, which parts it consist of, how to drive it, etc. The symbol (i.e., term) *car* represents the concept residing in our minds, and it is useful when we share this concept with others. A concept does not have to have its corresponding object. An example of this is the abstract concept *emotions*. Such concepts and their relationships form knowledge in our mind. Some knowledge can be specific to a domain or specialty, such as computer science, hence the development of specialized ontogies for those fields (see Fig. 3.2).

Ontology Definitions

Various researchers in the Ontology Engineering (OE) and Artificial Intelligence (AI) fields have provided definitions for *ontology*. Among these definitions, the most quoted one is from Gruber et al. [76]: An ontology is an explicit specification of a conceptualization. This definition was slightly modified by Borst et al. [18] as: Ontologies are defined as a formal specification of a shared conceptualization.

Studer et al. [209] provide a more complete and detailed definition, which covers both definitions above: An ontology is a formal, explicit specification of a shared conceptualization. *Conceptualization* refers to an abstract model of some phenomenon in the world by having identified

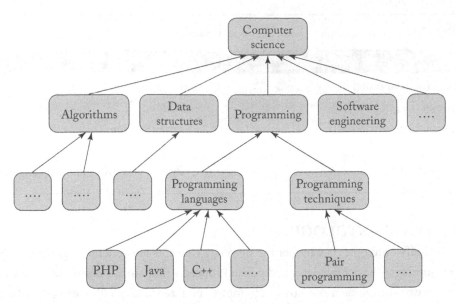

FIGURE 3.2: A portion of a computer science ontology [183].

the relevant concepts of that phenomenon. *Explicit* means that the type of concepts used, and the constraints on their use, are explicitly defined. *Formal* refers to the fact that the ontology should be machine-readable. *Shared* reflects the notion that an ontology captures consensual knowledge, that is, it is not private to some individual, but accepted by a group.

Ontology Components

Ontologies consist of common components. Classes or concepts are kinds of things or types of objects. Instances or objects are specific things. They can be either concrete (e.g., people, automobiles, animals) or abstract (e.g., numbers). For example, *Python* is an instance of the class *programming language*. Properties or attributes add characteristics and values to classes or instances. For example, the "Latest version" attribute of the "Python" instance has a value "3.2.2." A relationship specifies in what sense an object or a class is related to another. Two major relationships are *is-a* (subsumption) and *is-part-of* (meronomy). The example sentence in Table 3.1 shows a subsumption relationship between "Python" and "programming language." In "a keyboard *is-part-of* a laptop," an instance "keyboard" is a component of another instance "laptop."

The combinations of relationships provide semantics to the ontology. Other ontology components include axioms (i.e., assertions), which represent knowledge that is considered true. Based on axioms and rules, theorems can be deduced. Multiple axioms and (deduced) theorems comprise a theory. Other components of ontologies include events, restrictions, and function terms.

TABLE 3.1: Common ontology components and examples.

Name	Example
Classes (i.e., concepts)	Programming language
Instances (i.e., objects)	Python
Properties (i.e., attributes)	Latest version
Values	3.2.2
Relationships (i.e., relations)	Python *is-a* programming language

3.1.2   KINDS OF ONTOLOGIES

One way to classify ontologies is whether the ontology concepts are general or specific for a certain field. Upper ontologies have high-level and general concepts that are applicable across a wide range of domains, or worlds. Domain ontologies attempt to represent knowledge using specific terms in a certain knowledge domain. Specific classes and instances from domain ontologies can be mapped to general classes in an upper ontology. Another kind of ontology is a linguistic ontology. However, some consider this type of ontology not as an ontology but as a lexical database.

Upper Ontologies

A formal upper ontology is also called a foundation ontology. The terms in the upper ontologies are not specific to a certain domain. Therefore, upper ontologies can cover a wide range of concepts in multiple domains. They might have limitations in representing specific knowledge details because the same terms might be translated differently, depending on the knowledge domains that are being considered with respect to a particular upper ontology. Selected examples of standardized upper ontologies are:

Cyc.   Cycorp (www.cyc.com) built the Cyc ontology with a vision to create the world's first true artificial intelligence that has commonsense knowledge and the ability to reason about it. Cyc includes about 3,000 terms that are organized into 43 topical areas, such as fundamentals, times and dates, living things, actors, and actions, etc. Under these terms, there exist over 1 million assertions that were manually implemented in the CycL language.

The Standard Upper Ontology (SUO).   The IEEE initiated a joint effort to develop a large, general, and formal ontology [177]. The participants were from academia, industry, and government in several countries. From this effort, two ontologies emerged. They are the Information Flow Framework (IFF) Foundation Ontology and the Suggested Upper Merged

Ontology (SUMO). Not only these two ontologies, but also OpenCyc, 4D ontology, and Multi-Source Ontology (MSO) are competing to be a foundation of the standard.

Suggested Upper Merged Ontology (SUMO). Is a formal ontology using an ontology language called SUO-KIF [176]. It includes an upper-level ontology that has about 1000 terms, a Mid-Level Ontology (MILO) with about 2000 terms, and a dozen domain ontologies. In total, SUMO includes over 20,000 terms and 70,000 axioms. It is mapped to a lexical database, WordNet, and expanded using Wikipedia.

Instead of modeling a specific domain, linguistic ontologies describe semantic constructs by using words as grammatical units. They are built with different purposes. For example, WordNet is used as an online lexical database, and SENSUS as an ontology for machine translation.

WordNet. Is a large English lexical database created at Princeton University, based on psycholinguistic theories [133, 134]. It organizes words into synonym sets called "synsets," which represent underlying concepts. It also provides general and brief definitions for the synsets as well as a representation of the semantic relations among them. The types of relations include synonymy, antonymy, hypernymy (subclass-of), hyponymy (superclass-of), meronymy (part-of), and holonymy (has-a). WordNet is widely used in natural language processing and ontology enrichment.

SENSUS. The Natural Language group at ISI developed SENSUS[1] to provide a broad conceptual structure for machine translation tasks. The content of this ontology was obtained from various electronic knowledge sources and then organized into three regions. The upper region, that also is called the Ontology Base, contains general and essential items for linguistic processing. WordNet and an English dictionary are merged into the Ontology Base. The items in the middle region provide word senses in English. The lower regions contain more specific items, which are anchor points for different languages.

Domain Ontologies

Domain ontologies [137] represent specific concepts and relationships in a certain domain. The concept vocabularies are reusable in the same domain when developing another domain ontology. Numerous domain ontologies exist in areas such as science, e-commerce, enterprise, medicine, etc. Well-known examples include:

---

1. http://www.isi.edu/natural-language/projects/ONTOLOGIES.html

The United Nations Standard Products and Services Codes (UNSPSC). The United Nations Development Program (UNDP) and Dun & Bradstreet developed the UNSPSC[2] as a global commodity code standard, which organizes products and services in different segments. The coding system has a five-level taxonomy of products, which are Segment, Family, Class, Commodity, and Business Function. Each level has a two-digit number and a description.

Unified Medical Language System (UMLS) medical ontology. The United States National Library of Medicine developed UMSL[3] as a large database to integrate massive numbers of biomedical terms from various sources. It has three parts. The Metathesaurus part contains biomedical information for each of a couple of million terms. The Semantic Network part is a top-level ontology with biomedical concepts and relations. The Specialist Lexicon has syntactic information about biomedical terms to support natural language processing.

Chemicals Ontology [122]. Is composed of two ontologies, Chemical Elements and Chemical Crystals. The Chemical Elements ontology presents knowledge of the chemical elements in the periodic table, such as chemical names and their properties. The Chemical Crystals ontology models crystalline structures of the chemical elements. The Chemicals Ontology is used for education and scientific discoveries.

Ontology Examples by Formality

A spectrum of ontology examples is presented in Figure 3.3. The ones located on the right side are more formal or "heavyweight," and the ones on the left are more informal and "lightweight." For example, formal ontologies such as SUMO and Cyc are based on logics. They contain axioms, rules, and various relationships among concepts; therefore, reasoning is possible. Informal ontologies have limitations regarding inference since they are not based on a formal logic and only contain simple relationships such as *is-a* or *part-of*.

3.1.3 ONTOLOGY LANGUAGES

Ontology languages are used in constructing and reasoning ontologies. Various languages are shown in Figure 3.4. They were built from different disciplines. For example, a language based on the first order logic (e.g., KIF) was developed from the Artificial Intelligence field from the early 1990's. It has formal rules, axioms, and theorems, which allow deducing a new theorem based on what we know already. General Knowledge Representation languages and systems also were used in ontology construction. In the Software Engineering field, ontologies were built using the Unified Modeling Language (UML), which is not as expressive as logic-based languages, but is able to show important

---

2. http://www.unspsc.org/

3. http://www.nlm.nih.gov/research/umls/

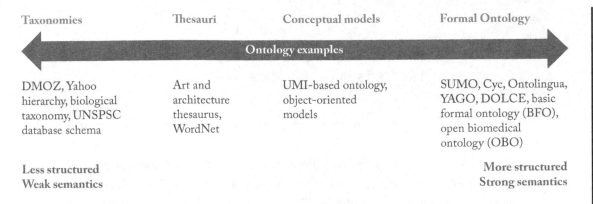

Taxonomies	Thesauri	Conceptual models	Formal Ontology
		Ontology examples	
DMOZ, Yahoo hierarchy, biological taxonomy, UNSPSC database schema	Art and architecture thesaurus, WordNet	UMI-based ontology, object-oriented models	SUMO, Cyc, Ontolingua, YAGO, DOLCE, basic formal ontology (BFO), open biomedical ontology (OBO)
Less structured **Weak semantics**			**More structured** **Strong semantics**

FIGURE 3.3: Ontology examples by their formality.

		Languages of ontology		
XML, relational model	Entity-relationship (ER), extended ER	RDF UML	Description logic, OWL, DAML+OIL	Higher order logic, first order logic
Informal **Less expressive**				**Formal** **More expressive**

FIGURE 3.4: Ontology language examples based on their formality and expressivity.

entities and their relationships. Entity-Relationship diagrams are used to construct ontologies in the Database field. These languages are useful in addressing the different needs of particular disciplines. Selected examples of ontology languages are described below:

Knowledge Interchange Format (KIF). Was developed for the ARPA Knowledge Sharing Effort [153]. It is based on first-order logic [67]. One of the related ontology languages is Ontolingua [55], which was built on top of KIF to address the difficulty in creating ontologies using KIF. Ontolingua is based on frames and first-order logic. It has LISP-style syntax and had wide acceptance in 1990s. Figure 3.5 presents an example of KIF. It asserts that the number obtained by raising a real number ?x with an even number exponent ?n is greater than zero.

Resource Description Framework (RDF). The World Wide Web Consortium (W3C) developed RDF (http://www.w3.org/TR/rdf-primer/) to represent information on the Web [115].

```
(=> (and (real-number ?x)
         (even-number ?n))
    (> (expt ?x ?n) 0))
```

FIGURE 3.5: An example of KIF representation.

It consists of three components: resources, properties, and statements. Resources are described with RDF expressions. A Uniform Resource Identifier (URI) and optional anchor identifiers refer to a unique resource on the Web. Properties define attributes and relations, which describe resources. Statements are composed of triples in RDF terminology, which have subjects, properties (i.e., predicates), and objects. The subjects are resources, and properties represent relationships or aspects of the resources between subjects and objects. For example, we can represent a sentence, *this coffee tastes bitter*, as RDF triples. The subject is *this coffee*, the predicate is *tastes*, and the object is *bitter*. A collection of RDF statements forms a directed multigraph. By using a query language such as SPARQL, we can infer specific knowledge from this RDF graph. Due to the need to define relationships between resources and properties, RDF Schema or RDFS was built. The combination of RDF and RDFS is referred to as RDF(S).

Web Ontology Language (OWL).   Building upon RDF(S), the OWL language was created to publish and share ontologies on the Web [39]. Like its predecessors, it has a layered structure: OWL Lite, OWL DL, and OWL Full. OWL Lite is intended to support users who need a classification hierarchy and simple constraints. OWL DL provides the maximum expressiveness and allows reasoning because of its correspondence with the description logic. OWL Full provides more flexibility to represent ontologies than OWL DL. It allows ontologies to augment the meaning of the pre-defined vocabulary. A class 'Flight' might be defined as a subclass of the class 'Travel' using OWL (Figure 3.6). Thus, attribute 'flightNumber' can have only one integer value, and the value for 'transportMeans' is 'plane'.

3.2   LITERATURE REVIEW

This section presents a literature review on ontology engineering as well as digital library initiatives related to the use of ontologies.

3.2.1   ONTOLOGY ENGINEERING

More and more ontologies are being created and used in academia, e-commerce, businesses, government, and so on. Due to the ability of ontologies to convey semantics, intelligent information systems and digital libraries that are based on ontologies might provide accurate information that users request. Uschold and Gruninger [223] present why ontologies and semantic-based technolo-

```
<owl:Class rdf:ID="Flight">
  <rdfs:comment>A journey by plane</rdfs:comment>
  <owl:intersectionOf rdf:parseType="Collection">
  <owl:Class rdf:about="#Travel"/>
  <owl:Restriction owl:cardinality="1">
    <owl:onProperty rdf:resource="#flightNumber"/>
    <owl:allValuesFrom rdf:resource="&xsd;;integer"/>
  </owl:Restriction>
  <owl:Restriction>
    <owl:onProperty rdf:resource="#transportMeans"/>
    <owl:hasValue rdf:datatype="&xsd;;string">plane</owl:hasValue>
  </owl:Restriction>
  </owl:intersectionOf>
</owl:Class>
```

FIGURE 3.6: An OWL definition of the class "Flight."

gies will play an important role in achieving seamless connectivity. They argue that getting "the right information to the right people at the right time" is the challenge of IT. For this, connecting people, software agents, and various IT systems is necessary. However, due to the lack of 'semantics' in the data streams, this connection may not be effective, as researchers and businesses have been focusing on technologies for supporting only physical and syntactic connectivity. In addition, the physical coupling among the systems becomes less flexible. Incorporating semantics from an ontology for digital libraries might allow system elements to connect with each other in a deeper and more conceptual manner, thus achieving seamless connectivity.

Once we know the importance of ontologies, a next question to consider is how we can develop an ontology to meet our needs. It is important that a domain ontology has an accurate and comprehensive coverage of that domain. To ensure high quality, most ontology development works are conducted either manually or in a semi-automatic way [70, 223]. One well-explained ontology development method was proposed by Noy and McGuinness [165]. They present an iterative methodology of ontology development using the Protégé-2000 ontology editing environment in the wine and food domain, as an example. The emphasis is on its three fundamental rules: there is no one correct way to model a domain; ontology development is an iterative process; and, concepts in the ontology should be close to objects and relationships in the domain of interest. In addition, they propose a seven-step process that explains the development details: (i) determine the domain and scope of the ontology; (ii) consider reusing existing ontologies; (iii) enumerate important terms in the ontology; (iv) define the classes and the class hierarchy; (v) define the properties of classes—slots; (vi) define the facets of the slots; and (vii) create instances. The authors conclude with the remark that one can assess the quality of created ontologies by taking into account how successful is their use in target applications.

Different development methods are sometimes merged together. Brusa et al. [20] merged the iterative method by Noy and McGuinness, as well as Methontology by Gomez-Perez et al., to develop a government budgetary ontology. They divide their ontology development into three phases. In the specification phase, the ontology goal and scope are determined. The domain of the ontology also is described. Motivating scenarios and competency questions are prepared. Then ontology granularity and type are decided. In the conceptualization phase, a domain conceptual model is defined. The authors used a Unified Modeling Language (UML) diagram to elaborate on the main relations among defined concepts, which is a common practice in the software engineering field. Relationships among classes and class attributes are identified. Instances are created. The last phase is implementation. The importance of modularizing the ontology for extensibility and reuse was discussed. The Protégé 3.1 ontology editor was used in their study.

To address the problem of time- and effort-intensive manual methods, Sanchez and Moreno [192] developed a semi-automatic methodology to extract information from web documents to construct an ontology. The procedure involves finding keywords that are representative of the domain of interest, fetching the resulting web documents using a publicly available search engine (e.g., Google), and filtering duplicate documents. Then an exhaustive analysis is performed to extract information from each document. After stemming and stop-word removal, statistical analysis helps to select the most representative keywords. The whole procedure iterates, adding new key phrases by joining newly found concepts and the original concept. The ontology is finally refined to obtain a more compact taxonomy and avoid redundancy. Other methods that are based on extracting information from text are provided by Balakrishna et al. [13] and Storey et al. [208].

Instead of creating ontologies from scratch, we may reuse already developed ontologies. One method is to merge more than one ontology into a single ontology to expand its coverage of a domain. Stumme and Maedche [211] introduce the method, FCA-MERGE, which is used to develop federated and autonomous web systems by merging specific ontologies. They apply techniques such as natural language processing and formal concept analysis to derive a lattice of concepts as a result of FCA-MERGE. Humans then explore and transform these concepts into a merged ontology. The other method is ontology mapping. In a distributed environment like the Semantic Web, several applications need to access multiple ontologies that have been developed. These ontologies might be mapped to a common layer, where information can be shared in semantically sound ways. In a survey paper, Kalfoglou and Schorlemmer [91] present a formal mathematical definition of ontology mapping, along with a review of 35 works, such as MAFRA, OIS, OntoMapO, and Information Flow (IF)-Map with some example cases. However, among these methods there is not a single method that is fully automatic. This is pointed out as one of the biggest challenges for ontology mapping when we consider the proliferation of ontologies and agent technologies.

3.2.2 ONTOLOGY AND DIGITAL LIBRARIES

Ontologies are used in digital libraries for many purposes: domain modeling (representation), content annotation, providing semantic concepts and relationships, formal description, and representation of all aspects of digital libraries.

Kruk et al. [109] conducted a study of the use of ontologies in digital libraries. They found that ontologies can be used in digital libraries under three different perspectives: bibliographic ontologies, structural ontologies, and community ontologies. Bibliographic ontology provides a uniform standard format for metadata description in digital libraries. Thus, it facilitates the process of integration of different digital libraries based on their metadata. Structural ontology provides a description of the structure of the content in the digital library. This empowers the content's metadata in the digital library with more semantics. There are several advantages of this ontology; it allows for universal access of content description and retrieval, and facilitates the addition of new structure and the modification of the structure of the content without modifying the content itself. Community ontology enriches the digital library with information about user profiles, relations, and interactions. Community ontology can combine the power of social network and Semantic Web features to enrich the user experience with the digital library by personalizing the digital library according to user interests.

Ontologies also are used to enhance performance of services in digital libraries. Scholar ontology [203] is an ontology that maintains a semantic network of scholars' interpretations, comments, and analyses of literature work. The ontology gives semantics over the existing research papers' metadata and allows for better engagement of researchers in analyzing and asserting their claims on papers related to their work.

In [57], an ontology describes the different scenarios of using an e-learning digital library. A personalization system was built based on an ontology for describing and organizing user profiles, user preferences, navigation profiles, user actions, and the relationships between all these information instances. The ontology also was used to describe the scenario of new functionalities that a user likes to add into the system. The new functionality is implemented by integrating Semantic Web services and ontologies.

Liu et al. [120] present their study on intelligent information retrieval services in DLs. Based on their ontology of scientific documents, user queries are expanded to include semantically relevant terms for better search results. Another study in this line of research is by Xu et al. [228]. As an attempt to go beyond keyword matching-based retrieval in DLs, they provide algorithms to incorporate the WordNet lexical database in constructing an ontology as well as in expanding queries.

Other studies of semantic searching are conducted by [46, 116, 201]. In JeromeDL, community-oriented services, as well as semantic empowered services, augment the traditional DL services [109]. The metadata of the DL resources are semantically "ontologized" into a bibliographic ontology called MarcOnt, and the resources are tagged and filtered by the community of people to support semantic and social searching. CallimachusDL [64] is another semantic-based DL, which provides faceted search. It also integrates both social media and multimedia elements in a semantically annotated repository.

3.3 ONTOLOGY ENGINEERING

There was a rapid proliferation of ontology developments beginning in the 1990's. Different groups pursued their own approaches. However, due to the lack of shared guidelines regarding development principles, processes, and methodologies, often these initiatives resulted in duplicate efforts and slow progress. In addition, the possibility of reusing and extending these ontologies for other applications was low. Accordingly, workshops on OE were held to explore and discuss the principles, rules and design decisions with the aim of identifying best practices.

Gómez-Pérez et al. [70] define ontological engineering as "the set of activities that concern the ontology development process, the ontology life cycle, and the methodologies, tools and languages for building ontologies." They elaborate on the activities to be performed in the Ontology Development process in Figure 3.7. The process consists of three parts: Management, Development, and Support. In this chapter, we focus on Development.

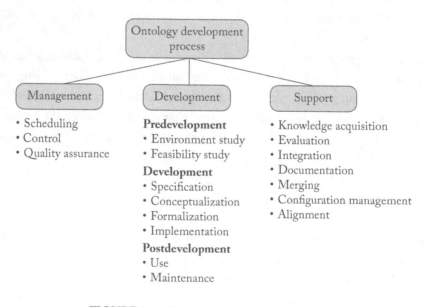

FIGURE 3.7: Ontology development processes.

3.3.1 METHODOLOGIES

The "Development" portion of Figure 3.7 is divided into three phases. In the pre-development phase, a study of the environment is carried out to identify the platform used as well as the application areas for the ontology. In the feasibility study, questions are asked regarding whether an ontology can be developed for that platform and application area. In the actual development phase, four activities are performed:

- *Specification*: goals, intended uses, and end-users are identified and documented;
- *Conceptualization*: domain knowledge becomes meaningful models at the knowledge level [162];
- *Formalization*: the conceptual model is transformed into a formal and semi-computable model; and
- *Implementation*: ontologies are built using an ontology language.

In the post-development phase, ontologies are updated through the maintenance activity, and used/re-used by other applications. Two examples of ontology development methods are presented below.

The Cyc Method

The Cyc knowledge base (KB) is one of the earliest ontologies. Its development started in the mid-1980's by manually adding more than a million assertions of common-sense knowledge about the world. For this, the following three-step processes were carried out [117].

- *Process I*: Manual extraction of common sense knowledge. This knowledge was acquired manually in three steps:
  - Encoding the knowledge required to understand books and newspapers: the knowledge that the authors of the books and articles expect that their readers already possessed was encoded.
  - Examination of articles that are unbelievable: this was to study the rationale that makes some articles unbelievable.
  - Identification of questions that anyone should be able to answer by having just read the text.
- *Process II*: Computer-aided extraction of common sense knowledge. Once enough common sense knowledge is gathered, tools that support natural language processing and machine learning might be used to search for new knowledge.
- *Process III*: Computer-managed extraction of common sense knowledge. Most work is performed by the system. Humans only recommend knowledge sources to the system.

In all three processes above, two activities were performed:

- *Activity 1*: Development of a knowledge representation and top level ontology.
- *Activity 2*: Representation of the knowledge of different domains.

There are several modules, which are integrated with the Cyc KB and CycL inference engine. For example, the WWW Information Retrieval module accesses the Cyc KB and extends it with the information available on the Web. These modules allow the Cyc KB to be applied in different contexts.

Methontology Method

This method is based on both software engineering and knowledge engineering approaches. It includes techniques for the activities in the ontology development processes (Figure 3.7) and an ontology life cycle based on evolving prototypes. Among the activities in "Development" in Figure 3.7, the conceptualization activity requires special attention to avoid propagating errors because the next activities, formalization and implementation, are strongly dependent on it. The conceptualization activity converts informal views of a domain into semi-formal specifications using tables and graphical representations. These representations are useful in bridging the gap between humans' perception of a domain and the ontology languages used for implementation. A total of 11 tasks under the conceptualization activity are defined as presented in Table 3.2.

At this point, an ontology conceptual model is developed. The relevant instances appearing in the concept dictionary are identified and described in an instance table. The name of the instance, related concept, and attribute values are added if they are known. These tables and graphical representations are further formalized and implemented using ontology editors. For example, the WebODE ontology editor can translate conceptual models into several ontology languages.

The Cyc ontology, which was developed by the Cyc method explained above, is proprietary. However, Cyc Corporation provides its opensource version, OpenCyc, along with its API and data dump. In the Cyc method, important concepts are identified manually, and then expanded using a semi-automatic means followed by refinement of them. The Methontology method has a foundation in software engineering, and thus, there exists a series of structured tasks to perform. It gradually builds ontology concepts, starting from the glossary of terms, into concept taxonomies, and finally, to a concept dictionary.

It seems that there is no single "standard" ontology development method, considering that ontologies are developed for diverse purposes in different domains. However, the two methods presented here would help in understanding the perspective of ontology development in general. To incorporate ontologies into DLs, especially for DLs in specific domains, we might have to develop

TABLE 3.2: Tasks under the conceptualization activity.

Task	Description
1	Build the glossary of terms: All the relevant terms in a domain, such as concepts, instances, attributes, relations, natural language descriptions, synonyms, and acronyms, are collected and organized in a table
2	Build concept taxonomies: Based on the glossary of terms, sets of disjoint concepts, which are the ones that cannot have common instances, are identified and their concept hierarchy is constructed
3	Build *ad hoc* binary relation diagrams: Diagrams that show relationships between pairs of concepts in the concept taxonomy are created
4	Build the concept dictionary: The concept dictionary shows concepts, their relationships, properties, and optionally instances, in a table
5	Define *ad hoc* binary relations in detail: Each relation in the concept dictionary is elaborated with its source concept, target concept, source cardinality, mathematical properties, and its inverse relation
6	Define instance attributes in detail: An instance attribute table is formed based on elaborating each attribute with its concept name, value type, range of values, etc.
7	Define class attributes in detail: A class attribute table is formed with each attribute name, value type, precision, cardinality, value, etc.
8	Define constants in detail: A constant table is formed based on detailed descriptions of constants
9	Define formal axioms: A formal axiom table, where each axiom is specified with its name, description, expression, concepts, variables, etc., is constructed
10	Define rules: After needed rules are identified, they are described in the rule table. Each rule will have its name, description, expression, concepts, etc.
11	Define instances

a corresponding ontology, unless we have access to an existing one. The presented methods might be used for such purposes.

3.3.2 TOOLS

Ontology development tools can be used to build an ontology from scratch. Basic features include editing and browsing of the ontology. Export/import for different formats, graphical editing, and documentation are often provided. Ontology merging tools identify conflicting concepts between two ontologies, so that users may resolve the issues semi-automatically. Ontology annotation tools

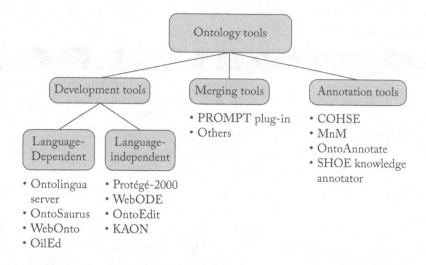

FIGURE 3.8: Ontology tools for building, merging, and annotation.

allow users to insert instances of concepts and relations into existing ontologies. Figure 3.8 shows the different ontology tools used for building, merging, and annotation. Swoogle is an example of ontology search engine. It provides a search interface for looking up online published ontologies. Protégé Ontology Library[4] provides a list of ontologies. The list contains ontologies from different domains and in different formats.

Inference engines make querying of ontologies easier. They are usually dependent on the ontology language used. Ontology learning tools extract concepts and relations from a textual corpus and can build a lightweight ontology semi-automatically. Natural language processing and machine learning techniques are used for this.

Two examples of ontology development tools are introduced.

Protégé Editor and Framework

The Protégé ontology editor and framework is widely used. It supports modeling ontologies in two ways with its Protégé-Frames editor and Protégé-OWL editor:

Frame-based ontology.   Concepts are organized in classes, which have subsumption relationships. A set of slots in a class describe properties and relationships. Also, a set of instances of
a class is associated with the class.

---

4. http://protegewiki.stanford.edu/wiki/Protege_Ontology_Library

OWL-based ontology.   OWL ontologies, suitable for the Semantic Web, include class descriptions, properties, and instances. Logical reasoning is supported by inference engines, which can be installed as plug-ins.

In addition, there is a WebProtégé ontology editor, which runs on a server to allow collaborative ontology building. The developed ontologies can be exported to various formats such as OWL, RDF(S), and XML Schema. The editor can be extended with plug-ins or a supported API to develop knowledge-based applications.

Sigma Ontology Development Environment

This system integrates multiple tools to develop formal ontologies. Its primary component is ontology editing and browsing employing the Knowledge Interchange Format (KIF) [66]. Two types of browsers exist. One shows a textual hierarchy while the other presents an automatic graph layout. An inference system that works with first-order logic and natural language/logic translators also is included. Some of the features are:

Language generation.   The formal statements written in SUO-KIF format can be paraphrased similar to a natural language. For example, a SUMO term "DiseaseOrSyndrome" is translated into *disease or syndrome*.

Natural language understanding.   The system can translate a restricted English sentence (i.e., present tense, singular, ambiguous words are assigned to the most popular sense, etc.) into KIF format, based on terms from the SUMO upper ontology. Details are presented in [140].

Inference, reasoning, proof, proof with equality.   A previously unknown fact might be deduced using Sigma's inference engine.

Although the Sigma tool is designed to work with various ontologies, more features are available when a standard ontology, Standard Upper Merged Ontology (SUMO) [164], is used. A number of domain ontologies from e-commerce, governmental organizations, biological viruses, etc. have been created to extend SUMO.

3.3.3   REASONING ONTOLOGY

Formal ontology languages have their own reasoning mechanisms as well as knowledge representations. There exists a tradeoff between the two. When a language is more expressive, the inference engine should create more complicated results with the corresponding mechanism. The inference engines have features like:

Automatic classifier (for the DL-based languages).   It computes the concept taxonomy from the ontology concept definitions.

Inheritance (simple or multiple) management. Concept attributes and relations are managed using the concept taxonomy.

Exceptions management. There might be conflicts in the property values of concepts. For example, a concept *bird* can have a property *flies* with a value *true*. Exception cases are *ostrich* and *penguin*. They are birds but cannot fly. An inference engine should deal with these situations.

3.4   ONTOLOGY APPLICATIONS

This section presents some initiatives that exploit ontologies to implement semantic-aware applications.

3.4.1   SEMANTIC WEB

W3C started the Semantic Web project as a way for providing semantics and standard formats for data. Their explanation of the Semantic Web [224] is:

> The Semantic Web is about two things. It is about common formats for integration and combination of data drawn from diverse sources, in contrast to the original Web that mainly supports the interchange of documents. It is also about language for recording how the data relates to real world objects. That allows a person, or a machine, to start off in one database, and then move through an unending set of databases which are connected not by wires but by being about the same thing.

The Semantic Web can enhance the user experience when interacting with the Web. It enables users to explore, share, and collect information on certain topics more easily. The main purpose of the Semantic Web is to enable machines to extract information and relations from webpages exactly as if a human read these webpages and deduced novel information and relations between them. The Web contains information about entities that users deal with every day. The Semantic Web provides formal and well-defined descriptions of these entities and promotes using these definitions in wherever it is referenced in the Web. This mechanism ensures that if an entity is mentioned in two different webpages that they will be using the same definition and thus promoting a common format of entities across the Web and facilitating the task of inferring semantic relations between webpages for the machine.

The Semantic Web enables a webpage's author to describe the semantic concepts of the webpage content by using ontologies. An entity in the webpage can be described by identifying the entity or concept in the ontology that corresponds to the semantics of the entity in the webpage. More semantics can be inferred using the relations between concepts in the ontology.

There are two types of ontologies: general and domain specific. Domain specific ontologies describe the entities existing in the domain and the relations between these entities. General ontologies describe concepts and relations existing across domains or integrate concepts and relations across different ontologies.

The information presented in a webpage can be easily inferred by any person reading it, but cannot be inferred by computers without the direct help of a person. Ontology plays the role of helping computers to infer information about webpages and to relate this information to other sources of information.

Some famous examples of Semantic Web projects that use ontologies are: DBpedia, FOAF, and SIOC. DBpedia is an effort to extract, store, link, and organize useful structured information from Wikipedia. It also allows linking other information sources to Wikipedia. FOAF is an ontology (Friend Of A Friend) that describes persons and relationships between them. SIOC is another ontology (Semantically Interconnected Online Communities) that describes online discussion communities (forums, blogs, and mailing lists) and the interconnection between them. The ontologies used in these projects are designed and provided in an open-standard machine readable format.

These projects help autonomous machine agents to consume these data, understand, query, and infer new concepts and relations from them. This would build the infrastructure for autonomous agents to produce content on the Web with the intervention of humans.

3.4.2   FOCUSED CRAWLING

The Web is a huge source of different types of data and information. Many entities are interested in collecting data from the WWW. Search engine companies and business companies, as well as marketing and advertising organizations, all seek information from the WWW, but for different needs and according to different perspectives. The huge evolving structure of the WWW made it difficult for the information seekers to use the traditional approaches of information retrieval where huge amounts of resources are used.

One of the most important services used in many applications on the WWW is crawling. Crawling is the process of retrieving webpages that are linked from a starting webpage(s). The starting webpages are called seeds. Crawling is used in search engines for indexing webpages on the WWW for faster search results. There are several issues in the crawling process such as: checking webpages for updates, permission for crawling, hidden web, avoiding loops, and parallel crawling.

Crawling can be used for building a customized collection, e.g., a collection of webpages that are related to a certain topic. This type of crawling is called focused crawling. Avoiding crawling the huge Web, however, requires more calculation while crawling identified webpages. A decision needs to be taken on every webpage visited in the crawling phase. This decision is based on some calculation that leads to either retrieving this webpage or skipping it, when not relevant to a topic. Figure 3.9 shows a possible architecture of a ontology-based focused crawler. The most important process in the focused crawler is ranking, where the relevance of the webpages is estimated.

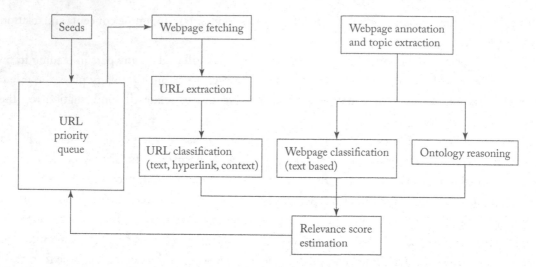

FIGURE 3.9: Architecture of ontology-based focused crawler.

There are several approaches for estimating the degree of relevance of a webpage to a certain topic. The topic is specified by a number of keywords. The text of the webpage is analyzed, using text analysis algorithms, and a score is given to the webpage according to the occurrences of the topic keywords in the webpage's text.

Another approach uses the URL text plus the webpage content. The URL text alone sometimes gives little indication regarding the topic of the webpage. Hence, one can supplement by adding in the anchor text or other context of the URL.

The representation of the topic of interest plays an important role in the performance of the focused crawling and the quality of the resulting webpages. A simple approach is using keywords or sample webpages. The performance of a focused crawler using keywords alone suffers from semantic problems, which lower the quality of the webpages collected. A word alone can have several meanings in different contexts and environments, which could mislead a focused crawler based only on keyword matching techniques.

An ontology can help solve the semantic problems faced by a focused crawler by better representing the topic of the domain (see Figure 3.9). The ontology can be used to determine whether the webpage is relevant or not. The text of the webpage is analyzed to get the semantics or the main concepts that represent it. Then, the concepts produced are compared to the concepts of the domain ontology based on the similarity between them. The result of the comparison is a score given to the webpage that shows how similar the concepts in this webpage are to the concepts in the ontology. In order to provide a fair comparison, the ontology should provide a fairly good coverage of the domain modeled. The ontology should contain most of the concepts that describe the domain. A good strategy for enhancing the ontology coverage is by learning during the crawling process. The learning is performed by adding to the ontology the concepts of the relevant webpages that do not exist in the ontology. Also, we can enrich the ontology by adding new concepts that are related to the existing concepts. An example of a source of related concepts could be Wikipedia, or WordNet, where entities that are connected to, related, or have similar meanings to the concepts in the ontology can be added to the ontology.

The quality of the webpages collected using focused crawling can be measured using two metrics: precision and recall. Precision is $\frac{RC}{TC}$ and recall is $\frac{RC}{AR}$, where RC is the number of collected webpages considered relevant to the topic specified, TC is the total number of webpages collected, and AR is the total number of webpages that are relevant to the topic specified.

3.5 CASE STUDY: CRISIS, TRAGEDY, AND RECOVERY (CTR) ONTOLOGY

The Crisis, Tragedy, and Recovery Network (CTRnet) project has been collecting news and online resources that are related to natural disasters (e.g., wildfires, floods, typhoons, and earthquakes) and man-made tragedies (e.g., campus shootings in the U.S. and internationally). The goal for the development of the CTRnet digital library is to collect, organize, and serve resources that can cover the disaster and emergency management domain comprehensively. Without knowing which concepts are important and how they are related with one another, we may not see the big picture. This might lead the CTRnet DL to collect and provide resources that are unbalanced in covering the domain. For this reason, we are developing a CTR ontology with in-depth coverage. The CTR domain is broad. Therefore, having solid domain knowledge will help to collect and organize resources. It also will help visitors navigating through information in the CTRnet digital library.

This case study shows an effort to develop a domain ontology, which will eventually be integrated into the CTRnet digital library. We describe a semi-automatic approach in detail, which involves the use of four existing disaster databases.

3.5.1 APPROACH
Semi-automatic Ontology Development
To ensure high quality, as well as to make the development effort scalable, it makes sense to create the ontology using a semi-automatic methodology that involves the least amount of human intervention, as well as computational effort such as Natural Language Processing (NLP) [13]. The ontology

building in this study has two parts. Part 1 is to merge multiple related ontologies, which have been built from existing disaster databases. Part 2 is to expand the ontology with related concepts.

Part 1. Merging Ontologies into a Global CTR Ontology

Our initial effort was to find online information sources about disaster management, where we can identify disaster-related concepts and their hierarchical relationships. The disaster databases we selected include:

- EM-DAT: The International Disaster Database [62];
- The Disaster Database from University of Richmond [169];
- Canadian Disaster Database [24]; and
- DesInventar Disaster Inventory System [171].

We started with the disaster classification in the Richmond database, and then merged it with the EM-DAT database. The process went smoothly, with the Richmond database providing more leaves and the EM-DAT elements comprising more high-level concepts. Next we merged the Canadian disaster database into the ontology, assigning each of its concepts to existing concepts in the draft ontology or creating a new concept in the ontology.

The overall hierarchy of the draft ontology was stable through this process, with most of the Canadian disaster database mapping to leaf concepts in the ontology. Finally, we merged the DesInventar disaster inventory system into the merged ontology that had been built from the other three databases. A large majority of DesInventar elements matched the partial union ontology. However, the concept of the 'cause' of a disaster was not included in any of the other databases. At first, we decided to exclude this element from the merged ontology, due to the lack of consensus across databases. However, DesInventar includes an extensive set of slots to be filled for every disaster, so, we later adopted them for integration with the ontology. The resulting CTR ontology has a total of 185 concepts. The number of man-made disaster concepts is 140. Figure 3.10 presents the highest-level concepts in the current CTR ontology.

This was not a trivial task, due to the ambiguities of natural language as well as different scopes and hierarchical structures of the disaster databases. Although ontology merging algorithms have been developed [210], human involvement is still a necessity to ensure accuracy.

Part 2. Enriching the CTR Ontology

Figure 3.11 illustrates a process whereby concepts in the merged CTR ontology might be expanded with related concepts. First, a group of concepts is selected from a region in the ontology. These concepts should have close relationships. For example, they are from the 'volcanic eruption' part of the ontology. The Concept and Term Expansion Module (CTEM) accepts these concepts as input and generates potentially related terms. Humans then identify appropriate concepts from

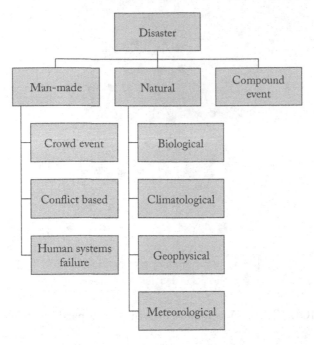

FIGURE 3.10: Highest-level concepts from the current CTR ontology.

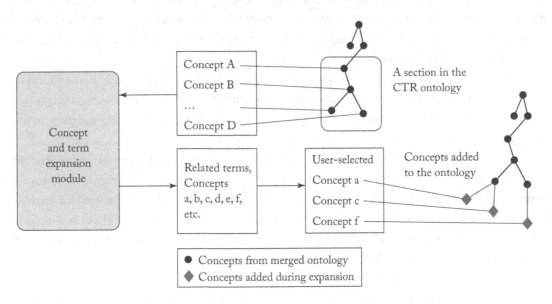

FIGURE 3.11: An ontology concept expansion process.

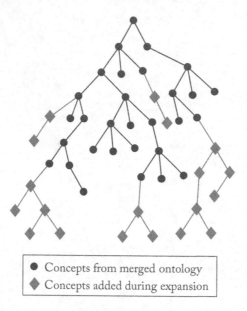

FIGURE 3.12: A conceptual diagram of an expanded ontology.

the generated result and add them to the existing ontology hierarchy. By iterating this process for different regions of the ontology, we might successfully broaden the coverage of the CTR ontology. As we mentioned above, we follow this semi-automatic ontology development approach to ensure high-quality ontology expansion.

A conceptual diagram of an expanded ontology is shown in Figure 3.12. Black round dots represent concepts that are from the disaster databases, while red diamonds represent concepts newly added through the expansion process. We may iterate the enriching process using the incrementally expanded ontology.

One use of the ontology is in query expansion. A user-entered query is augmented with ontology concepts, which are closely related to the query, possibly with weights to ensure the expansion does not shift the focus of the query unduly. The ontology also will be used for browsing. Browsing in a collection of content is a default feature in a digital library. If these two browsing features, i.e., browsing the ontology and content, are integrated, then one can move around the ontology concepts, following links from them to relevant content, or move around the content, moving back to the ontology, etc.

In the case of the Ensemble project (http://computingportal.org/), our proposal argued that the integration of browsing by ontology and by content would help. For example, an educational resource might be developed in a computer science (CS) database course. That would be linked in the ontology to the database area of concepts. A teacher in a library and information science (LIS) program, or information technology (IT) or business program, might want to teach database concepts in a course that is not connected with CS. Unless the educational resource is connected with the ontology, and the teacher uses that ontology, they might not find the useful educational resource.

The ontology also will be used to include different types of events (community and government events) in an NSF-funded project: IDEAL (http://www.eventsarchive.org/), the sequel of the CTRnet project.

3.6 SUMMARY

In this chapter, we presented concepts related to the use of ontologies. First, we introduced the widely adopted definitions as well as provided an overview on common practices regarding the creation, development, and use of ontologies, especially in DL applications. Furthermore, we presented a case study focusing on the creation of the Crisis, Tragedy, and Recovery (CTR) ontology.

3.7 EXERCISES AND PROJECTS

3.1 How can end-users work effectively with large ontologies that are integrated into a digital library?

3.2 List and explain four activities that are performed during the ontology development phase.

3.3 Explain the benefits and disadvantages for each of the steps of merging and mapping ontologies.

3.4 Other than the 'Assessment by humans' approach, which approach can be used to evaluate an ontology's context/application level?

3.5 Pick your favorite digital library. Identify three different ontologies that would be important in that DL.

3.6 For each ontology mentioned previously, identify possible services and users. How can ontologies help different users of a digital library?

3.7 Suppose you want to create each ontology mentioned previously. Identify possible strategies to be used in the development process.

3.8 Using the Protégé ontology editing environment available at http://protege.stanford.edu, create one of the ontologies mentioned previously.

3.9 Use the ontology created in the previous exercise to enhance the services of your favorite digital library.

3.10 How can we best extend the 5S framework to define other ontology-related concepts, such as query expansion, ontology-based semantic annotation, and ontology-aided browsing?

CHAPTER 4

Classification

Venkat Srinivasan and Pranav Angara

Abstract

When interacting with a large collection of documents, being able to browse them by topic can be particularly useful. Topical taxonomies have been developed across several domains to organize and make easily accessible diverse kinds of information. In this chapter we present our work on machine-learning-based techniques for categorizing electronic theses and dissertations into a topical taxonomy to facilitate faceted browsing and searching.

4.1 INTRODUCTION

Advances in electronic publishing, coupled with increased access to the Internet, have paved the way on a scale never seen before, for production and dissemination of books in electronic formats, as well as book-sized documents (henceforth referred to as long documents) like legal reports and Electronic Theses and Dissertations (ETDs). Not only is this type of born-digital content being produced at a rapid rate, but also there are numerous efforts to digitize existing paper collections. In the context of books, for example, the Million Books project involving Carnegie Mellon University and others, and Google's efforts on digitizing millions of books, are two significant efforts to make accessible a large collection of e-books based on what currently is only available on paper. The Networked Digital Library of Theses and Dissertations (NDLTD Union Catalog [168]) already includes over three million metadata records for ETDs.

One very exciting and critical use for these emerging collections of open access (or at least easily accessible) large-sized documents is in support of research and scholarship. Long documents like ETDs and e-books are richer in information content than short papers. User-friendly modes of access to vast collections of such documents will be of invaluable aid to the scholarly community, as well as the general public.

However, even though such collections of long documents are growing at a rapid rate, techniques for managing and providing access to them have rarely progressed beyond decades-old efforts based on fulltext searching and browsing. Large ETD collections, for example, are being made accessible through the NDLTD website,[1] mostly via a keyword search and browse interface. There is very little use of advanced text analysis techniques or classification techniques, for example. Evaluation studies suggest that effectiveness and usability, as measured in various ways, is low [17, 73, 74].

In this chapter, we present advanced text analysis-based techniques, particularly based on text classification, which have been proposed to develop a DL that makes vast collections of ETDs more accessible and usable for the scholarly community, and for the public in general. Consistent with the overall theme of the book, we also show how the 5S formalisms help in this regard.

The chapter is organized as follows. In the rest of this section we discuss the usefulness of this effort, and some of the research questions we address. In Section 4.2, we briefly review some prior and related work in the field of text classification, and also provide relevant definitions and background. In Section 4.3, we discuss the relevant 5S formalisms, and how they apply to this particular problem situation. In Section 4.4, we discuss in detail the ETD classification and the DL building process.

4.1.1 MOTIVATION

ETDs form an important testbed for several reasons. They are a key part of global scholarship, and are valuable resources, with comprehensive coverage of the topic of study. Each ETD summarizes specialty-related literature, and has a large bibliography section. There is local quality control, and some are reviewed by external experts. Rarely is research described elsewhere in enough detail so reproducibility of science can be tested. Given these advantages, easier access to ETDs would be a valuable aid to scholarly activities.

It is in this context of ETDs that we have developed our research methodology, and thereby bring into the spotlight an important genre that now can be accessed only with fulltext search through production systems like Scirus[2] or Google Scholar. More specifically, we are interested in developing methods for providing improved access to vast collections of ETDs to aid research and development activities of the scholarly community.

We are classifying ETDs into a topical taxonomy to facilitate browsing and searching. Taxonomies have been used for many years and in many disciplines to group (similar) information together into (similar) categories. Taxonomies may mirror the mental model that humans use to organize information. Identifying constituent topics of an information rich and (likely) multi-topic

---

1. http://www.ndltd.org/find

2. http://www.scirus.com/, which terminated operation in 2014.

identifier	cai:VTETD:etd-11172009-055013
datestamp	2009-12-16
All	
VTETD	
dc:title	A Comparison of Criteria used in Gifted Identification in the Commonwealth of Virginia
dc:creator	Palmer, Karen Smith
dc:subject	Educational Leadership and Policy Studies
dc:description	In the Commonwealth of Virginia, gifted education plans are submitted to the state every five years for state approval. The plans must indicate the use of a minimum of four criteria out of the eight criteria provided by the Commonwealth in the identification process. The concept of using multiple criteria stems from research. Research has shown that the criteria used in the identification of gifted students affect the number of identified students as well as the proportions of the underrepresented (Donovan & Cross, 2002). Research has also shown that the use of multiple criteria leads to a higher proportion of underrepresented students identified (Callahan, Hunsaker, Adams, Moore, and Bland, 1995). The purpose of this study was to compare the gifted identification criteria used within the Commonwealth of Virginia's public school divisions and analyze the effects of the criteria on the percentages of underrepresented gifted within the divisions. In this study, the researcher analyzed the numbers of each minority in the total populations against the total gifted minority populations to identify those divisions that were proportional for traditionally underrepresented minorities. All aspects of the gifted identification process for each division were then analyzed. The aspects were then used to compare the proportional divisions to the non-proportional divisions for commonalities in the identification process. Findings revealed that there were no divisions with reported minorities that were proportional in all traditionally underrepresented ethnicities. In addition, no one specific standardized measure was successfully used in identifying non-traditionally gifted minorities in all ethnic groups. The implication that can be drawn from this research is that despite all attempts to put research into practice by using multiple criteria in the identification of the gifted, there is no one criterion that ensures the proportional identification of underrepresented minorities.
dc:contributor	Dr. Carol Cash
dc:publisher	V
dc:date	2009-12-08
dc:type	text
dc:format	application/pdf
dc:identifier	http://scholar.lib.vt.edu/theses/available/etd-11172009-055013/
dc:source	http://scholar.lib.vt.edu/theses/available/etd-11172009-055013/
dc:language	en
dc:rights	unrestricted
dc:rights	I hereby certify that, if appropriate, I have obtained and attached hereto a written permission statement from the owner(s) of each third party copyrighted matter to be included in my thesis, dissertation, or project report, allowing distribution as specified below. I certify that the version I submitted is the same as that approved by my advisory committee. I hereby grant to Virginia Tech or its agents the non-exclusive license to archive and make accessible, under the conditions specified below, my thesis, dissertation, or project report in whole or in part in all forms of media, now or hereafter known. I retain all other ownership rights to the copyright of the thesis, dissertation or project report. I also retain the right to use in future works (such as articles or books) all or part of this thesis, dissertation, or project report.

FIGURE 4.1: A sample ETD record in the NDLTD Union Catalog.

document, and subsequently mapping the ETD to the corresponding node(s) in the taxonomy, will make navigating the huge ETD collection easier.

4.1.2   ETDS AND NDLTD

The source of ETDs in this study is the NDLTD Union Catalog. The NDLTD initiative, which was started in the 90s, sought to expand electronic publication of student research, and make ETDs accessible from around the world. Our testbed is a collection of ETDs harvested using metadata from the NDLTD Union Catalog [168].

The Union Catalog consists of metadata records for ETDs from contributing member institutions (universities) around the world. As of March 2010, the Union Catalog consisted of metadata records for 820,000 ETDs in various languages. By 2013 the number exceeded three million. It is the single largest cumulative source of information on ETDs available on the Internet. The metadata format used is known as the Dublin Core [225], which helps with describing electronic resources, and consists of the following 15 fields for each resource: Title, Creator, Subject, Description, Publisher, Contributor, Date, Type, Format, Identifier, Source, Language, Relation, Coverage, and Rights. A sample metadata entry for an ETD in the Union Catalog is shown in Figure 4.1. An increasing number of ETDs also are described with an extended version of the Dublin Core developed to more fully describe theses or dissertations, ETD-MS.[3]

---

3. http://www.ndltd.org/standards/metadata

The Union Catalog also contains ETDs in languages other than English. For our study however we are focused on ETDs that are in English.

4.1.3   PROBLEM SUMMARY

A definition of the problem is as follows: Given a large collection of ETDs, and a topical taxonomy, identify the node in the taxonomy that each of the ETDs will be mapped into, depending on its topic(s).

In this chapter, we present some of our work so far toward this goal. We specifically focus on the use of metadata information associated with an ETD to aid in identifying the category of the ETD. We also limit ourselves to identifying the major topic of the ETD, leaving the task of identifying other topics as future work. Likewise, we leave to future work the assignment of one or more categories to the separate sections of an ETD, which might be of particular interest for multidisciplinary research.

4.1.4   RESEARCH QUESTIONS

We will investigate the following research questions in the context of this chapter:

- *How much information does the metadata associated with ETDs provide toward category identification?*

- *Which of the metadata fields are most useful in category identification?*

- *Which automated text categorization algorithms perform best at this task?*

4.1.5   CONTRIBUTIONS OF THIS PROJECT

The following are the major contributions of our work on ETD categorization.

- The literature accessible for aid with scholarly work so far has been limited to books, research papers, etc. Our work with ETD categorization is expected to make vast collections of ETDs more accessible to the scholarly community and the general public.

- By associating ETDs with topics that are organized systematically according to a widely used (and hence familiar) topical taxonomy like DMOZ, the ETD collections could be easier to navigate and knowledge discovery made easier, as compared to when all that is possible is searching by keywords.

- Tools from our work can be used for automated categorization of books and ETDs—a task currently being done by trained catalogers. Libraries and universities are expected to save money spent toward these efforts. Furthermore, in cases when no catalogers are available, works could still be categorized.

4.2   RELATED WORK

While text classification has received considerable attention in the research community [200], hierarchical text classification has seen only limited interest. In this section, we discuss some representative works from the literature relating to hierarchical text categorization.

In order to aid the users' understanding of the material presented in this chapter, we first provide some relevant, but informal, definitions from the text classification field. Formal definitions of these terms are provided in Section 4.3.

4.2.1   DEFINITIONS

Text Classification.   Refers to the process of identification of class(es) or topical categories of text documents from among k existing (and pre-defined) categories.

Supervised Learning.   Supervised learning refers to a suite of machine-learning techniques wherein the computer or the algorithm *learns* by means of examples provided to it. Learning typically is defined according to the task at hand, for example learning to identify hand-written characters, or identifying e-mails as spam or non-spam.

Classifier.   A classifier is a supervised machine-learning algorithm that learns through examples to identify documents as belonging to one or more of k existing classes.

Training Set.   A training set is a set of documents that are labeled with the respective topical categories to which they belong. These documents serve as examples to *train* the classifier to learn to identify the categories of documents based on word occurrence patterns.

Feature Selection.   Words occurring in a document are referred to as *features* of the document. Feature selection is a process that eliminates non-informative words (words that are unlikely to be helpful in identifying the category of the documents) in a principled way using various statistical measures (χ^2, odds ratio, mutual information, etc.).

Evaluation.   Refers to the process of evaluating the effectiveness of the classifier that has been induced or trained using the training data. The commonly used evaluation metrics are precision, recall, and the $F1$ measure (defined below).

Precision.   Generally a classifier is trained on a certain fraction of the training data and evaluated on the data that has been held out. Precision is the fraction of documents from the heldout data set whose category is correctly identified by the classifier after having been trained by the training data.

Recall.   Recall is the ratio of true positive (documents of a class correctly identified), to the sum of the true positive and false negative (documents of a class wrongly discarded) documents identified by the classifier.

*F*1 **Measure.**   Refers to the harmonic mean of precision and recall (as computed below). Sometimes it is reported to give one single evaluation measure instead of multiple ones.

$$F_1 = \frac{2 \times Precision \times Recall}{(Precision + Recall)}$$

4.2.2   HIERARCHICAL TEXT CLASSIFICATION

Fundamentally, hierarchical text classification methods differ according to the following dimensions:

- type of taxonomy chosen;
- methods for feature selection;
- methods for training set selection;
- type of classifier used; and
- evaluation metrics.

Many of these methods use a top-down, or *pachinko machine*, method for doing the classification [30, 97]. This method involves inducing a classifier for every (internal) node in the tree in order to distinguish between the child nodes of this node. The classification proceeds in a top-down fashion, starting at the root node, where each classification decision decides which path along the tree will be followed. The classification proceeds in this manner, until the document processing reaches the leaf nodes.

The following sections describe some notable efforts in the area of hierarchical text categorization. Additional details for these methods are summarized in Table 4.1. The "Performance" column reports the results of the evaluation carried out by the authors of the cited works.

4.2.3   NAÏVE BAYES CLASSIFIER

One of the first attempts at hierarchical text classification was by Sahami et al. [97]. The taxonomy chosen was a "toy" taxonomy, 2 levels deep, that consisted of 10 nodes in total. The document collection chosen for experiments was a subset of the documents from the Reuters-22173 news stories collection that mapped to the nodes in the selected taxonomy.

They trained a Naïve Bayes classifier for each internal node of the taxonomy, after performing feature-space reduction using Information Theoretic measures. Subsequently, a top-down hierarchical classification approach is used to classify test documents. They reported substantial improvements over the conventional flat classification approach.

4.2.4   NEURAL NETWORKS CLASSIFIER

Srinivasan et al. [188] developed a Neural Networks-based classifier building on the Hierarchical Mixture of Experts (HME) model [89]. The HME model is a supervised feedforward network that

TABLE 4.1: Hierarchical text classification approaches

Author	Classifier	Taxonomy	Training Set	Performance
Sahami et al. [97]	Naïve Bayes	10	1000	0.81 (Precision)
Srinivasan et al. [188]	Neural Networks	120	300,000	0.30 (Precision)
Liu et al. [121]	SVM	246,279	792,601	0.24 (F_1)
Frank et al. [63]	Centroid based	4214	868,836	0.55 (Precision)
Cai et al. [23]	SVM	1172	14,690	0.34 (Precision)
Dumais et al. [51]	SVM	163	10,000	0.5 (F_1)

can be used for classification or regression. This model uses a divide and conquer principle to reduce the categorization problem into smaller sub-problems (one classification decision, on a reduced feature set, at each node). Using this approach, they train an array of neural network classifiers.

The taxonomy used is MeSH (Medical Subject Headings) and the document collection is a set of medical literature records obtained from the MEDLINE collection.[4] However, they only use the title and abstract of the article for training and testing purposes. The training-testing split is 30%–70%.

χ^2, odds ratio, and mutual information are used for feature selection [129]. The metric used for evaluating the performance of the classification algorithm is the F_1 measure [129].

4.2.5 SEARCH-BASED STRATEGY

Xue et al. [229] propose a two-stage search-based classification algorithm. In the first stage, candidate categories for a test document are identified. This is done by comparing the document with the entire training set (using a k-nearest neighbor approach [129]), and then selecting the nodes corresponding to the nearest k training documents as the possible candidate categories for this new document. In the next stage, a statistical-language model-based classifier is developed to perform the hierarchical top-down classification.

The dataset chosen for analysis is a subset of DMOZ.[5] Incidentally, they do not perform any feature selection to reduce the feature space. They measure the F_1 measure at various levels of the category tree, and report 0.8 as the best obtained F_1 measure (at level 1), and 0.2 as the worst (at level 9).

---

4. http://www.nlm.nih.gov/databases/databases_medline.html

5. http://www.www.dmoz.org

4.2.6 COMPARATIVE ANALYSIS

Ceci et al. [30] present a comparative analysis of various types of classifiers used in hierarchical text categorization. They choose a centroid-based classifier, Naïve Bayes, and SVM for experimentation and comparison. They also study and contrast various methods for building training sets for a node in a taxonomy. One method involves using the training documents of a node and all of its children as the positive training set for that node, and those of its siblings (and all of their children) as the negative training set. Another method involves using only the documents corresponding to that node as the positive training set, and the documents for its sibling nodes (not their children) as the negative training set.

Ceci et al. draw several interesting conclusions from their experimentation. Based on the results of their baseline analysis (flat classification), they conclude that SVMs are the best performing classifiers across all datasets they tested. They also found that certain types of classifiers (centroid-based ones, in particular) do not perform well when doing hierarchical classification.

4.2.7 SCALABILITY ANALYSIS

While several researchers attempt to do hierarchical text categorization, not many report the computational costs for the methods developed. What is fairly obvious from the work so far, though, is that the computational cost is proportional to the number of categories, and increases to a very high level as the size of the taxonomy increases.

Liu et al. [121] report that it took two months for their classification experiments on the entire Yahoo! directory to finish while running on a cluster consisting of ten powerful machines. Yang et al. [230] provide a formal analysis of computational complexity of various classifiers and also study their applicability in the context of hierarchical classification. They obtain tighter bounds (as a function of the size of the taxonomy) on the running times of various algorithms. The ideas and framework they provide can readily be used for analysis of running times and the scalability of hierarchical classification algorithms as they are being developed in a research setting.

4.3 5S FORMALISM

Formal definitions of terms and concepts in the context of hierarchical multi-label text classification are presented below, given in relation to the 5S discussion in Book 1 of this series.

4.3.1 STREAMS

Streams in the context of our work are no different from those defined elsewhere in the book. Streams consist of text, video (static or dynamic), or audio material associated with an ETD. ETDs also comprise structured streams as shown in Figure 4.2 (adapted from Gonçalves et. al. [72]) that model the structure inherent in ETDs.

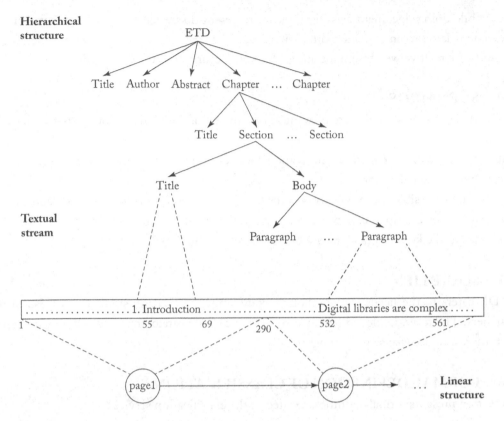

FIGURE 4.2: ETD structured stream. (Adapted from [72])

4.3.2 STRUCTURES

The taxonomy that is under use (DMOZ) comprises a structure. It is defined as a set $(T, \leq_h)$ where T represents the set of nodes in the taxonomy and $\leq_h$ is a partial ordering on the nodes of the taxonomy such that $\forall p, q \in T$, $p \leq_h q$ implies that p is the ancestor of q in the taxonomy.

4.3.3 SPACES

The document set D is a collection of digital objects d_i (ETDs in our case). Each digital object by itself is a tuple such that $d_i = (h, SM, ST, StructuredStream)$, where $h \in H$ is a unique handle for an ETD, SM is the text/audio/video/image stream associated with an ETD, ST is a structural metadata specification, and structured streams are as presented above.

Let $C = \{do_1, do_2, \ldots, do_k\}$ be a collection, i.e., a set of digital objects identified by k handles in H. A metadata catalog DMC for C is a set of pairs $(h, dm_1, \ldots, dm_k)$, where $h \in H$ and the dm_i are descriptive metadata specifications.

While doing document classification, we represent documents as vectors in a vector space. A document is represented by a t-dimensional vector $d_i = (w_{i1}, w_{i2}, ..w_{in})$, where the term w_{in} represents the relative weight (importance) of a word occurring in the document.

4.3.4 SCENARIOS

Two important usage scenarios are relevant in the context of the Digital Library that we have built here. In the first scenario, the users browse by topics (nodes) in the taxonomy to navigate to a node of interest. In the second scenario, the navigation could be performed by metadata fields (for example by department name, keywords, etc.).

Another possible usage scenario is browsing by both nodes in the taxonomy and metadata fields. A user, for example, may want to browse ETDs in science (a node in the taxonomy) that contains a specific keyword (a metadata field) of interest, e.g., RNA.

4.3.5 SOCIETIES

The DL caters to the needs of the scholarly community, particularly students, but also of other researchers. The tools developed herein also aid in automatic cataloging of ETDs and are hence of direct interest to librarians and catalogers.

4.3.6 FORMAL DEFINITION OF CLASSIFICATION

This section presents formal definitions related to the classification service.

Definition 4.1 Feature selection is a scenario made up of transition events that begin from a state of having a *token feature sequence* and end with a state having *a subset of the token feature sequence*.

Definition 4.2 A training set is a structured stream.

Definition 4.3 A classifier is a labeling function from a token to one or more entries in the structured stream.

Definition 4.4 Supervised learning is a scenario made up of transition events from a state of having a *token feature sequence* and ending with a state of having a *trained classifier*. Supervised learning is a process that finds a labeling function to map tokens in a text stream to entries in a classification scheme.

Definition 4.5 Text classification is a service that takes in a stream, and produces a structured stream. This service usually consists of a set of scenarios such as *supervised learning* and *category assignment*, each of which is composed of a sequence of scenarios, such as *preprocessing* and *feature selection*. Prior to feature selection after tokenization, *stop word removal* and *stemming* may be performed.

4.3.7 HIERARCHICAL CLASSIFICATION

In light of the definitions presented in the preceding sections, the hierarchical classification problem can be formally defined as a function $\mathcal{F} : D \to 2^T$, where D is the set of documents in the collection, T is the set of nodes in the taxonomy, and $\mathcal{F}$ is the mapping function (classifier) such that some quality metric m is optimized (maximized or minimized). Additionally $t \in \mathcal{F}(d) \Rightarrow \forall t' \leq_h t : t' \in \mathcal{F}(d)$. In other words, if a document is mapped by the classifier to a particular node in the taxonomy, then, by default, the document belongs to all the ancestor nodes of this node as well.

4.4 CASE STUDY: HIERARCHICAL CLASSIFICATION OF ETDS

ETD categorization is a multi-step process. The steps of our approach to ETD categorization are described in detail below, summarized in Figure 4.3.

4.4.1 BUILDING A TAXONOMY

The first step is to identify a suitable taxonomy for ETDs. While there exists at least one existing taxonomy for ETDs (the one developed by ProQuest[6]), it was found to be unsuitable for our purposes, mainly since it is very general and not deep enough to cover very specialized categories within a domain. A narrow taxonomy that contains only general terms as a specific category is unlikely to be of much help in browsing. Similarly, a taxonomy that is very deep and specific is not of much help, since users are unlikely to navigate to a node that is very deep in the tree (in this case, searching would be preferred).

The taxonomy that has been used for this work is the one provided by DMOZ.[7] DMOZ is often referred to as the "yellow pages of the internet" and has been extensively used for categorizing webpages and facilitating searching, and also browsing by topics. The DMOZ category tree by itself is very large, with in excess of 500,000 nodes. Therefore, it is unusable by itself for ETD categorization

For the purpose of this work though, we limit ourselves to categorizing only up to two levels deep in the DMOZ taxonomy. The top level of the taxonomy consists of the "root" node. The next level (children) consists of the following topics (after suitably pruning the taxonomy): arts, business, computers, health, science, society.

4.4.2 CRAWLING ETD METADATA

NDLTD's Union Catalog provides Dublin Core metadata for over three million ETDs. Much of this data was harvested and stored locally. Title, abstract, and keyword fields were combined to form a single string (more on this later below).

---

6. http://www.proquest.com

7. http://www.www.dmoz.org

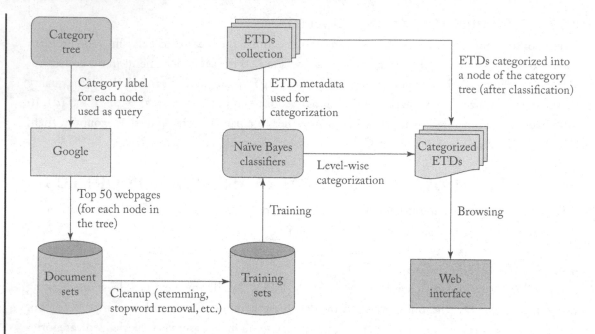

FIGURE 4.3: ETD categorization pipeline.

4.4.3 CATEGORIZING ETDS

The next step is to assign ETDs to their respective topic (or node) in the category tree. We explored various hierarchical categorization algorithms, and decided to use the top-down supervised classification algorithm proposed by Koller et al. [97]. However, since we are only classifying into two levels in the tree, our technique essentially reduces into a flat classification task.[8]

The detailed steps are in the following sections, and are summarized in Figure 4.3.

Building the Training Set

Given the taxonomy, we first build a collection of training documents for each node. We build this document set by using the (enhanced) category label of the node as a query to a web search engine and retrieving the top 50 hits. We then crawl these webpages, and remove the HTML tags. Each document is subject to stopword removal and stemming, and once this is done, the stemmed words are used as features and a Naïve Bayes classifier is trained to distinguish between different child categories.

---

8. We are currently working on doing categorization at the lower (more specific) levels in the category tree.

Training the Classifier

Using the training set above, we build and train a Naïve Bayes classifier for the root node of the DMOZ category tree to distinguish between its children. Specifically, we train the classifier to distinguish between Arts, Business, Computers, Health, Science, and Society categories.

Categorization

Once the training has been done, the classifiers are used to map ETDs to their respective topic in the tree. As mentioned above, we make use of only the metadata information associated with each ETD, viz. title, subject, and description fields of Dublin Core, to categorize it suitably. The categorization is done in a level-wise manner. At every level in the category tree only one classification task is done. Since we are doing the categorization into a tree that is only two levels deep, we had to build only one Naïve Bayes classifier for assigning ETDs into one of the six major areas, as mentioned.

We selected ETDs from eight different universities (or consortia, as in Ohio) and categorized them (when possible) into the second level of the DMOZ category tree. Results are presented in Table 4.2. While strictly speaking this does not produce a hierarchy-based ETD browsing system, once our work on classification into deeper levels of the DMOZ category tree is complete, as mentioned above, we will have a fully functional system ready.

Training of the classifiers is done offline, and is quite efficient. Training on 300 documents (50 documents for each of the 6 categories) took less than 5 min, on a desktop computer with Dual Core Intel 2.80 GHz processors with 1 GB memory, and running Ubuntu Linux. Categorization

TABLE 4.2: ETD categorization for ETDs from eight major U.S. universities in Union Catalog.

Name of the University	Total No. of ETDs	Art	Pct (%)	Business	Pct (%)	Computers	Pct (%)	Health	Pct (%)	Science	Pct (%)	Society	Pct (%)
						Category							
MIT	29804	653	2.19	1847	6.20	6507	21.83	375	1.26	7141	23.96	555	1.86
Virginia Tech	11,976	742	6.20	627	5.24	2665	22.25	1218	10.17	3317	27.70	340	2.84
OhioLINK	8020	1056	13.17	350	4.36	1267	15.80	1322	16.48	2887	36.00	345	4.30
Rice	6685	937	14.02	235	3.52	1181	17.67	145	2.17	2412	36.08	62	0.93
NCSU	5026	283	5.63	245	4.87	1419	28.23	512	10.19	1436	48.47	114	2.27
Texas A&M	4834	302	6.25	363	7.51	1363	28.20	566	11.71	2115	43.75	125	2.59
Caltech	4774	58	1.21	52	1.09	1392	29.16	29	0.61	3096	64.85	18	0.38
Georgia Tech	3582	32	0.89	133	3.71	1348	37.63	85	2.37	1233	34.42	23	0.64
TOTAL	74,701	4063		3852		17,142		4252		24,637		1582	

is also very efficient; to categorize over 74,000 ETDs (Table 4.2), took less than 30 min. Average precision and recall values were 0.9 and 0.88, respectively.

4.5   SUMMARY

In this chapter, we have presented our work on building a minimalistic and functional DL of ETDs categorized by topics for faceted browsing. We also presented the use of the 5S formalism in this setting to aid in understanding the construction of classification services in DL systems.

Hierarchical classification of documents remains an active area of research. We are currently extending our work on ETD classification by leveraging the fulltext of ETDs, in addition to metadata, for category identification. We are classifying the ETDs into a widely used and familiar taxonomy, Library of Congress Classification (LCC). Ultimately, we hope to make available a DL that contains all (freely available) ETDs from the Union Catalog, organized by topics as specified by LCC.

4.6   EXERCISES AND PROJECTS

4.1 Explain the benefits and disadvantages of using ontologies for constructing an ETD classification service.

4.2 Explain the benefits and disadvantages of using categorized collections when implementing digital library services.

4.3 Pick your favorite digital library. Identify three different classification services that would be important in that DL.

4.4 Suppose you want to implement the classification services mentioned previously, identify possible strategies to be used in the development of such services.

4.5 Using the machine learning approaches (e.g., Naïve Bayes, SVM, and kNN) available in the WEKA (Waikato Environment for Knowledge Analysis) library (http://www.cs.waikato .ac.nz/ml/weka/), categorize the collection of your favorite digital library. Which method provides the best results? What is the impact of the training set size on the results?

4.6 Use the categorization created in the previous exercise to enhance services of your favorite digital library.

4.7 Familiarize yourself with LCC[9] and NDLTD Union Catalog's listing of ETDs by university.[10] Select 1 or more universities from the list (except Virginia Tech, NCSU, FSU, and LSU), and navigate to the main page with ETD listings of these universities. From there, get the list of departments that each have more than 50 ETDs listed in the ETD collection. For each such department, identify the *most specific* node(s) in the LCC that the ETDs from that department would be mapped into. For example, Virginia Tech Computer Science department's ETDs would be mapped into LCC category QA75.5-76.95. Your final results should contain a mapping of at least 5,000 ETDs to LCC categories.

4.8 Section 4.3 briefly describes the 5S's as used in the context of a hierarchical text classification problem. Using this as a starting point, elaborate on the 5S's in the context of this problem.

4.9 How can we best extend the 5S framework to define the hierarchical classification of digital objects according to an ontology?

4.10 Assume you have 1 million ETDs and 3,000 LCC categories, and enough training data to build 3,000 classifiers for those categories. Assume you have a program that will split ETDs into chapters. Assume you have made runs to build classifiers for:

1. each ETD using the metadata only;
2. each ETD using the fulltext of the whole work;
3. each chapter of each ETD, using the fulltext of the chapter.

Please explain how you would use all this to aid those interested in discovering topically interesting ETDs, including methods and interface descriptions.

---

9. http://www.loc.gov/catdir/cpso/lcco/
10. http://alcme.oclc.org/ndltd/servlet/OAIHandler?verb=ListSets

CHAPTER 5

Text Extraction

Sung Hee Park, Venkat Srinivasan, and Pranav Angara

Abstract

To support many digital library activities, it is useful to extract data, information, and knowledge from text. Text processing (including tokenization), natural language processing, and machine learning are key technologies involved. When one begins with large and/or composite documents, document segmentation (e.g., identifying sections, or finding a figure and separating its label and illustration) also is a necessary precursor, and can directly address needs for extracting images and captions.

In this chapter, we cover formal and practical aspects related to the implementation using machine learning of text extraction services in digital libraries. A case study on reference string parsing illustrates the promise and complexity of a text extraction service. This requires feature extraction, training, and classification of extracted entities.

5.1   INTRODUCTION

This section presents text-extraction services, covering definitions, research areas, and common problems and challenges.

5.1.1   RATIONALE AND SCOPE

Text extraction is useful in supporting many digital library activities. The term *text extraction* refers to identifying entities of interest from character strings found in any media type, such as text documents, video sequences, or images. However, in this chapter we focus on text information extraction from documents. Both the input documents and extracted text may vary in size: from a big chuck of text, e.g., chapter, section, or paragraph, to a word or part of sentence, e.g., a particular part of speech (POS, such as a noun or verb) or a named entity such as a person, institution, location, time, date, or monetary amount.

5.1.2   RESEARCH TOPIC

Text extraction is related to topics such as 1) *pattern recognition*, 2) *classification*, and 3) *structuring*. Pattern recognition is a research area that focuses on finding repeated patterns in the input, usually based on the use of a classification technique. Classification is a technique that assigns input elements to a corresponding specific class. Classification can be further divided into general classification and sequence tagging.

Additionally, structuring is a text-processing technique commonly used for document processing, analysis, and engineering. Its objective is to tag (each part of) a plain text (an input) with an entry from a predefined tagset. Examples of such tags or labels are based on allowable parts of speech, or on the set of tags in a markup language like HTML.

These three research topics refer to activities that are closely related to text extraction. For example, structuring helps with breaking text into pieces, which makes segmentation easier. Furthermore, in some cases, such as transforming a plain text file to a more presentable HTML form, structuring works down to a fine level. In those cases, extraction may just involve separating out each of the lowest-level types of tagged items, e.g., finding all the proper nouns.

For another example, text extraction often seeks to find character strings that fit into a particular pattern, like a phone number, address, or person name; pattern recognition applies in such cases. Likewise, classification often is a key part of text extraction, since identifying a character string of interest frequently is based on it fitting into a class or category of interest.

5.1.3 PROBLEMS AND APPLICATIONS

Text extraction can be defined as a classification problem in which the extracted text should be tagged with a predefined tagset. One application of text extraction to digital libraries is document segmentation, e.g., finding chapters, sections, and all levels of sub-sections of a PDF version of a thesis. Three other applications related to sequence tagging are part of speech (POS) tagging, bibliographic information extraction, and reference metadata tagging. Information extraction can be applied to digital libraries to extract information from digital objects that can be added to metadata records, as shown in Figure 5.1.

5.2 RELATED WORK

General Information Extraction (IE) techniques from documents have been widely researched. Naomi Sager directed work on an early IE system in the Linguistic String Project, focused on the medical domain [190]. The Message Understanding Conference (MUC), sponsored by the U.S. Defense Advanced Research Projects Agency (DARPA), encouraged IE research from 1987 to 1998 [75]. At MUC-7, there was an evaluation of extraction of useful information from news messages about airplane crashes and rocket/missile launches. MUC encouraged a focus on extracting four types of elements: named entities, co-references, template elements, and template relations. Subsequently, the Automatic Content Extraction (ACE) evaluation project was organized by the National Institute of Standards and Technology (NIST) from 2000–2008. An aim of the ACE

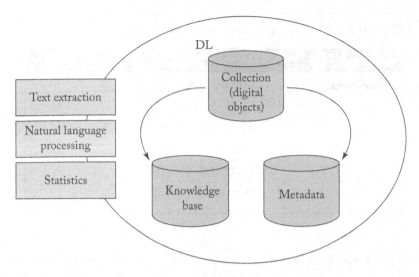

FIGURE 5.1: Text extraction in digital libraries.

program was the development of technologies to extract entities from language data and then infer relations among them. Those two programs, MUC and ACE, also contributed to the development of a variety of indicators for deep evaluation [172]. In recent years, text extraction has become a popular tool. For example, a great deal of knowledge is being extracted automatically from the WWW [54].

In this section, we review prior work regarding text information extraction in terms of: 1) classification algorithms and 2) feature selection in classification. In the next section, we look into formalization.

5.2.1 ALGORITHMS

Much research has addressed improving canonical representation extraction performance. Such studies can be categorized into two types of approaches: 1) rule or other knowledge-based approaches [3, 34, 38]; and 2) machine learning approaches [36, 83, 84, 231]. Table 5.1 summarizes prior work, making clear which approaches are supervised or unsupervised.

Rule-Knowledge-Based Approaches

Rule-based approaches to canonical reference representation extraction are classification methods that exploit rules to mark tokens in the questioned sequence with proper semantic labels. These approaches are particularly appropriate in situations where human experts in the specific area also would apply rules.

Some prior research has successfully applied rule-based approaches to reference metadata extraction. However, that has been done in a limited problem space (e.g., less than ten reference

TABLE 5.1: Comparison of text extraction approaches

Approach	Author & Year	Uns/Su
Rule-based	Day et al. (2006) [38]	S
	Cortez et al. (2007) [34]	U
	Afzal et al. (2010) [3]	U
Machine learning	Councill et al. (2008) [36]	S
	Hong et al. (2009) [84]	S
	Hetzner (2008) [83]	S

output styles, two or three disciplines). For example, Day et al. [38] adopted a rule-based approach using a knowledge representation frame, INFOMAP, with respect to six output styles. Their frame describes the layout appearance of semantic labels such as *author*, *title*, *publisher*, and *year*. Ding et al. [47] used different templates designed to deal with the specific citations from digital contents.

Cortez et al. [34] proposed a knowledge-based approach for extracting citation metadata in a flexible way, called FLUX-CiM, using blocking, matching, binding, and joining processes. Unlike other knowledge/ontology-based approaches such as [34, 38], this method used a knowledge base to gather frequencies of terms that occur in each field, like *authors*, *titles*, *journals*, etc. To evaluate the effectiveness of the method on output style-free extraction, three disciplines were used: computer science, health science, and social science. The accuracy of using term frequency (TF) in each of these disciplines is 96%, 94%, and 97%, respectively. TF here was helpful in improving the accuracy for the disciplines. However, TF, which they used as a primary feature, is likely to be dependent on discipline. It may be worthwhile also to investigate the utility of another value associated with terms, namely inverse document frequency (IDF).

In addition, Embley et al. [53] used a conceptual model like Ding's template-based approach, not only in citation parsing but also in general information extraction.

A general disadvantage of rule-based approaches is that it is not easy to extract rules. Although previous research has shown that rules are effective in the case of limited numbers of output styles and disciplines [34, 38], they are not easily adapted in solutions that are discipline-independent and that involve style-free complexity.

Machine Learning Approaches

Figure 5.2 shows a concept map for machine-learning-based text extraction. Thus, machine learning approaches have been used for sequence labeling. Examples include: hidden Markov models

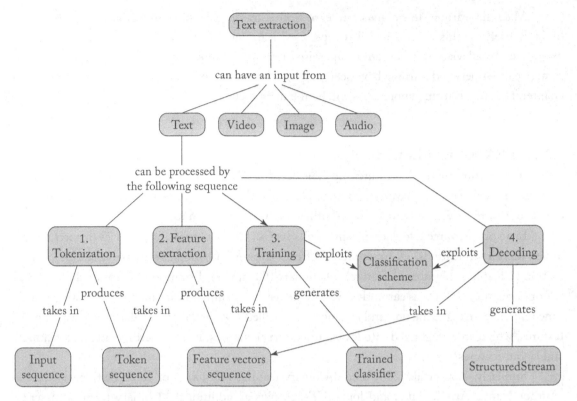

FIGURE 5.2: Text extraction through machine learning from the 5S perspective.

(HMM) [83], conditional random fields (CRF) [84, 36, 178, 186, 123], and Support Vector Machines (SVMs) [79, 163].

Machine learning approaches generally fit into two main categories: *kernel function–based*, such as support vector machines, and *probabilistic graphical models*, such as CRF, HMM, and the Maximum Entropy Markov Model (MEMM). Fundamentally, SVM is a binary classifier, but it has been extended to solve the sequence labeling problem. Thus, SVM^{struct} is one of the support vector machine implementations for sequence labeling [87]. Probabilistic graphical models can be grouped further into *generative models* and *discriminative models*. A generative model is a probabilistic graphical model in which an input sequence generates an output sequence. Generative models calculate a joint probability $P(X, Y)$, whereas a discriminative model, e.g., CRF, directly calculates a conditional probability of $P(Y|X)$, where X is an input sequence and Y is an output label sequence. An example classifier for a single classification is a naïve Bayesian network. HMM [181] is a typical generative model for a sequence data segmenter and labeler.

Machine learning techniques can learn from a training dataset. Since these sets are labeled by human effort, this process is called supervised learning; it often is both time consuming and expensive. To alleviate this burden in supervised learning methods, some efficient methods called semi (weak)-supervised learning have been proposed and evaluated [128, 86, 118]. In the rest of this chapter, machine learning approaches will be the main focus.

5.2.2   FEATURE SELECTION

With classification methods, features are considered to play a critical role, as they can be used to discriminate between data belonging to one class, and data belonging to other classes. Novel and effective features have been proposed and utilized in text extraction tasks.

In an open-source reference-parsing tool, *ParsCit*, Councill et al. [36] used 23 features named Token identity (3 features), N-gram prefix/suffix (9 features), Orthographic case (1 feature), Punctuation (1 feature), Number (1 feature), Dictionary (6 features), Location (1 feature), and Possible editor (1 feature). *ParsCit* is currently used in CiteSeerX. In similar fashion, in the lightweight real-time reference-string extraction and parsing system called *FireCite*, Hong et al. [84] used a set of 10 features, which are categorized into lexical (dictionary) features, local features, contextual features, and layout features.

Similarly, Zou et al. [234] used 14 binary features consisting of three dictionary features (Author Name, Article Title, and Journal Title), plus an additional 11 binary features, describing local and orthographical information (e.g., pagination pattern, name initial pattern, four digit year pattern, etc.). Yu and Fan [231] used 15 features in total: nine local features (ALLCHINESE, CONTDIGITS, ALLDIGITS, SIXDIGITS, CONTDOTS, CONTAINS@, SINGLECHAR, NAME, EMAIL), three layout features (LINE_START, LINE_IN, LINE_END), and three lexicon features (FAMILYNAME, AFFILIATION, ADDRESS) for metadata extraction from Chinese research papers. On the other hand, Peng et al. [178] investigated state transition, unsupported vs. supported, local, layout, and lexicon features.

Table 5.2 shows the summary of the methods and features used in related studies and their performance. One of several machine learning methods such as CRF, SVM, HMM, and housemade-methods were empirically selected to fit to each application and sometimes compared one to another. The most popular method was CRF, which looked similar to or better than other methods such as SVM and HMM.

Local and lexical features were mainly used and layout features were optionally used but contextual features were rarely used. The evaluation for investigating which features are useful was conducted only in Peng's study [178]; other studies did not mention feature engineering.

TABLE 5.2: Summary of evaluation in related studies

Studies	Methods / Features	Application / Datasets used in evaluation (F1 measure)
ParsCit (2008) [36]	CRF	
	Local, lexical, contextual, layout features	Cora (.95), CiteSeerX (.87), Flux-Cim (.94)
FireCite (2009) [84]	FireCite: Lightweight reference string parser devised by authors	Reference string extraction
	Local, lexical, contextual, layout features	Flux-Cim (.94)
Zou et al. (2010) [234]	CRF, SVM	Medical article reference parsing
	Local, lexical features	600 medical article data; CRF (.97), SVM (.97)
Yu et al. (2007) [231]	CRF, HMM	Chinese paper header extraction
	Local, lexical, layout features	Chinese research paper data set; CRF (.96), HMM (.87)
Peng et al. (2006) [178]	CRF	Paper header extraction
	Local, lexical, layout features	Cora; Local + layout (.934), Local (.888), Local + lexical (.899), Local + Layout + Lexical (.93)

As we can see in Table 5.2, most of the studies neither mentioned how they selected the features they used and their effectiveness, nor evaluated the effectiveness of the features that they chose, except in Peng's study [178]. Lessons we have learned from this review are that a variety of features must be made and chosen to fit the application.

That is why further work is needed for feature engineering, which means identifying what features are useful among different applications. In Section 4.1, *Feature Engineering* of his dissertation [173], Park intensively investigated an effective feature selection method via his newly proposed fine-feature engineering. Because of limited space, we did not include the details of the fine-feature engineering. For more detail, refer to Park's dissertation [173].

To ensure beneficial use of features, automatic reference metadata-labeling methods have used the following four types of features: 1) local features (dictionaries), 2) lexical features,

TABLE 5.3: Features for canonical representation extraction.

Features	Description	References
Local features	Non-lexical information about the token	[36, 84, 234, 231, 178]
Lexical features	Information about the meaning of the words within the token	[36, 84, 234, 231, 178]
Contextual features	Lexical or local features of a token's neighbors	[36, 84]
Layout features	Relative position of a word in the entire reference string	[36, 231, 84, 178]

3) contextual features, and 4) layout features. High-level classification of existing features is described in Table 5.3.

Local Features

Local features represent orthographic information about a token (e.g., a single capital letter surrounded by spaces, acronyms, and numbers). For example, among the local features, one single capital letter followed by a dot would appear to be the initial of a middle name or a first name in the *author* field, while numerals would appear in the *pages* or *year* attributes.

Lexical Features

Lexical features represent information about the semantic category of a token. For instance, New York is a city name and May is the fifth month of a year. A lexical feature of the token New York can be LOCATION and similarly a lexical feature of May can be MONTH.

Contextual Features

Contextual features are state transition features. From a probabilistic perspective, they can be defined as the probability of transition from a state at time $t - 1$ to a state at time t, i.e., $P(y_t|y_{t-1})$ where y_{t-1} is the state at time $t - 1$, just before the state at time t. For example, the probabilities will differ in the two cases where the current state lexical feature is TITLE, and either the previous state is AUTHOR or YEAR.

Layout Features

Layout features reflect the relative positions of a word in a reference sequence. They are similar to contextual features, in terms of structural information. But layout features encode physical position, whereas contextual features are concerned with semantic transitions. Layout features can be binary features or can have real values between 0 and 1.

5.3   FORMALIZATION

In this section, we give informal and formal definitions related to text extraction and explain how some concepts in this relate to 5S constructs.

5.3.1   INFORMAL DEFINITIONS

Text extraction is a pipeline service which produces structured streams from plain streams, using spaces and structures.

Societies.   First, a specific society may set some constraints on the streams and structures. For example, university librarians are interested in ETDs and references in them, as well as classification schemes for bibliographical information found in such scholarly documents. The societies that are likely to be interested in text extraction research include those working on: 1) natural language processing, 2) pattern recognition, or 3) artificial intelligence.

Streams.   Two main types of streams are of interest: 1) video/image/text documents, and 2) general structured streams. For perspective, see Figure 5.3.

Scenarios.   From the scenarios point of view, information extraction from text consists of a pipeline of scenarios involving: 1) tokenization, 2) feature extraction, 3) training, and 4) tagging/classification/segmentation.

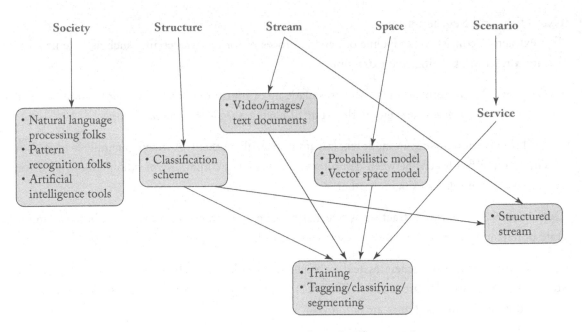

FIGURE 5.3: Text extraction from the 5S perspective.

Structures. For each domain of interest, a **classification scheme** is necessary, so it can be used to guide the conversion of a plain input stream into a suitably structured stream.

Spaces. To classify the segments of the input stream using proper labels, digital libraries may use metric spaces to calculate, for each label, the similarities between an unknown data item and a centroid or other representative of the training data. The following types of spaces can be used: probabilistic or vector.

The relationship among informal definitions is illustrated in Figure 5.3.

5.3.2 FORMAL DEFINITIONS
Classification Schemes
Definition 5.1 A **classification scheme** is a structure.

A classification scheme can be described using a set of labels, assigned to a graph representation of the relationships between the concepts and categories in a specific domain. For example, taxonomies and ontologies can be considered as classification schemes. In the case of text information, the semantics of a classification scheme indicate the category or categories to which an information unit should be assigned. For example, parts of ETDs can be described using a logical structural classification scheme made up of chapters, sections, subsections, paragraphs, etc.

Extraction and Segmentation
Text extraction consists of a pipeline of general processes for text processing, such as tokenization, feature extraction, training, and extraction.

Definition 5.2 **Tokenization** is a scenario made up of transition events that begin from a state of having a *character sequence* and end with a state of having a *sequence of tokens stream*.

Tokenization divides an input text stream into smaller tokens. A token generally is a word. A tokenizer identifies tokens between delimiters such as blank, comma, semi-colon, colon, or space, and separates the tokens from each other.

Definition 5.3 **Feature extraction** is a scenario made up of transition events that begin from the state of having a *token sequence* and end with a state of having a *token feature sequence*.

Feature extraction generates feature vectors, considering each token of a token sequence stream. In some cases, feature selection (Def. 4.1) may be employed to reduce the number of features, so that the most important ones are employed.

Definition 5.4 **Text segmentation** is a service that takes a stream as input and produces a structured stream.

Recall that a structured stream is defined with labels and a labeling function in the 5S definition. A *structured stream* generated by a text segmentation service is a *structured stream* such that *pre-defined labels* (e.g., title, author, and introduction) are assigned to the *input stream* by a *classifier/labeling function* trained in the training phase, meeting constraints of the classifier, such as finding a global minimum of the classifier. For logical document structuring, one type of text segmentation, a classifier should be learned prior to segmenting a document with bibliographical labels.

Definition 5.5 **Text extraction** is a service that takes a stream as input, and produces a substructured stream.

A *substructured stream* generated by a text segmentation service is part of a *structured stream* such that *pre-defined labels* (e.g., reference string, non-reference string) are assigned to the *input stream* by a *classifier/labeling function* trained in the training phase, meeting constraints of the classifier, such as finding a global minimum of the classifier. Once a structured stream has been generated, we can extract some part of the stream with a specific label (e.g., reference string) for a reference extraction application.

Figure 5.4 illustrates all the definitions above and their flows in a diagram. These services, such as text segementation and extraction, usually consist of a set of scenarios, such as *training* defined in Def. 4.4 and *decoding*, each of which is composed of a sequence of scenarios, such as *tokenization* (Def. 5.2), *feature extraction* (Def. 5.3), and *learning/decoding*. For better efficiency, prior to feature extraction after tokenization, **stop word removal** and **stemming** may be performed.

5.4 CASE STUDIES

In this section, two connected case studies, related to the construction of digital libraries of Electronic of Theses and Dissertations (ETDs), are described. Document segmentation is discussed in the first subsection below, in terms of dividing a long (multi-page) document into small parts, e.g., chapters and sections. In the second subsection below, reference section extraction is explained; this involves extracting the reference section from a text document. For more details on these two cases, please see [206] and [172], respectively.

5.4.1 DOCUMENT SEGMENTATION

We used several open-source tools in order to segment documents and extract images (see Table 5.4). In the following subsections, we discuss our methodology in detail. The various steps are shown in Figure 5.5.

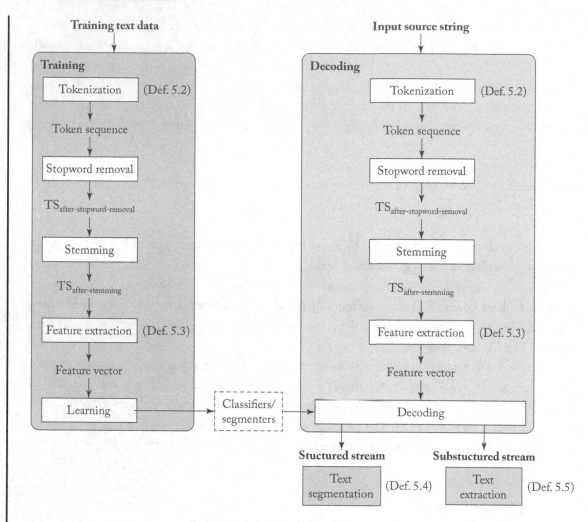

FIGURE 5.4: Flow chart of text extraction.

Extracting Chapters

In order to get the text from ETDs, we used the well-known *pdf2xml* tool. It decodes the structure of PDF documents and produces very fine grained information (metadata) about every token (word) that occurs in a PDF file. Sample metadata produced for an example token in a PDF file, such as the font used, is shown in Figure 5.6. As can be seen, this output is not readily usable. Instead of producing lines or paragraphs that occur in PDF files as output, it generates tagged tokens (words). A page in a PDF file is treated as a co-ordinate space, with the origin (0,0) being at the top left

TABLE 5.4: Open source software used		
Tool	**Source**	**Function**
pdf2xml [40]	SourceForge	Extract font related metadata
pdfimages [61]	XPDF (Linux)	Extracts images (in PPM/PBM format) from PDF files
pnmtojpeg [221]	Linux utility	Converts PPM and PBM images into JPEG

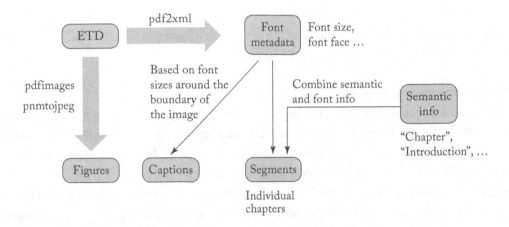

FIGURE 5.5: Steps in text and image extraction.

```
<TOKEN sid="p1_s8" id="p1_w4" font-name="liberationserif" symbolic="yes"
 bold="no" italic="yes" font-size="9" font-color="#000000"
rotation="0" angle="0" x="121.843" y="36.381" base="44.4" width="19.485"
height="9.963">name</TOKEN>
```

FIGURE 5.6: XML metadata for the token 'name' occurring in a PDF file.

corner of the page. Every token is encoded as a point in XY space, relative to the origin (as seen in 'x', 'y' in Figure 5.6).

In order to identify chapter boundaries, we first wrote parsers to decode the *pdf2xml* output and to identify Title Case (TC) tokens. We define TC tokens as those tokens that are likely to be chapter titles. ETDs, though, commonly contain fonts with heterogeneous sizes and characteristics. Hence, identifying TC tokens is not straightforward. In order to do this, we detect candidate TC tokens that occur near the top of a page, and use these to identify chapter boundaries. Often, ETDs

TABLE 5.5: Major reference styles used in ETDs

Style	Example
Bracketed	[Fox2011]
Bracketed	(Fox2011)
Numeric	[1]

have one or more words like "Introduction", "Summary", "Chapter", "References", etc. in chapter headings. We use this cue also to identify TC tokens.

Extracting Images and Captions

In order to extract images from PDF files, we make use of *pdfimages*, which comes bundled in Linux, as part of the XPDF package. We process the PDF file page by page, and extract images that occur in each page. We also are interested in extracting image captions. Hence, once a page is found to contain image(s), we extract the XML metadata information for the page using *pdf2xml*. Using this metadata information, we identify the XY location of the image(s) on the page and identify small-sized texts in the neighborhood of the images as possible image captions. The images extracted by *pdfimages*, however, occur in PPM, PNM, or VEC formats. In order to convert them to JPEG (for ease of display on the Web), we use *pnmtojpeg*.

Extracting Other Miscellaneous Information

As an addon, we also attempted to extract individual entries in the bibliography section and their corresponding references within the body of the ETD. We identified 3 major styles used in ETDs (see Table 5.5) and wrote parsers to scan through the body of the ETD to identify locations of citations to references.

Web Prototype Design

We developed a Web prototype using the content management system Drupal [50]. We used several Drupal modules, like those for taxonomy, image gallery, etc. (see Table 5.6) in order to achieve the desired functionality. Users can browse by chapter, page, figure, reference, etc. (see Section 5.4.1).

Results

Web Demo. Our web demo allows for browsing by separate streams (chapters, images, etc.), as well as presents a unified view of the entire document. The screenshots in Figure 5.7

TABLE 5.6: Drupal modules

Module Name	Function
Views	Image gallery
Taxonomy	Taxonomy for browsing by chapter
Vocabulary	Creating navigation block for taxonomy

show the use of the taxonomy and image gallery features. The web demo can be accessed at http://zappa.dlib.vt.edu/etd/ (as of July 2013).

Evaluation.   One critical issue in the development of such a system, besides its usability, is the performance of the backend methods. In order to understand the accuracy of our text, image, and caption extraction methods, we ran several experiments. To evaluate the accuracy of the document segmentation technique, we randomly selected 10 ETDs each from the engineering, arts, business, and mathematics disciplines from the Virginia Tech ETD collection. Our algorithm achieved an accuracy of 70%, 50%, 70%, and 60%, respectively, on this data set. We consider the algorithm to be accurate when it successfully identifies every single chapter boundary for an ETD. For example, in this case, our algorithm perfectly identified every single chapter boundary in 7 out of the 10 engineering ETDs we had selected. If we relax the criterion a bit, and allow for identification of some but not all chapters in ETDs, the accuracy in relaxed matching can go higher than for perfect matching. Nevertheless, the performance of our algorithm is, in total, 62.5%, perfectly segmenting 25 out of all 40 ETDs used in the experiment.

Evaluating the performance of our image and captions extraction tool is a little harder. One problem is that *pdfimages* extracts certain extra ghost images from ETDs. These are just small-sized spurious PPM or VEC files, and, without visual inspection, it is hard to tell whether it is a real image extracted from the ETD or just some ghost image. We observed, however, that in the case of ETDs in our collection, the ghost images are mostly less than 1KB in size. So, in order to perform a reasonable evaluation of our method, we ignore all extracted image files that are less than 1KB. Another problem is that *pdfimages* segments the images themselves under certain circumstances. For example, when the image is a flowchart, *pdfimages* extracts certain segments separately, and returns multiple images instead of the entire flowchart as a whole. To get a rough estimate of the performance of our image and caption extraction tool, we selected 10 ETDs at random from the Virginia Tech ETD collection, and extracted images (and captions) from them. These ETDs were found to contain a total

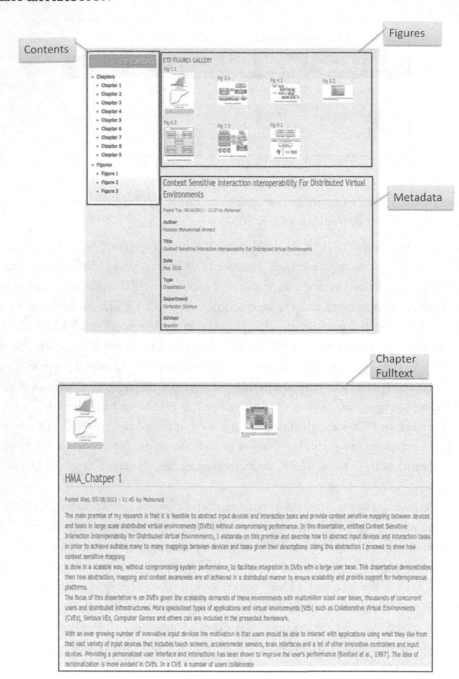

FIGURE 5.7: Web demo screenshots.

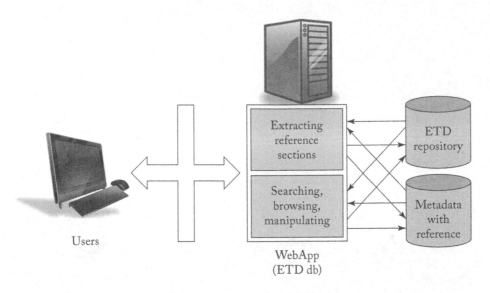

FIGURE 5.8: System architecture for a reference section extraction.

of 91 images, out of which we were able to recover 36 images. The rest of the images either could not be recovered at all, or were recovered only partially or were segmented. Of these 36 images, we were able to extract captions for 24 of them. More experimentation (including user studies) is needed to get better estimates. Clearly, more advanced methods are needed for this extraction task.

5.4.2   REFERENCE SECTION EXTRACTION

Automatic reference section extraction is a module of the ETD-db system for exposing references to the public. Figure 5.8 illustrates its system architecture. The automatic reference section extraction consists of the following: conversion of the ETD PDF file into a text file (e.g., using *pdf2txt*), feature extraction, learning (training), and reference section extraction (see Figure 5.9).

PDF2Txt

The Apache PDFBox is an open-source, Java-based library that supplies components for working on and manipulating PDF files. In the context of our project, the operations required dealing with stripping content from a PDF document and writing it to a text file. The version used in this project was 1.4.0. Figures 5.10 and 5.11 show an example of a chapter reference and an end reference, respectively.

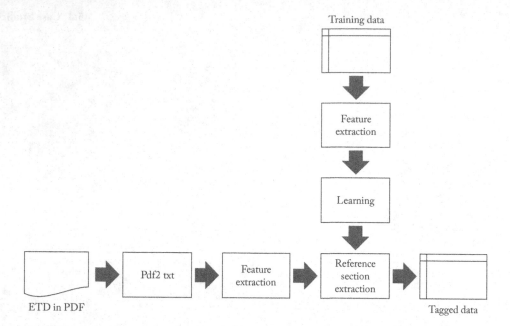

FIGURE 5.9: Dataflow diagram of a reference section extraction.

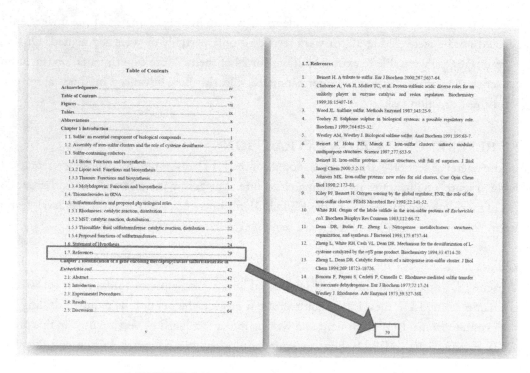

FIGURE 5.10: An example of a chapter reference.

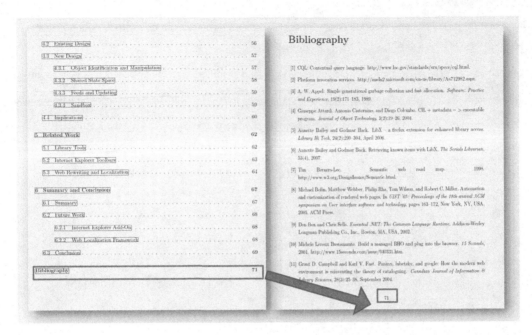

FIGURE 5.11: An example of an end reference.

TABLE 5.7: Feature sets

Feature Name	Descriptions	Examples
Word local features	28 different string patterns	Types of punctuation, capitalization, etc.
Line feature	2 patterns in a line	Number of words in the line, percentage of capitalized words
Contextual feature	8 patterns of a neighborhood	Class (REF or NON-REF) of neighbor lines before and after the current line

Feature Extraction

Features that we use can be categorized into three types: word local features, line features, and contextual features. Table 5.7 describes each feature with simple examples. Twenty-eight different string patterns (e.g., types of punctuation, capitalization, etc.) are used as word features.

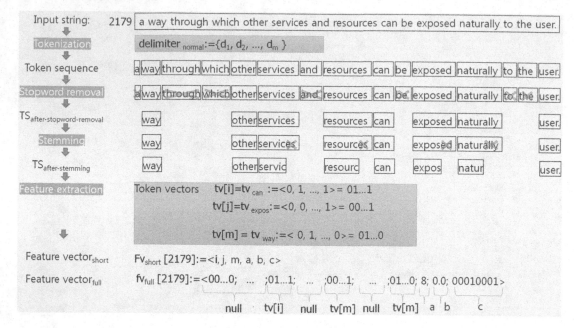

FIGURE 5.12: Steps of feature extraction.

For more detail with examples, see Figure 5.12. Through a typical example, it is easy to understand what is a datum for training and how features and tokens are related and represented. First, the input is a line of text string, e.g., line number 2179: *a way through which other services and resources can be exposed naturally to the user*. See Figure 5.13 to find where the example line is located in the article text. The input string is divided into a sequence of tokens by delimiters $D = \{d_1, d_2, \ldots, d_m\}$. For better performance, the token sequence is filtered and shortened by stopword removal and stemming. Each token is transformed to a token vector by features defined to capture the token characteristics. A token vector is represented by a bit string for patterns it does or does not have (e.g., $< 0, 1, 0, 0, 1, 0, 0, 0, \ldots, 0, 0, 1, 0 >$). A feature vector is based on a line of tokens with token vectors for the tokens it has and a null vector for all of the tokens it lacks. For better efficiency, the feature vector is represented by a list containing each token index corresponding to the token vector, instead of a bit string representing a token vector. For training data, each line is labeled as 'REF' if it is a reference, or as 'NON-REF' otherwise.

Training

After extracting features, a machine-learning-based classifier is trained to identify reference sections from texts. First, some lines from a reference section and from the body of the text are extracted to

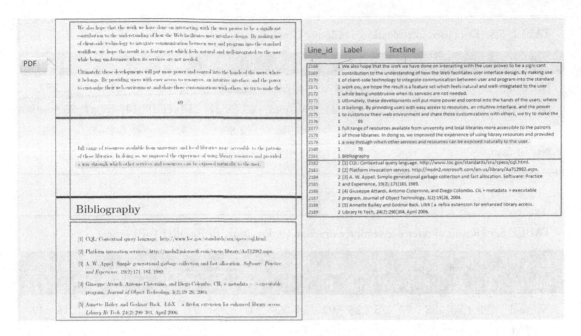

FIGURE 5.13: An example of a training data set.

train a classifier we use in deciding whether or not a line is a reference string. Figure 5.13 illustrates the training text lines corresponding to a reference section and the body of the text, respectively. A reference section is localized by the red box on the left-hand side and labeled as "2" on the right-hand side. Similarly, the body of the text is localized by the blue box on the left-hand side and labeled as "1" on the right-hand side of Figure 5.13. For training, features also should be extracted. Then, the feature vectors are created to measure the similarity between each line in the vector space. In particular, there exists a class tag (i.e., 'REF' or 'NON-REF') indicating if that line is a reference or not, as an attribute of each feature vector.

Reference Section Extraction (Classification)

By using the mentioned training mechanism, our system can "learn," over time, various patterns that references follow. Once a classifier object is trained, any feature vector can be tested against obtained models to see if it "matches" any previous patterns. To implement this, we use WEKA (Waikato Environment for Knowledge Analysis), an open-source, machine-learning toolkit. The operations provided by WEKA are applicable to the machine-learning techniques employed by our software. The version used in this project was 3.7.3.

TABLE 5.8: Data used in evaluation, randomly sampled

Items	Doc1	Doc2	Doc3	Doc4	Doc5	Doc6
No. of lines	4,818	4,899	2,237	6,178	2,369	2,254
No. of reference lines (location)	324 (end)	291 (end)	63 (end)	214 (end)	145 (end)	73 (end)
Percentage of reference lines	6.7%	5.9%	2.8%	3.5%	6.1%	3.2%
No. of features	5,185	5,493	3,208	6,061	3,393	4,097

TABLE 5.9: Result of reference section extraction (P=Precision, R=Recall, F1=F1 score).

Docs	Doc1			Doc2			Doc3			Doc4			Doc5			Doc6		
Metric	P	R	F1	P	R	F1	P	R	F1	P	R	F1	P	R	F1	P	R	F1
Normal + SVM	.99	.80	.88	.97	.75	.85	.92	.54	.68	1.0	.83	.91	.86	.65	.74	.83	.35	.49
Simple + SVM	1.0	.74	.85	.97	.66	.78	.92	.38	.54	.99	.67	.80	.89	.51	.65	.95	.26	.41

Evaluation

We evaluated our machine learning approach to reference section extraction. We used six documents randomly selected from the VT ETD-db system, and marked their reference sections and non-reference sections, manually. Table 5.8 shows the statistics of documents used in this evaluation. In the first column of the table, *No. of lines* indicates the number of total lines in the text, *No. of reference lines* indicates the number of reference lines in the text, *Percentage of reference lines* indicates the ratio of reference lines to the total lines in the text, and *No. of features* indicates the number of features used in the training. Incidentally, all reference sections were found at the end of documents.

We evaluated two tokenization methods: Support Vector Machines (i.e., with a normal tokenizer and a simple tokenizer) and one existing method, ParsCit. Our "normal tokenizer" considers delimiters (space, tab, carriage return, period (.), comma (,), semicolon (;), colon (:), single quotation mark ('), double quotation mark ("), parentheses (()), and question mark (?)). Our 'simple tokenizer' drops period, comma, semicolon, colon, double quotation mark, and parentheses, as compared with the normal tokenizer. ParsCit is based on heuristics using regular expressions. Table 5.9 shows precision, recall, and F1-score of these two tokenizer methods of interest, run against six test datasets. For more details on metrics, see definitions in Section 4.2.1.

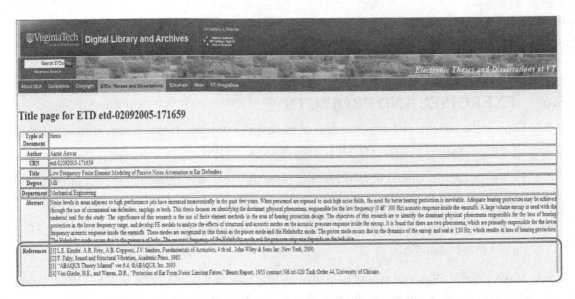

FIGURE 5.14: VT ETD-db with reference metadata

When we informally performed experiments on extracting chapter-reference sections by picking some documents with chapter references, ParsCit failed (it reported that the "Citation text cannot be found: ignoring"). The ETD selected used "Literature Cited" as the reference section header in each chapter. ParsCit probably does not include "Literature Cited" as a starting word of a reference section. Even though we did an experiment with chapter reference sections starting with 'References', ParsCit extracted only the references in the last chapter; it also had some extraction errors where it failed to find the end of the reference section. When we performed an experiment considering contextual features, against document 6 (which showed the worst performance), the performance was improved, resulting in: precision, 0.973; recall, 0.986; and F1, 0.979.

Figure 5.14 illustrates VT ETD-db with Reference Metadata. 'References' after an 'Abstract' are included to show the users the references to which the ETD refers.

5.5 SUMMARY

In this chapter, we presented concepts, related work, formal aspects based on the 5S formalism, and case studies associated with text-extraction services. Text extraction is a necessary process for extending metadata (i.e., special descriptive structures), to be more comprehensive and precise. Text extraction is one type of a pattern recognition problem. Specifically, it involves structuring using classification techniques. We also looked into other techniques related to reference-metadata extraction based on sequence tagging, which is a type of text extraction. Furthermore, we formally described text extraction from the 5S perspective. Finally, we discussed two small studies in terms of the 5S-related concepts for text extraction: 1) document-section segmentation, and 2) reference-section extraction.

5.6 EXERCISES AND PROJECTS

5.1 Explain the benefits and disadvantages of using text-extraction techniques to enrich metadata records in digital libraries. Which services are improved?

5.2 Pick your favorite digital library. Identify three different text-extraction services that would be important in that DL.

5.3 When information is extracted from text automatically, imprecision may be introduced. How should that be handled?

5.4 Make a list of clues that would help identify the start of a portion of a thesis or dissertation that has its set of references. Note that this may be a chapter with a number or letter, but might not, and might be before or after the appendices, etc.

5.5 Make a list of clues that would help identify the start of a section at the end of a chapter that has end-of-chapter references.

5.6 Make a list of clues that would help identify the start of a new chapter in a thesis or dissertation.

5.7 Make a list of clues that would help identify a figure in a thesis or dissertation, and would help ensure that the caption number, caption text, and figure content (in its entirety) are each extracted correctly.

5.8 Table 5.3 lists some types of features to help with extraction. Which of these would you expect would be most useful, relative to the others? Why? Are there types of documents where your assessment might not apply; if so, what are they?

5.9 Study the operation of your preferred tool for working with references. You might consider EndNote, BibTeX, or some other system. How might you develop a program that takes the surface or rendered form of the references in a published thesis or dissertation, and converts them to the corresponding EndNote or BibTeX representation. Hint: consider how reverse engineering and parsing methods might fit together.

5.10 Reflect on the previous question again, but now consider how the use of some type of knowledge base might help in this process. Give a list of all such knowledge bases and explain where they might fit in the processing.

Text

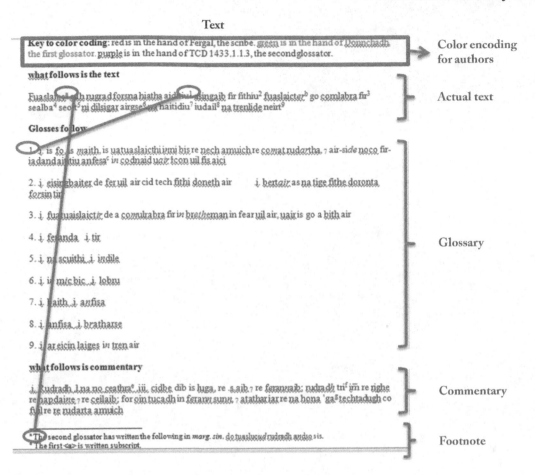

FIGURE 5.15: Digital library for Irish Law Corpus.

5.11 Figure 5.15 shows a snippet of the input files used for building a digital library for an Irish Law Corpus.[1] Based on the text-extraction concepts learned in this chapter, how would you automatically segment the data shown into its respective components in the DL?

---

1. Thanks for this idea go to Charlene Eska, Virginia Tech.

CHAPTER 6

Security

Noha ElSherbiny

Abstract

Security is an important issue in digital library design. Security weaknesses in digital libraries, coupled with attacks (as studied in connection with Cybersecurity) or other types of failures, can lead to confidential information being inappropriately accessed, or loss of integrity of the data stored. These in turn can have a damaging effect on the trust of publishers or other content providers, can cause embarrassment or even economic loss to digital library owners, and even can lead to pain and suffering or other serious problems if urgently needed information is unavailable. In this chapter, security requirements that are essential for any digital library are explored, along with models and mechanisms to provide them.

6.1   INTRODUCTION

Computer security is a broad term that refers to the protection of computer systems from threats. There are various domains of security, such as network security, information security, physical security, personnel security, operational security, and Internet security. In this chapter, we are concerned with information security and logical aspects of security. This closely relates to the currently 'hot' topic of Cybersecurity.

From the previous chapters, we saw how varied and rich the content of digital libraries can be, as well as the complexity of their architecture. Some of the content stored in a digital library may be free for use, while other content is not. There are many different actors working with a digital library; each of these may have different security needs [33]. Thus, a digital library content provider might be concerned with protecting intellectual property rights and the terms-of-use of content, while a digital library user might be concerned with reliable access to content stored in the digital library. Requirements based on these needs sometimes are in conflict, which can make the security architecture of a digital library even more complex.

The architecture must be designed so that security concerns are handled holistically. A security system designer must view the whole architecture and consider all of the applicable security factors when designing a secure digital library. The nature of a security attack often may differ according to

TABLE 6.1: Definition for five security services

Security Service	Definition
Authentication	The assurance that the communicating entity is who it claims to be.
Access Control	The prevention of unauthorized use of a resource (i.e., this service controls who has access to a resource, under what conditions access can occur, and what those accessing the resource are allowed to do).
Confidentiality	The protection of data from unauthorized disclosure.
Data Integrity	The assurance that the data received is exactly as sent by an authorized entity (i.e., contains no modification, insertion, deletion, or replay).
Non-repudiation	Provides protection against denial by one of the entities involved in a communication of having participated in all or part of the communication.

the architecture of the digital library; a distributed digital library has more security weaknesses than a centralized digital library.

In this chapter, we provide an overview on security requirements that need to be taken into account when designing and implementing digital libraries. Existing security models and mechanisms also are introduced.

6.2 BASIC CONCEPTS

According to the X.800 recommendation for the security architecture for OSI [207], there are five main security services that are required to provide system security (see Table 6.1).

Support of the security of digital libraries is not limited to these five services. As discussed in previous chapters, digital libraries cover broad areas of information systems; therefore, there are other services to consider. These are discussed below.

Availability refers to a property that allows the system to be accessible and usable upon demand by an authorized system entity.

Privacy is concerned with the collection and distribution of data and the legal issues involved.

Identity Management is a process where every person/resource is assigned unique identifier credentials, which are used to control access to any system/resource via the associated user rights and restrictions of the established identity.

Trust. An entity is said to "trust" a second entity when the first entity assumes the second entity behaves exactly as the first entity expects.

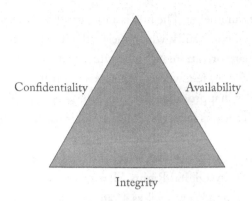

FIGURE 6.1: CIA triad.

Intellectual property rights involve the protection of digital content from disclosure, unauthorized distribution, or copying. Some types of intellectual property rights include copyrights, patents, and trademarks.

All these security requirements are essential to protect digital libraries from different security attacks.

6.3   RELATED WORK

The CIA triad is a common model used to describe the security of information systems [182]. As shown in Figure 6.1, there are three properties in the triad: confidentiality, integrity, and availability. These three properties are necessary to provide a secure system.

Security also can be described using the DELOS reference model [27], which defines a 3-tier architecture. There are security issues relating to each of the three tiers; on the DL tier, issues of intellectual property rights, digital rights management, data confidentiality, and data integrity affect the digital content. On the Digital Library Systems (DLS) tier, availability and access control are security issues because the DLS is the interface between the DL and the users. The user interface of the digital library, the DLMS, is at issue in the third tier.

According to the DELOS reference model, there are six main concepts in a digital library universe: content, user, functionality, architecture, quality, and policy. Each of these concepts has security issues that affect it. These issues are explored below.

6.3.1   CONTENT

The content of a digital library includes the information objects that a digital library provides to the users. Some of the security issues involved are integrity and access control. Integrity requires that each object/resource has not been altered or changed by an unauthorized person. Access control encompasses two security requirements. The first is authentication, where the user must log into the system, while the second is confidentiality, which means that the content of an object is inaccessible to a person unless they have authorization. Not all digital libraries are free; often content is provided to digital library users for a certain fee, whereupon access control is needed to protect the content. Furthermore, some content is inappropriate for some users, or targeted to particular user groups; there are a whole host of such reasons for access control. Logical attacks such as hacking and message tampering can affect the integrity and confidentiality of the content. Improved information access in digital libraries has raised many issues that affect the management of digital libraries. Content Management, or more specifically Digital Rights Management, refers to the protection of content from different logical security attacks, as well as a range of issues relating to intellectual property rights and authenticity.

Digital Rights Management (DRM)

DRM provides content protection by encrypting the content and associating it with a digital license [220]. The license identifies each user allowed to view the content, lists the content of the product, and states the rights the user has to the resource in a computer readable format using a digital rights expression language (DREL) or extensible Rights Markup Language (XrML), that also describes constraints and conditions.

There are seven technologies used to provide DRM [59]. Table 6.2 below summarizes the DRM components and supporting technology.

Each of these components involves mechanisms used to provide DRM:

Encryption. Encryption techniques such as symmetric and asymmetric ciphers can be used to provide access control; public-key encryption is used in payment systems that control how and by whom the content is used. Symmetric ciphers using DES, 3DES, AES, and RC4 algorithms require the use of a shared secret key to encrypt data before it is sent. At the receiver's end, the cipher text is decrypted using the same secret key. Symmetric ciphers depend on both the sender and receiver knowing the shared key. Asymmetric ciphers use a pair of keys, public and private, for each of the sender and the receiver. The public keys of both the sender and the receiver are known but the private key is kept secret. If encryption is performed using the public key, then only the private key can be used for decryption and vice versa.

Passwords. Stored strings must be matched by users desiring access.

Watermarking. Characters or images are added to reflect ownership. Steganography is used to conceal data inside audio, video, or images [88]. Different watermarking techniques have different aims; some watermarks might be visible while others are invisible. Some water-

TABLE 6.2: DRM components and protection technologies. (Adapted from [59])

Component	Protection Technology
Access and usage control	Encryption (e.g., symmetric, asymmetric), passwords
Protection of authenticity and integrity	Watermarks, digital signatures, digital fingerprints
Identification by metadata	Allows description of an object in suitable categories, covering the digital content, rights owner, and conditions
Specific hardware and software	Includes all hardware and software used by the end device through which the digital content is being played, viewed, or printed
Copy detection systems	Search engines, which search the network for illegal copies and use watermarking
Payment systems	Can be seen as a certain type of protection technology as it requires user registration, or credit card authorization, which also requires a trust relationship between the content provider and the customer
Integrated e-commerce systems	DRMS must include systems, which support contract negotiation, accounting information, and usage rules

marks are reversible [136]; it depends on the desired use of the watermark and what is being protected.

Digital signature. Asymmetric encryption can be used. Likewise, hash algorithms such as MD5 and SHA can be used to create a signature [207].

Digital fingerprint. Digital fingerprints are a more powerful technique involving digital signatures and watermarking. The creator of the content creates a unique copy of the content marked for each user; the marks are user-specific, hence called fingerprints. Should a user illegally distribute the content, the creator can use search robots to find those copies [199].

Copy detection systems. Search engines also can help locate such copied objects. Copy-detecting browsers can protect digital content too.

Payment systems. Users must divulge personal information to pay for content. Installing payment systems can help protect digital content.

There is no standard mechanism for providing DRM, mainly due to the lack of regulations [33]. However, there are various systems and protocols introduced to provide content management and support fair usage policies.

6.3.2 PERFORMANCE

There is a tradeoff between security and performance. Nadeem and Javed [151] used a Pentium-4, 2.4 GHz machine running the Microsoft Windows XP operating system, to encrypt 20,527 bytes to 2,323,398 bytes of data using DES, 3DES, and AES. For 20,527 bytes of data it took 2 seconds to encrypt using the DES algorithm and 4 seconds to encrypt using the AES algorithm [151]. It can be seen that the more complex the encryption algorithm, the longer it takes to encrypt the data. In another study, encrypting data with the RSA algorithm using a key size of 1,024 took 0.08 ms/operation on an Intel Core 2, 1.83 GHz processor under Windows Vista in 32-bit mode, while using a key size of 2,048 (which gives much greater security) took 0.16 ms/operation [37].

6.3.3 USER

Users in a digital library refer to "the various actors (whether human or machine) entitled to interact with digital libraries" [27]. Digital libraries connect the different actors with the information they have and allow the users to consume old, or generate new, information. Security issues relating to the users of a digital library intersect with content issues discussed above. A main logical security issue relating to users and content is access control. Different access control requirements arise for distributed systems [218] to ensure both confidentiality and authentication:

- Access control must be applied and enforced at a distributed platform level, so should be scalable and available at various levels of granularity.

- Access-control models should allow a varied definition of access rights depending on different information and must be dynamic where changes to policies are easily made and easy to manage.

- "Access-control models must allow high-level specification of access rights" [218].

Digital library users may need to be authenticated before they can access content in a digital library. Global/universal identification may not suffice. A service provider that provides content taking into account a non-identity-based criteria like age will not benefit from global identification because there is no way to verify the authenticated user's personal information. Usernames and passwords are not efficient ways to provide authentication.

One of the most widely used authentication protocols is Kerberos [161]. It follows a client/server model, which secures communication with servers on a local network. Developed at MIT in the 1980s to provide security across a large campus network, it is based on the Needham-Schroeder protocol and has been standardized and included in many operating systems such as UNIX, Linux, Windows 2000, NT, and XP. Kerberos is used as an authentication protocol in cases where attackers monitor network traffic to intercept passwords. It secures communication, provides single sign-on and mutual authentication, and does not send a user's password in the clear on an unsecured network. An alternative solution suitable for digital libraries [227] is to represent information about an individual using credentials. Credentials are "abstract objects which contain statements expressing knowledge or information from a definite context." Credentials do not specify direct information about a client and their attributes; they describe the local environment and context in which the requests originate [32].

Digital credentials can be used as a means of authentication in providing DL access control [227]. Two agents can be used to assist in the management—a personal security assistant and a server security assistant—to manage digital credentials using a client/server model. The server must notify the client of the credentials required for the current request. The client must have some trust in their server to give credentials, which raises privacy issues. The personal security assistant is used to obtain credentials on behalf of the client, store the credentials, parse and interpret the required credentials, and manage the acceptance policies [227]. A server security assistant is available to specify the credential acceptance policies and their usage.

There is a tradeoff between flexibility and security that must be considered when choosing an access-control model, as is discussed below.

Access Matrix Models (AMM)

This conceptual model specifies the rights that each subject possesses for each object [218]. Actions on objects are allowed or denied based on the access rights specified. There are two implementations of the AMM:

- An *Access Control List* (ACL) provides a direct mapping of each object the subjects are allowed to access, and their usage rights (owner, read, or write).

- A *Capability List* defines the objects each subject is allowed to access and the usage rights.

Access control lists and capability lists are not suitable for distributed systems. Their limitations lead to multiple problems [152]. ACLs provide limited expressibility of policies. Any change in the policies will propagate in the system/application. Authentication in a system that uses ACLs solely is a problem because using username and password in a distributed system is not practical. In a distributed system, administration of the system should be decentralized by delegation to reduce the overhead. The owner of the object specifies a policy in an ACL. If an overall policy is specified by an entity higher than the object owner, then conflicts may occur in the access rights. The number of administrative entities in a distributed system can be very large. Not all the administrators may have trust amongst themselves, resulting in incorrectly defined policies. For example, admin A may trust B but not C, however B may trust C. If A were to define a policy for B then it would be implicitly applicable to C, causing problems.

Role-Based Access Control (RBAC)

Role-based access control involves policies that regulate information access based on the activities the users perform. Such policies require the definition of roles in the system: "a set of actions and responsibilities associated with a particular working activity" [193]. Permissions are assigned to roles instead of individual users. Specifying user authorization involves two steps: first, assigning the user to a role, and second, defining the access control that the role has over certain objects. RBAC is easier to manage and is more extensible than Access Control Lists.

However RBAC does not flexibly handle constraints, where a user with a specific role may need specific permission on an object. An example of an RBAC architecture addressing key limitations is OASIS [12], for use in distributed systems. Role management in OASIS is decentralized and service specific. OASIS is integrated with an event-based middleware that notifies applications of any environmental changes. Roles are parameterized by applications and services to define their client roles, and to enforce policies for role activation and service invocation within each session. Role membership certificates (RMC) are returned to each user on successful login, to be used as a credential to activate other roles [12]. RBAC is suitable for use with digital libraries because it supports decentralized architectures and varying roles, however RBAC does not allow for the definition of different roles in a collaborative group.

Task-Based Access Control (TBAC)

Task-based access control extends subject/object access control by allowing the definition of domains by task-based contextual information [218]. Steps required to perform the task are used to define access control. The steps are associated with a protection state containing a set of permissions for each state, which change according to the task. TBAC uses dynamic management of permissions. TBAC systems are limited to defining contexts in relation to activities, tasks, or workflow progress. Since it is implemented by recording usage and validity of permissions, TBAC requires a central access-control module to manage permissions activation and deactivation in a just-in-time fashion.

Team-Based Access Control (TMAC)

RBAC does not address cases where group members of different roles want to collaborate in a single group. The Team-Based Access Control (TMAC) model defines collaboration by user context and object context. "User context provides a way of identifying specific users playing a role on a team at any given moment" [218], while object context defines the objects required. TMAC offers the advantages of RBAC, along with the ability to specify fine-grained control on users and on object instances.

A scalable access-control data structure can be used with large collections, applying concepts of team-based access control, focusing mainly on the access-control data structure, and employing an access-control framework called Document Access Control Method (DACM) with a Document Storage System (DocSS) [69]. DACM allows the decentralized administration of privileges, the definition of different rule sets to control a single collection, and different delegation patterns as models. Current object access-control policies use an array of rules to record the privileges each subject is allowed, with regard to each object. This is impractical to manage in the large data collections found in digital libraries. DACM solves this problem by finding symmetries in a permission function to allow a brief expression without losing important distinctions.

Content-Based Access Control (CBAC)

Another approach to access-control models involves defining models according to content. This approach is applicable in digital libraries and distributed systems [1], where the access rights to the user are dynamic and may change with each login. Content-based access-control policies are very well suited for digital libraries and distributed systems. Recent research has proposed different models; most use digital credentials for authentication, but vary in the definition/storage of the policy. An important content-based access-control model [58] introduces the Digital Library Authorization System and the Digital Library Authorization Model (DLAM).

Subject, object, and privilege sets cannot be used to define policies in digital libraries, mainly because DLs are dynamic with large collections of data and subjects. CBAC defines access-control policies based on subject qualifications and characteristics. DLAM provides a means to specify the qualifications and characteristics of subjects. It uses content-dependent and independent access control and allows the definition of policies with varied granularity.

6.3.4 FUNCTIONALITY

The concept of functionality encompasses the services that a digital library offers to its users. The minimum functions of a digital library include adding new objects to the library and searching and browsing the library, as well as other functions relating to DL management. A security attack that can affect the functionality of the digital library is a Denial of Service attack, which can affect the performance of the system and prevent users from accessing the system.

6.3.5 ARCHITECTURE

Digital libraries often are complex forms of information systems, interoperable across different libraries, and, so, require an architectural framework mapping content and functionality onto software and hardware components [27]. There are various models for architecture, e.g., client-server, peer-to-peer, and distributed. All of these require protection of the communication channels between two parties, where sensitive data might be transferred [96]. Securing the connections involves different layers—Internet, transport, or application layer—depending on the architecture of the system.

The distributed model is scalable and flexible. It is useful when building a digital library with changing content from different sources and offers potential for increased reliability. The security requirements for a distributed digital library are challenging, since the content and operations are decentralized. Fault tolerance and error recovery are issues that affect a distributed system. Replication is used to increase the availability of the system. While this approach solves problems with denial-of-service attacks, it complicates the protection of the content because one or more replicas of the content exist. Consistency must be maintained, which requires special efforts when updates are frequent; on the other hand, having multiple replicas can help with recovery when one copy is corrupted [127].

The client-server model does not have the same security problems as a general distributed model, however, it presents a major security weakness, the server being a single point of failure. Attacks can be concentrated on one server rather than on the multiple replicas of a distributed model.

6.3.6 QUALITY

The content and behavior of a digital library is characterized and evaluated by quality parameters [73]. Quality is a concept not only used to classify functionality and content, but also used with objects and services [7, 139]. Some of the parameters are automatically measured and are objective while others are considered subjective, in the sense that they are measured through user evaluations [213].

6.3.7 POLICY

Policy is the concept that represents the different regulations and conditions that govern the interaction between the digital library and users. Policy supports both extrinsic and intrinsic situations [27], and their definition and modification. Examples of security issues relating to policies include providing DRM, privacy, and confidentiality of the content and users, defining user behavior, and collection delivery.

An important security issue relating to policy is trust. For example, there may be various contributors to a digital library, each of whom wishes to protect their content; if there is trust between the contributors and the DL managers then they will be more willing to share their content. There are three basic models of trust [64].

Implicit Trust Model. In this model, there is no explicit way to validate the credentials of the communicator. It is sometimes called the assumptive trust model. For example, A receives an email from B, A knows both the email address and domain name, therefore A assumes that

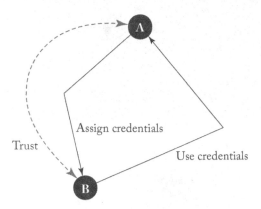

FIGURE 6.2: Explicit trust.

B is the sender and trusts B. However there is no way to prove that B actually sent that email and it was not a replayed message. In current electronic transactions, implicit trust is not a reliable model for use.

Explicit Trust Model.   In the explicit trust model, credentials are used to validate the communicating entities. For example, in Figure 6.2, A issues B a credential such as a username and password. B then uses this username and password to log onto the system. Here we have explicit trust, where A trusts B because of the credentials it just verified, and B trusts A, the issuer of the credentials.

Intermediary Trust Model.   This model is commonly used in distributed and peer-to-peer systems, where the trust is "transmitted" through intermediaries. For example, from Figure 6.3 we can see that A and B have explicit trust, and B and C have explicit trust. Therefore a third trust is inferred: A and C have intermediary trust.

Digital libraries should be secure. This is an important quality that affects all aspects, as has been shown previously using the DL characterization of the DELOS Reference Model [27]. Many of the security issues discussed affect more than one concept, suggesting the overlapping of issues between digital library concepts.

6.4   FORMALIZATION

In other chapters of this series of books, we explored how 5S can be used to define various aspects of digital libraries.

In [71], how an XML-based 5S language (5SL) can be used to create detailed specifications for minimal DLs is described. Such specifications are organized into five models, one for each of

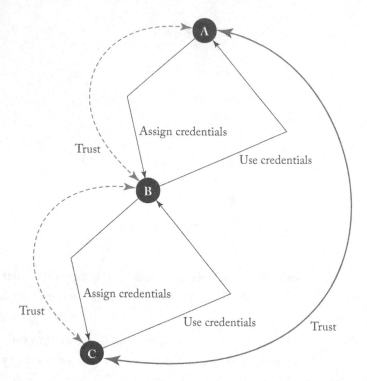

FIGURE 6.3: Intermediary trust model.

the Ss. Many of the elements of a minimal DL can be defined based on a single one of the Ss, so fall within that single model. But others require more elaborate definitions that rely on two or more of the Ss, and for convenience, are placed within the single model for the S that is most important for that element.

One of the hypotheses of this book series is that any digital library, and probably any information system, can be formalized using 5S. Accordingly, the security-related aspects of digital libraries (and other information systems if this hypothesis is correct) can be described if we have 5S-based definitions for all of the security-related concepts involved, and suitably extend the models developed for 5SL [71]. The subsections below should help provide an intuitive grasp of how such a formalization might proceed. Having discussed the different security requirements that are needed in a digital library, we now look at how each of them maps to the 5S formalism.

6.4.1 STREAMS

The streams model describes the different formats of the digital content that is to be stored in the digital library. As discussed in the previous section, publishers or suppliers (related to the societies model) of the digital content must have certain access rights defined for each digital object. A major security threat is the improper disclosure of content, meaning that a person has violated an access right defined for the digital object. To prevent this attack, we need to provide data confidentiality based on which data is protected from unauthorized disclosure. Encryption of the data is a mechanism used to provide data confidentiality. As discussed in the prior section, there are various encryption methods available for use. Another security vulnerability in the streams model is the modification of data; again, digital content access rights might not allow a certain user to modify the contents of a digital object. Any change in the content would be a violation of the access rights defined. Therefore, to detect modifications made to the digital object, we must have data integrity, which is the assurance that the data received is exactly as sent by an authorized entity [207] (i.e., contains no modification, insertion, deletion, or replay). There are various methods to provide data integrity, some of which are hash functions, such as SHA-1 and MD5, or message authentication codes (MAC), such as DAA and keyed Hash MAC (HMAC). These mechanisms can be used with encryption methods to provide data confidentiality.

Illegal use of data is another security attack that can occur in the structure model. An attacker may have gained access to a resource by legal means, but then abuses his privileges by illegally using the data, such as making a copy of the document. Here, an attacker would be violating his access rights; this can be prevented by providing access control, as well as protecting the intellectual property rights of the data. A term is used to describe the protection of content from the different logical security attacks and issues relating to intellectual property rights and authenticity: DRM—see Section 6.3.1.

Thus, to address security issues, additional types of streams should be described in the stream model, such as encrypted versions of other streams. Likewise, these should be related to various scenarios (attacks, disclosures, modifications, and encryption activities). Other connections exist with the remaining Ss, such as the use of structures in characterizing digital content access rights.

6.4.2 STRUCTURES

The structure model covers the organization of the digital content and its metadata in the digital library. Again, disclosure is another security threat where the data objects may be revealed, violating a predefined access right. To combat this attack we can use access control, data confidentiality, and authorization services on its own, or a group of them together. Authorization is a desired service of the digital library: giving permission to use a resource by defining its access rights. Access control is another required security service; it is the prevention of unlawful use of a resource [207] (i.e., this service controls who has access to a resource, under what conditions access can occur, and what those accessing the resource are allowed to do). In the previous section, various access-control models were described; any of these models can be used to provide access control. Another security vulnerability in the structure model is the catalog data. The catalog data has all the information about the metadata; any change in the content would cause a variety of problems. An attacker might change the access rights of certain documents, causing a violation of the access rights defined by the owner of the resource. Therefore, to detect modifications made to the catalog data, we must have data integrity. Again, this can be provided by using hash functions, encryption techniques, or MAC. Another important feature that is required is data consistency, which is the integrity, validity, and accuracy of data between applications. In the structure model, organization tools are used to describe the structure in the digital library. An attacker may use these tools to change the relationships between certain entities, which would make the model inconsistent. By applying the same mechanisms described for data integrity, we can provide data consistency for the structure model.

6.4.3   SPACES

The spaces model includes a description of the 2D space commonly used as part of the user interface. Related security concerns deal with attacks on, or captures of, the flows of data connected, which include keystrokes, mouse clicks, and what is displayed (e.g., text, graphics, images, video), typically in frames and windows on computer screens. Scenarios that may be involved include authentication, encryption/decryption, logging, and recovery using those logs. Clearly, many of the security approaches discussed above have some aspect that involves the user interface.

Another use of spaces in digital libraries involves supporting access to content, e.g., leveraging use of vector spaces, probability spaces, or related use of feature vectors. Clearly, modification of content (streams) will lead to changes in derived representations using any of these spaces. Further, attacks on indexes, inverted files, or related supporting structures will negatively influence the operations that make use of space-based representations.

Yet another application of spaces in DLs is the placement of physical units in the 3D world, as in the locating of computers in a distributed system. Since latency grows with physical distance traversed by data, response time can lengthen if remote rather than local systems are forced to respond to requests. Denial-of-service (see next subsection) attacks on nearby servers, thus have a strong impact on the perceived performance of a distributed system, even if most of the system continues to operate. On the other hand, when there are multiple replicas of data scattered around the world, recovery is likely if a small number of copies are destroyed or corrupted by attack [127], since multiple simultaneous attacks at far-flung locations are very difficult to arrange, and since backup copies often are physically dispersed and secured.

6.4.4   SCENARIOS

Scenarios describe how the digital library actors behave and how the services of the digital library are carried out. Another security attack is denial of service (DoS), which would prevent the digital library from providing any services to its users. Availability is a security requirement that describes a system property that allows authorized users to access and use the system upon demand. There are various types of DoS attacks; pingflood attack involves sending large amounts of ICMP echo command (ping) data packets to the server to attempt to overload it. A counter mechanism requires a network administrator to obtain the IP address of the attacker and block access to the network. TCP smurf is another DoS attack. It involves the attacker communicating with the victim using the victim's IP address. This causes confusion on the victim's network resulting in a flood of traffic sent to the victim's network device. Firewalls can be used to prevent TCP smurf. A similar DoS attack is UDP fraggle, which is also used to confuse the victim's network, but using UDP. Again UDP fraggle can be prevented by having a firewall or simply by blocking any ports that could be used for fraggle such as port 7, echo port, or port 17. Distributed denial-of-service (DDoS) attack is more complex than the other attacks discussed; it involves ping flood but from various computers. The computers attacking might not be aware they are being used; a Trojan or a virus might have given a hacker control over the devices. There is no simple solution to overcome DDoS attack, but buying an intrusion detection system would help prevent the attack.

6.4.5 SOCIETIES

As discussed before, the society model describes the entities that make up the community of the digital library. In this section, we present typical security attacks that affect digital library societies.

Masquerade is another security attack where an attacker falsifies his identity, pretending to be someone else. This is a major problem because certain users may be allowed access to certain content while others are not; if an attacker masquerades as an entity that is allowed to access certain content, then a violation of the access rights of the content occurs.

Authentication is the guarantee that the entity communicating is who it claims to be, thus preventing masquerade. Another form of masquerade that occurs on a lower level (Network Layer of TCP/IP) is IP address spoofing. IP spoofing is the creation of Internet protocol (IP) packets with a fictitious source IP address to hide the identity of the sender or impersonate another computer system, thus possibly gaining access to confidential content. Providing authentication in the system by using packet filtering can prevent IP spoofing.

A different security attack is misuse of privileges, where a user violates the access rights of a digital object. This can be prevented by providing access control, using any of the methods discussed previously.

Another security attack could be session hijacking, which is the use of a session to gain unauthorized access to information or services. Mainly, it refers to the theft of an HTTP cookie, which a user uses to authenticate to a remote server. Here authentication is an important feature, but it is not enough to authenticate the user at the start of the session; authentication should continue throughout the session. A mechanism to prevent session hijacking is encryption of the traffic between the communicating entities, such as with SSL.

Authentication bypass is a security threat where an attacker could perform some action that is restricted to authenticated users without providing authentication. This could lead to various other vulnerabilities, such as disclosure of protected data or modification of data. Authentication bypass is easy to avoid by providing authentication of the user. We need to ensure the credentials submitted are valid before performing any action. Mechanisms such as Kerberos and the X.509 authentication service verify the user's identity just before the data exchange starts. Source/sender non-repudiation is preventing sender or receiver repudiation.

Repudiation is the "denial by one of the entities involved in a communication of having participated in all of or part of the communication" [207]. This is a problem when a user denies communicating in an e-commerce environment. Some digital libraries may require payment to access certain information; the payment process must be secure and must prevent any repudiation by the user. Non-repudiation is a desired requirement that can be satisfied by having users digitally sign any transaction. In the case of payment, an authorized third party may be used to handle the communications, such as PayPal.

6.4.6 CONNECTING THE Ss

Table 6.3 shows the different security attacks that can occur at each of the 5Ss, what service is required to prevent or detect the attack, and what corresponding mechanism is required to provide that service.

The security services mentioned above are related to one another. For example, by definition, in order to have access control, one must have authentication of the user and confidentiality of the data. Therefore access control involves authentication and confidentiality. Other broad terms such as intellectual property rights include having copyrights on content or more broadly having DRM. Figure 6.4 shows a concept map of the different security issues of a digital library and how they all relate to each other. The remainder of this subsection highlights some of the most important relationships.

Secure digital libraries require data consistency of the content and the catalog of the digital library. Data consistency as defined before is the integrity, validity, and accuracy of data between applications. Here, data integrity is of the different digital library components and is a security requirement that can prevent replay attacks, data insertion, data modification, and data deletion.

Another security issue in digital libraries is availability, which is a security requirement used to prevent DoS attacks. The possible types of DoS attacks that can occur on a digital library are DDoS attack, ping flood, TCP smurf, and UDP fraggle. Intellectual property rights is a major security concern in digital libraries, since the content stored on the digital library might not be free; the

TABLE 6.3: The possible security attacks that can occur at each of the 5Ss

5S	Security Attack	Security Service
Streams	Disclosure	Data Confidentiality
	Modification of Data	Data Integrity
Structures	Disclosure	Access Control + Data Confidentiality + Authorization
	Modification of catalog data	Data Integrity + Data Consistency
	Illegal use of data	Digital Rights Management + Privacy + Authorization
Spaces	Disclosure	Data Confidentiality + Authorization
	Modification of data	Data Integrity
Scenarios	Denial-of-Service Attacks: Ping flood / TCP smurf / UDP fraggle / DDoS	Availability
	Disclosure	Access Control + Data Confidentiality + Authorization
Societies	Masquerade	Authentication
	IP spoofing	Authentication
	Session hijacking	Access Control + Authentication
	Authentication bypass	Access Control + Authentication
	Source/sender repudiation	Non-repudiation
	Misuse of privilege	Access Control

creator of the content might wish to enforce certain access rights on the content. The content might have copyrights that determine how the content is to be used.

DRM is a sub-category of intellectual property rights, which refers to the protection of content from the different logical security attacks and issues relating to intellectual property rights and authenticity. In order to enforce DRM, certain sub-requirements are needed, for example, digital signatures and access control. These can be used to preserve the authenticity of the object. Access control as stated above is basically having data confidentiality and authentication of the user, along with a series of access usage definitions for each of the objects. These definitions describe who can access a resource, under what conditions, and what can be done with the resource. As seen in the DELOS reference model an important aspect of digital library design involves the different

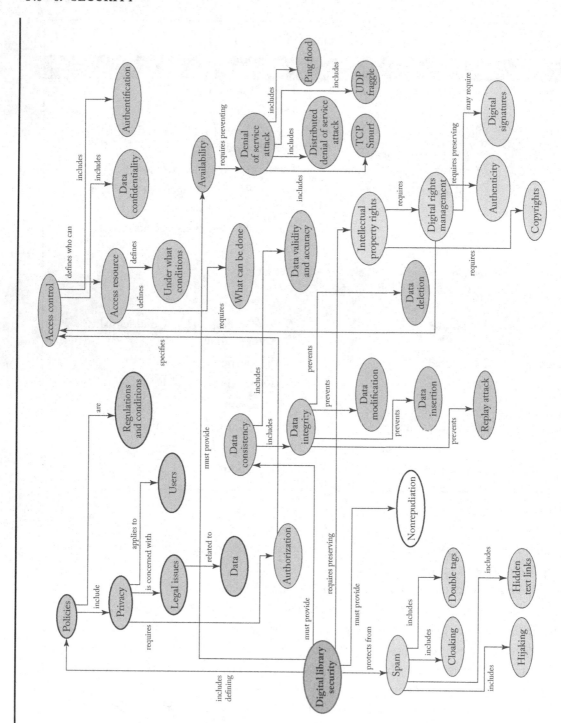

FIGURE 6.4: Concept map of the issues related to digital library security.

policies, including the security policies. Security policies are the different regulations and conditions that govern how a system stores, manages, protects, and distributes sensitive information. There are various security policies in digital libraries that define the terms and conditions for use of the digital library; some policies may define the privacy issues relating to a digital library. This includes the privacy from the user's perspective as well as the collection and distribution of the data. There are various legal issues concerning privacy, especially the personal information being stored, e.g., in certain digital libraries that store sensitive personal information about people, their salaries, and their income. DL designers must make sure that the personal information is confidential and not available to anyone, or may risk facing legal charges.

6.5 CASE STUDIES

One short and one long case study follow.

6.5.1 CTRNET/IDEAL

In the Crisis, Tragedy, and Recovery network (CTRnet) project (http://www.ctrnet.net), Professor Donald Shoemaker, from the Sociology Department at Virginia Tech, described the sensitive nature of some of the content. Survey results, which may include sensitive information such as the income of studied subjects, must not be revealed to just anyone. Certainly some members of the study group may view such data. For others, derived or aggregate data could give an abstract view of the study findings without revealing sensitive personal information. An example of privacy violation could result when personal information could be deduced after multiple queries are conducted, using the digital library search agent. All such privacy issues would need to be addressed. An important aspect of privacy is authorization, which, in turn, requires specifying access control.

Another security issue that affects such digital libraries is spam. During the discussion with the CTRnet project members, it was stated that spam was a serious security issue. The digital library offers forums for victims of crises or tragedies to exchange ways to deal with grief and recovery. The DL is free to any user; it is only required that they create an account the first time they use the DL if adding content. Spammers, unfortunately, have been using the forums to publish adverts and other spam messages.

After the conclusion of funding for the CTRnet project in August 2013, work commenced on the newly funded IDEAL (Integrated Digital Event Archiving and Library) project (http://www.eventsarchive.org). This continues the work on CTRnet, but also expands to support work with other types of events, e.g., those connected with governments and communities. With such broadened scope, additional analysis of security-related concerns will be explored.

6.5.2 CINET

CINET (http://ndssl.vbi.vt.edu/CINET), cyber infrastructure for network science, is a Web portal/service, which provides a common repository for managing both data and models, through a digital library that maintains metadata and provides users with tools to analyze and run these models. CINET hides the details of computation and data management, thereby minimizing the learning effort required. It allows easy extension by integrating off-the-shelf network analysis suites for analysis and visualization; this means new algorithms can be added easily over time. CINET aims to foster research, teaching, and collaboration by building a broad user base, from multiple disciplines, including incorporation into courses on network science at many different universities.

CINET has five partners: Argonne, Indiana University, University of Houston, University of Chicago, and Virginia Tech, which provide clusters and grids, on which to run the computations. The architecture of CINET (see Figure 6.5) is distributed, where the computing resources are at the various partners' sites. The middleware manages the repository and is responsible for running the models and graphs using the selected computing resources. A user interface is available to facilitate the interaction with the system. Thus, there are various interfaces for the users.

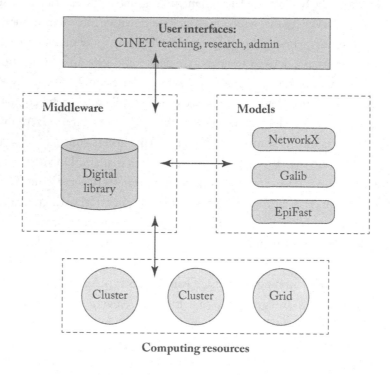

FIGURE 6.5: Architecture of CINET.

The 5S model can be used to describe the CINET digital library, along with the necessary security features.

Streams

CINET stores in the repository graphs and models of networks; both (in encoded form) are examples of streams. Some of these graphs are not for public use, e.g., they are provided by researchers who wish to keep the models confidential. Confidentiality is an important security issue, to ensure the content is protected from unauthorized disclosure. Integrity also would be an important issue, requiring detection of changes in the streams.

Structures

The metadata of the models and graphs stored are examples of structures in CINET. This information may not be available to everyone. Again, as in the streams model, confidentiality and integrity of the content are important security issues to consider.

DRM is also an important issue. The ownership, access rights, and copyrights of the content stored in the digital library must be preserved, otherwise the trust between the content providers and the CINET system will be lost. Similarly, authorization would be required to ensure the access control of the content stored.

Spaces

The availability of the portal is an important security issue in CINET. Different users have different views of the system; all the interfaces must be available for users at all times. CINET has a distributed architecture, with different computational resources at different sites. These resources need to be protected from DoS attacks, as well as other attacks on the communication channels.

Scenarios

CINET has various scenarios that might have vulnerabilities that need protection.

Log-in. Any society member in CINET will need to log into the CINET system before he/she is given access to add or make changes to the resources. In this scenario identity management and authentication are the security issues to consider.

Using Resources. CINET users work with the different resources available; they can run tests and visualizations on the existing data using the CINET computational resources or they can use graphs they have supplied, or algorithms that they have written themselves. This scenario has various security concerns. First, there is access control: who has the right to access what content in the repository, as well as who has the right to execute on the grid. Second, there is the issue of trust: can the content the user is providing be trusted to run on the computational resources? A user can be an "untrusted" user and run a virus on the grid.

Also, the communications channel must be secure, to prevent any changes to be made to the data being sent to/from the grids; therefore data integrity is an issue to consider.

Thus, the security issues involved in the scenarios model are: access control and authorization, identity management, authentication, trust, and data integrity.

Societies

The CINET societies involve various entities. CINET is used for educational purposes and therefore part of the CINET societies are the students that will use the portal, as well as professors and lecturers; they will have teaching materials to conduct certain courses. The security issues involved here are mainly identity management, authentication, and access control. Professors may wish to authenticate the students that use their resources, therefore authenitcation and identity management is required. The CINET system also should require authentication of the professors and students in order to give them access and privileges to appropriate resources.

CINET is maintained by administrators that ensure the services are running and who are improving the system; these administrators are also part of the society. Not only would they need to authenticate their credentials in order to access the system, but also, they would have different access rights depending on the role(s) that they play. This applies to the partners that offer their resources to run the computations; they are also part of the society.

The CINET repository is constantly updated by contributors. These contributors are varied; some of them require their content to be paid for, while others offer it to the public for free. These contributors are another example of societies. Again, access control and authentication are an issue here, but so is privacy; some entities using CINET may wish to remain anonymous.

Another example of societies is the algorithms and programs that are run on the CINET resources. These are not necessarily human, but are still part of the societies model. Authentication is important to validate who can use the resources; there needs to be a mechanism to detect bots, spammers, and other harmful programs that would use the CINET computational resources inappropriately.

Therefore, the security issues involved in the societies model are: access control and authorization, identity management, authentication, and privacy.

6.6 SUMMARY

Digital libraries should be secure. This is an important quality that affects all aspects, as has been shown above using the DL characterization of the DELOS Reference Model.

The 5S framework supports societies and their needs, covering all aspects mentioned above about users and related policies. Since societies cover software actors, agents, components, modules, etc., this also encompasses related architectural issues. Thus, security with regard to societies covers issues like client/server, commerce, identity, peer-to-peer, privacy, rights, roles, teams, and trust. Scenarios cover functions, operations, requirements, services, and tasks. Examples include access, access control, authentication, browsing, copying, DoS attacks, encryption, payment, recovery, searching, usage, and watermarking. Spaces cover distributed aspects, as well as representations related to 1D, 2D, 3D, and higher dimensional spaces. These include feature, measure, metric, probability, vector, and topological spaces. They are used throughout computer and human systems. Structures cover all types of organization, including data structures and databases, with lists (e.g., access control or capability), graphs, and networks. Structures are overlaid on other constructs in the 5S framework, especially on streams. Thus, documents are structured streams, while protocols involve scenarios applied to structured communication streams. Structures and streams cover all types of content, and many security issues related, including DRM, fingerprints, and watermarks.

Clearly, DL security support can be complicated, but the above discussion should help readers organize their thinking and make sure that DL systems meet security requirements. The security requirements presented should be considered when designing and implementing digital libraries. In that regard, application can be made of the discussion above of the most adopted security models and mechanisms.

6.7   EXERCISES AND PROJECTS

6.1 Pick your favorite digital library. Identify three different security attacks that would be dangerous in that DL.

6.2 Pick your favorite digital library. Identify three different security services that would be important in that DL.

6.3 What are the common problems faced when making an existing digital library completely secure?

6.4 Consider the security services listed in Table 6.3. What open-source software could be used for each of those services?

6.5 What is the best way to support security in a digital library when most content is freely accessible and only a small amount of the content has special security requirements?

6.6 How would you go about adding to CTRnet and IDEAL to address the security concerns explained?

6.7 How would you go about adding to CINET to address the security concerns explained?

6.8 DRM is widely deployed, even on small personal devices. How can a small personal digital library be enhanced with security support in a minimal way, without including the overhead needed when working with larger (distributed) systems?

Bibliography

[1] N. Adam, V. Atluri, E. Bertino, and E. Ferrari. A content-based authorization model for digital libraries. *Knowledge and Data Engineering, IEEE Transactions on*, 14(2):296–315, Mar/Apr 2002. DOI: 10.1109/69.991718. 139

[2] (ADS) Advanced Distributed Learning. Sharable Content Object Reference Model (SCORM), available at http://www.adlnet.org/, 2004. 5

[3] M. Afzal, H. Maurer, W. Balke, and N. Kulathuramaiyer. Rule based Autonomous Citation Mining With TIERL. *Journal of Digital Information Management*, 8(3), 2010. 107, 108

[4] M. Agosti, H. Albrechtsen, N. Ferro, I. Frommholz, P. Hansen, N. Orio, E. Panizzi, A. M. Pejtersen, and U. Thiel. DiLAS: a digital library annotation service. In *International Workshop on Annotation for Collaboration—Methods, Tools and Practices*, pages 91–101, 2005. 34

[5] M. Agosti and N. Ferro. Annotations on digital contents, available at http://www.is.informatik .uni-duisburg.de/wiki/images/d/de/agosti-ferro-ijodl-2005.pdf, 2005. 34

[6] M. Agosti and N. Ferro. A formal model of annotations of digital content. *ACM Transactions on Information Systems (TOIS)*, 26(1):1–55, 2008. DOI: 10.1145/1292591.1292594. 35, 38, 40

[7] M. Agosti, N. Ferro, E. A. Fox, M. A. Gonçalves, and B. L. Moreira. Towards a reference quality model for digital libraries. In *First International Workshop on Digital Library Foundations*, 2007. 140

[8] M. Agosti, N. Ferro, and N. Orio. Annotating Illuminated Manuscripts: an Effective Tool for Research and Education. In *JCDL '05: Proceedings of the 5th ACM/IEEE-CS Joint Conference on Digital Libraries*, pages 121–130, 2005. DOI: 10.1145/1065385.1065412. 35

[9] D. W. Archer, L. M. Delcambre, F. Corubolo, L. Cassel, S. Price, U. Murthy, D. Maier, E. A. Fox, S. Murthy, J. Mccall, K. Kuchibhotla, and R. Suryavanshi. Superimposed information architecture for digital libraries. In *ECDL '08: Proceedings of the 12th European conference on Research and Advanced Technology for Digital Libraries*, pages 88–99, Berlin, Heidelberg, 2008. Springer-Verlag. DOI: 10.1007/978-3-540-87599-4_10. 31, 33, 44

[10] C. Awre. User-author centered multimedia building blocks. *Managing compound objects within Fedora*, 2007. Knowledge Exchange Group—Enhanced E-theses Project Deliverable 9, available at http://igitur-archive.library.uu.nl/DARLIN/2010-0526-200241/UUindex.html (last accessed on 09/20/10). 3, 12

[11] C. Awre. Legal issues of compound ETDs. In *Knowledge Exchange Group—Research paper—Enhanced E-theses Project Deliverable 9.1*, available at http://igitur-archive.library.uu.nl/DARLIN/2010-0526-200238/UUindex.html (last accessed on 05/05/11), 2009. 2

[12] J. Bacon, K. Moody, and W. Yao. Access control and trust in the use of widely distributed services. In *Proceedings of the IFIP/ACM International Conference on Distributed Systems Platforms, Heidelberg*, Middleware '01, pages 295–310, London, UK, 2001. Springer-Verlag. DOI: 10.1007/3-540-45518-3_16. 138

[13] M. Balakrishna, D. I. Moldovan, M. Tatu, and M. Olteanu. Semi-automatic domain ontology creation from text resources. In N. Calzolari, K. Choukri, B. Maegaard, J. Mariani, J. Odijk, S. Piperidis, M. Rosner, and D. Tapias, editors, *LREC*. European Language Resources Association, 2010. 72, 83

[14] D. Bargeron, B. A. J. Brush, and A. Gupta. A common annotation framework. Technical report, Microsoft Corporation: MSR-TR-2001-108, 2001. 35

[15] J. Bekaert, P. Hochstenbach, and H. V. de Sompel. Using MPEG-21 DIDL to Represent Complex Digital Objects in the Los Alamos National Laboratory Digital Library, available at http://www.dlib.org/dlib/november03/bekaert/11bekaert.html. *D-Lib Magazine*, 9(11), November 2003. 4

[16] T. Berners-Lee, J. Hendler, and O. Lassila. The Semantic Web. *Scientific American*, 284(5), May 2001. DOI: 10.1038/scientificamerican0501-34. 36

[17] D. C. Blair and M. E. Maron. An evaluation of retrieval effectiveness for a full-text document-retrieval system. *Communications of the ACM*, 28(3), March 1985. DOI: 10.1145/3166.3197. 90

[18] W. Borst. *Construction of Engineering Ontologies*. Ph.D. thesis, University of Twenty, Enschede, The Netherlands, 1997. 64

[19] D. Braggins. Fingerprint sensing and analysis. *Sensor Review*, 21(4):272–277, 2001. DOI: 10.1108/02602280110406909. 13

[20] G. Brusa, M. L. Caliusco, and O. Chiotti. Building ontology in public administration: A case study. In *International Workshop on Applications and Business Aspects of the Semantic Web*, 2006. 72

[21] G. Buchanan, J. Gow, A. Blandford, J. Rimmer, and C. Warwick. Representing aggregate works in the digital library. In *JCDL '07: Proceedings of the 2007 conference on Digital libraries*, pages 247–256, New York, NY, USA, 2007. ACM Press. DOI: 10.1145/1255175.1255224. 35

[22] I. S. Burnett, F. Pereira, R. V. de Walle, and R. Koenen. *The MPEG-21 Book*. John Wiley & Sons, 2006. DOI: 10.1002/0470010134. 4, 5

[23] L. Cai and T. Hofmann. Hierarchical document categorization with support vector machines. In *CIKM '04: Proceedings of the thirteenth ACM international conference on Information and knowledge management*, pages 78–87, New York, NY, USA, 2004. ACM. DOI: 10.1145/1031171.1031186. 95

[24] P. S. Canada. Canadian Disaster Database. http://www.publicsafety.gc.ca/prg/em/cdd/srch-eng.aspx, 2011. [Online; accessed 26-September-2011]. 84

[25] K. S. Candan, H. Liu, and R. Suvarna. Resource Description Framework: metadata and its applications. *ACM SIGKDD Explorations Newsletter*, 3:1, 2001. DOI: 10.1145/507533.507536. 36

[26] L. Candela, D. Castelli, N. Ferro, Y. Ioannidis, G. Koutrika, C. Meghini, P. Pagano, S. Ross, D. Soergel, M. Agosti, M. Dobreva, V. Katifori, and H. Schuldt. The DELOS Digital Library Reference Model—Foundations for Digital Libraries. Version 0.98, 2008. http://www.delos.info/files/pdf/ReferenceModel/DELOS [last visited July 4, 2012]. 10

[27] L. Candela, D. Castelli, Y. Ioannidis, G. Koutrika, P. Pagano, S. Ross, H. J. Schek, and H. Schuldt. Deliverable D1.4.2: A reference model for digital library management systems interim report, DELOS digital library, available at http://www.delos.info/index.php?option=com_content& task=view&id=345, 2006. 133, 136, 139, 140, 141

[28] A. Carkacioglu and F. Yarman-Vural. SASI: A new Texture Descriptor for Content-Based Image Retrieval. *IEEE International Conference on Image Processing*, 2:137–140, 2001. DOI: 10.1109/ICIP.2001.958443. 19, 25

[29] CCSDS. Reference Model for an Open Archival Information System (OAIS): Recommendation for Space Data System Standards: CCSDS 650.0-B-1. Technical report, Consultative Committee for Space Data Systems, January 2002. 4

[30] M. Ceci and D. Malerba. Classifying web documents in a hierarchy of categories: a comprehensive study. *Journal of Intelligent Information Systems*, 28(1):37–78, February 2007. DOI: 10.1007/s10844-006-0003-2. 94, 96

[31] K. Cheung, A. Lashtabeg, and D. J. SCOPE: A Scientific Compound Object Publishing and Editing System. *The International Journal of Digital Curation*, 2(2):4–18, 2008. DOI: 10.2218/ijdc.v3i2.55. 3

[32] N. Ching, V. Jones, and M. Winslett. Authorization in the digital library: secure access to services across enterprise boundaries. In *Research and Technology Advances in Digital Libraries, 1996. ADL '96, Proceedings of the Third Forum on*, pages 110–119, May 1996. DOI: 10.1109/ADL.1996.502521. 137

[33] G. Chowdhury and S. Chowdhury. *Introduction to Digital Libraries*. Facet Publishing, 2003. 131, 136

[34] E. Cortez, A. da Silva, M. Gonçalves, F. Mesquita, and E. de Moura. FLUX-CIM: flexible unsupervised extraction of citation metadata. In *Proceedings of the 7th ACM/IEEE-CS Joint Conference on Digital Libraries*, page 224. ACM, 2007. DOI: 10.1145/1255175.1255219. 107, 108

[35] F. Corubolo, P. B. Watry, and J. Harrison. Location and format independent distributed annotations for collaborative research. In *Research and Advanced Technology for Digital Libraries, 11th European Conference*, pages 495–498, 2007. DOI: 10.1007/978-3-540-74851-9_50. 33

[36] I. G. Councill, C. L. Giles, and M.-Y. Kan. ParsCit: an open-source CRF reference string parsing package. In *International Conference on Language Resources and Evaluation (LREC)*, available at http://www.lrec-conf.org/proceedings/lrec2008/summaries/166.html, 2008. 107, 108, 109, 110, 111, 112

[37] W. Dai. Crypto++ 5.6.0 benchmarks, March 2009, http://www.cryptopp.com/benchmarks.html. 136

[38] M. Day, R. Tsai, C. Sung, C. Hsieh, C. Lee, S. Wu, K. Wu, C. Ong, and W. Hsu. Reference metadata extraction using a hierarchical knowledge representation framework. *Decision Support Systems*, 43(1):152–167, 2007. DOI: 10.1016/j.dss.2006.08.006. 107, 108

[39] M. Dean and G. Schreiber. *OWL Web Ontology Language Reference*. W3C, available at http://www.w3.org/TR/owl-ref/, 2003. 70

[40] H. Dejean. Pdf2xml Converter. http://sourceforge.net/projects/pdf2xml/index.html, 2013. [Online; accessed 30-December-2013]. 117

[41] L. Delcambre, D. Maier, S. Bowers, M. Weaver, L. Deng, P. Gorman, J. Ash, M. Lavelle, and J. A. Lyman. Bundles in captivity: An application of superimposed information. In *Proceedings of the 17th International Conference on Data Engineering (ICDE), Heidelberg, Germany*, pages 111–120. ICDE, 2001. DOI: 10.1109/ICDE.2001.914819. 33

[42] L. Delcambre, D. Maier, and R. Reddy. Structured maps: Modeling explicit semantics over a universe of information. *International Journal of Digital Libraries*, 1(1):20–35, 1997. DOI: 10.1007/s007990050002. 33

[43] L. M. Delcambre, D. Archer, S. Price, U. Murthy, E. A. Fox, and L. Cassel. Superimposing a strand map over a database lecture, 2008. Presented at the 39th SIGCSE technical symposium on Computer science education. 47

[44] L. M. L. Delcambre and D. Maier. Models for superimposed information. In *ER '99: Proceedings of the Workshops on Evolution and Change in Data Management, Reverse Engineering in Information Systems, and the World Wide Web and Conceptual Modeling*, pages 264–280, London, UK, 1999. Springer-Verlag. DOI: dx.doi.org/10.1007/3-540-48054-4_22. 31, 32, 33

[45] Digital Library Federation. Metadata Encoding and Transmission Standard (METS), available at http://www.loc.gov/standards/mets/, 2009. 4

[46] L. Ding, T. Finin, A. Joshi, R. Pan, R. S. Cost, Y. Peng, P. Reddivari, V. Doshi, and J. Sachs. Swoogle: a search and metadata engine for the semantic web. In *CIKM '04: Proceedings of the thirteenth ACM international conference on Information and knowledge management*, pages 652–659, New York, NY, USA, 2004. ACM. DOI: 10.1145/1031171.1031289. 73

[47] Y. Ding, G. Chowdhury, and S. Foo. Template mining for the extraction of citation from digital documents. In *Proceedings of the Second Asian Digital Library Conference, Taiwan*, pages 47–62. Citeseer, 1999. 108

[48] M. Doerr, S. Gradmann, S. Hennicke, A. Isaac, C. Meghini, and H. V. de Sompel. The Europeana Data Model (EDM). In *IFLA 2011: World Library and Information Congress: 76th IFLA General Conference and Assembly, Gothenburg, Sweden*, 2010. 12

[49] P. Dourado, P. Ferreira, and A. Santanchè. Representação unificada de objetos digitais complexos: Confrontando o ras com o ims cp. In *III Workshop de Bibliotecas Digitais.*, 2006. 4, 6

[50] Drupal. Available at http://www.drupal.org/. 118

[51] S. Dumais and H. Chen. Hierarchical classification of web content. In *SIGIR '00: Proceedings of the 23rd annual international ACM SIGIR Conference on Research and Development in Information Retrieval*, pages 256–263, New York, NY, USA, 2000. ACM. DOI: 10.1145/345508.345593. 95

[52] ECO4R. Exposing Compound Objects for Repositories. http://www.eco4r.org, 2010. 12

[53] D. Embley, D. Campbell, Y. Jiang, S. Liddle, D. Lonsdale, Y. Ng, and R. Smith. Conceptual-model-based data extraction from multiple-record Web pages. *Data & Knowledge Engineering*, 31(3):227–251, 1999. DOI: 10.1016/S0169-023X(99)00027-0. 108

[54] O. Etzioni, M. Cafarella, D. Downey, A.-M. Popescu, T. Shaked, S. Soderland, D. S. Weld, and A. Yates. Unsupervised named-entity extraction from the web: An experimental study. *Artificial Intelligence*, 165(1):91–134, 2005. DOI: 10.1016/j.artint.2005.03.001. 107

[55] A. Farquhar, R. Fikes, and J. Rice. The Ontolingua Server: a tool for collaborative ontology construction. *Int. J. Hum.-Comput. Stud.*, 46(6):707–727, 1997. DOI: 10.1006/ijhc.1996.0121. 69

[56] Federal Bureau of Investigation (FBI). The Integrated Automated Fingerprint Identification System - IAFIS. http://www.fbi.gov/about-us/cjis/fingerprints_biometrics/iafis/iafis, 1999. 14

[57] N. Ferran, E. Mor, and J. Minguillón. Towards personalization in digital libraries through ontologies. *Library management*, 26(4/5):206–217, 2005. DOI: 10.1108/01435120510596062. 73

[58] E. Ferrari, N. Adam, V. Atluri, E. Bertino, and U. Capuozzo. An authorization system for digital libraries. *The VLDB Journal*, 11(1):58–67, August 2002. DOI: 10.1007/s007780200063. 139

[59] M. Fetscherin and M. Schmid. Comparing the usage of digital rights management systems in the music, film, and print industry. In *Proceedings of the 5th international conference on Electronic commerce*, ICEC '03, pages 316–325, New York, NY, USA, 2003. ACM. DOI: 10.1145/948005.948047. 134, 135

[60] F. Fonseca, M. Egenhofer, C. Davis, and G. Câmara. Semantic granularity in ontology-driven geographic information systems. *Annals of Mathematics and Artificial Intelligence*, 36(1-2):121–151, 2002. DOI: 10.1023/A:1015808104769. 10

[61] FooLabs. Xpdf Download. http://www.foolabs.com/xpdf/download.html, 2013. [Online; accessed 30-December-2013]. 117

[62] Center for Research on the Epidemiology of Disasters CRED. EM-DAT: The International Disaster Database. http://www.emdat.be/, 2011. [Online; accessed 26-September-2011]. 84

[63] E. Frank and G. W. Paynter. Predicting library of congress classifications from Library of Congress subject headings. *Journal of the American Society for Information Science and Technology*, 55(3):214–227, 2004. DOI: 10.1002/asi.10360. 95

[64] A. Garcia-Crespo, J. M. G. Berbis, R. C. Palacios, and F. G. Sanchez. Digital libraries and Web 3.0. The CallimachusDL approach. *Computers in Human Behavior*, 27(4):1424–1430, 2011. DOI: 10.1016/j.chb.2010.07.046. 74

[65] R. Gartner. METS as an 'Intermediary' Schema for a Digital Library of Complex Scientific Multimedia. *International Journal of Computer Vision*, 31(3):24–35, September 2012. DOI: 10.6017/ital.v31i3.1917. 2

[66] M. R. Genesereth. Knowledge Interchange Format. In *2nd International Conference on Principles of Knowledge Representation and Reasoning*, pages 599–600, 1991. 79

[67] M. R. Genesereth and R. E. Fikes. Knowledge Interchange Format, Version 3.0 Reference Manual. Technical Report Logic-92-1, Stanford University, Stanford, CA, USA, 1992. 69

[68] A. Gerber and J. Hunter. Authoring, editing and visualizing compound objects for literary scholarship. *Journal of Digital Information (JoDI)*, 1(1), 2010. 10, 11

[69] H. M. Gladney. Access control for large collections. *ACM Trans. Inf. Syst.*, 15(2):154–194, April 1997. DOI: 10.1145/248625.248652. 139

[70] A. Gómez-Pérez and D. Manzano-Macho. An overview of methods and tools for ontology learning from texts. *Knowledge Eng. Review*, 19(3):187–212, 2004. DOI: 10.1017/S0269888905000251. 71, 74

[71] M. A. Gonçalves and E. A. Fox. 5SL: a language for declarative specification and generation of digital libraries. In *JCDL '02: Proceedings of the 2nd ACM/IEEE-CS Joint Conference on Digital Libraries*, pages 263–272, New York, NY, USA, 2002. ACM Press. 25, 141, 142

[72] M. A. Gonçalves, E. A. Fox, L. T. Watson, and N. A. Kipp. Streams, structures, spaces, scenarios, societies (5S): A formal model for digital libraries. *ACM Transactions on Information Systems*, 22(2):270–312, 2004. DOI: 10.1145/984321.984325. 3, 96, 97

[73] M. A. Gonçalves, B. L. Moreira, E. A. Fox, and L. T. Watson. What is a good digital library? - defining a quality model for digital libraries. *Information Processing & Management*, 43(5):1416–1437, 2007. 90, 140

[74] M. Gordon and P. Pathak. Finding information on the World Wide Web: the retrieval effectiveness of search engines. *Inf. Process. Manage.*, 35(2):141–180, 1999. DOI: 10.1016/S0306-4573(98)00041-7. 90

[75] R. Grishman and B. Sundheim. Message Understanding Conference-6: A Brief History. In *Proceedings of COLING*, volume 96, pages 466–471, 1996. DOI: 10.3115/992628.992709. 106

[76] T. R. Gruber. A translation approach to portable ontology specifications. *Knowledge Acquisition*, 5(2):199–220, 1993. DOI: 10.1006/knac.1993.1008. 64

[77] V. A. Gruzman and V. I. Senichkin. Hypermedia models. *Autom. Remote Control*, 62(5):677–694, 2001. DOI: 10.1023/A:1010213803542. 10

[78] F. Halasz and M. Schwartz. The Dexter Hypertext Reference Model. *Communications of the ACM*, 37(2):30, 1994. DOI: 10.1145/175235.175237. 34, 42

[79] H. Han, H. Zha, and L. Giles. A model-based k-means algorithm for name disambiguation. In *Second International Semantic Web Conference (ISWC-03) Workshop on Semantic Web Technologies for Searching and Retrieving Scientific Data.*, Workshop on Semantic Web Technologies for Searching and Retrieving Scientific Data, 2003. DOI: 10.1.1.4.3484. 109

[80] L. Hardman, D. C. A. Bulterman, and G. van Rossum. The Amsterdam hypermedia model: adding time and context to the Dexter model. *Commun. ACM*, 37(2):50–62, 1994. DOI: 10.1145/175235.175239. 34, 42

[81] B. Haslhofer, R. Simon, R. Sanderson, and H. van de Sompel. The Open Annotation Collaboration (OAC) Model. Technical Report arXiv:1106.5178v1 [cs.DL], arXiv CoRR, June 2011. 35

[82] HDF. Hierarchical Data Format- v.5-1.8.10. http://www.hdfgroup.org/, 2012. 4

[83] E. Hetzner. A simple method for citation metadata extraction using hidden Markov models. In *Proceedings of the 8th ACM/IEEE-CS Joint Conference on Digital Libraries*, pages 280–284. ACM, 2008. DOI: 10.1145/1378889.1378937. 107, 108, 109

[84] C. Hong, J. Gozali, and M. Kan. FireCite: Lightweight real-time reference string extraction from webpages. In *Proceedings of the 2009 Workshop on Text and Citation Analysis for Scholarly Digital Libraries*, pages 71–79. Association for Computational Linguistics, 2009. DOI: 10.3115/1699750.1699762. 107, 108, 109, 110, 111, 112

[85] R. E. Jenkins and N. M. Burkhead. *Freshwater Fishes of Virginia*. American Fisheries Society, Bethesda, Maryland, 1993. 31, 50, 53

[86] F. Jiao, S. Wang, C. Lee, R. Greiner, and D. Schuurmans. Semi-supervised conditional random fields for improved sequence segmentation and labeling. In *Proceedings of the 21st International Conference on Computational Linguistics and the 44th annual meeting of the ACL*, pages 209–216. Association for Computational Linguistics, 2006. DOI: 10.3115/1220175.1220202. 110

[87] T. Joachims, T. Hofmann, Y. Yue, and C. Yu. Predicting structured objects with support vector machines. *Communications of the ACM*, 52(11):97–104, 2009. DOI: 10.1145/1592761.1592783. 109

[88] N. Johnson and S. Jajodia. Exploring steganography: Seeing the unseen. *Computer*, 31(2):26–34, February 1998. DOI: 10.1109/MC.1998.4655281. 134

[89] M. I. Jordan and R. A. Jacobs. Hierarchical mixtures of experts and the EM algorithm. *Neural Comput.*, 6(2):181–214, 1994. DOI: 10.1162/neco.1994.6.2.181. 94

[90] J. Kahan and M.-R. Koivunen. Annotea: an open RDF infrastructure for shared web annotations. In *WWW '01: Proceedings of the 10th international conference on World Wide Web*, pages 623–632, New York, NY, USA, 2001. ACM. DOI: 10.1145/371920.372166. 35

[91] Y. Kalfoglou and W. M. Schorlemmer. Using formal concept analysis and information flow for modelling and sharing common semantics: Lessons learnt and emergent issues. In *13th International Conference on Conceptual Structures*, pages 107–118, 2005. DOI: 10.1007/11524564_7. 72

[92] J. F. Karpovich, A. S. Grimshaw, and J. C. French. Extensible file system (ELFS): an object-oriented approach to high performance file I/O. *ACM SIGPLAN Notices*, 29(10):191–204, 1994. DOI: 10.1145/191081.191112. 4

[93] A. Kerne. Recombinant information workshop, available at http://ecologylab.cs.tamu.edu/workshops/ht05recombinant.html, 2005. 34

[94] A. Kerne, E. Koh, B. Dworaczyk, M. J. Mistrot, H. Choi, S. M. Smith, R. Graeber, D. Caruso, A. Webb, R. Hill, and J. Albea. combinformation: a mixed-initiative system for representing collections as compositions of image and text surrogates. In *JCDL '06: Proceedings of the 6th ACM/IEEE-CS Joint Conference on Digital Libraries*, pages 11–20, New York, NY, USA, 2006. ACM. DOI: 10.1145/1141753.1141756. 34

[95] A. Kerne, E. Koh, S. M. Smith, A. Webb, and B. Dworaczyk. combinformation: Mixed-initiative composition of image and text surrogates promotes information discovery. *ACM Trans. Inf. Syst.*, 27(1):1–45, 2008. DOI: 10.1145/1416950.1416955. 34

[96] U. Kohl, J. Lotspiech, and S. Nusser. Security for the digital library-protecting documents rather than channels. In *Database and Expert Systems Applications, 1998. Proceedings. Ninth International Workshop on*, pages 316–321, Aug 1998. DOI: 10.1109/DEXA.1998.707419. 139

[97] D. Koller and M. Sahami. Hierarchically classifying documents using very few words. In *ICML '97: Proceedings of the Fourteenth International Conference on Machine Learning*, pages 170–178, San Francisco, CA, USA, 1997. Morgan Kaufmann Publishers Inc. 94, 95, 100

[98] N. Kozievitch, J. Almeida, R. da S. Torres, A. Santanchè, and N. Leite. Reusing a Compound-Based Infrastructure for Searching Video Stories. In *12th IEEE International Conference on Information Reuse and Integration (IRI)*. IEEE, 2011. DOI: 10.1109/IRI.2011.6009550. 13, 25

[99] N. P. Kozievitch. Complex Objects in Digital Libraries. In *JCDL '09: Proceedings of the 9th ACM/IEEE-CS Joint Conference on Digital Libraries*, Doctoral Consortium, available at http://www.ieee-tcdl.org/Bulletin/v5n3/Kozievitch/kozievitch.html, last accessed on 05/05/11, 2009. 4, 38

[100] N. P. Kozievitch. *Objetos Complexos em Bibliotecas Digitais: Analisando o Gerenciamento de Componentes de Imagens*. Ph.D. thesis, Instituto de Computação, Unicamp, Campinas, SP, Julho 2011. 13

[101] N. P. Kozievitch, J. Almeida, R. da S. Torres, N. A. Leite, M. A. Gonçalves, U. Murthy, and E. A. Fox. Towards a Formal Theory for Complex Objects and Content-Based Image Retrieval. *JIDM*, 2(3):321–336, 2011. 12, 13

[102] N. P. Kozievitch and R. da S. Torres. Describing OAI-ORE from the 5S framework perspective. In *Proceedings of the role of digital libraries in a time of global change, and 12th international conference on Asia-Pacific digital libraries*, ICADL'10, pages 260–261, Berlin, Heidelberg, 2010. Springer-Verlag. DOI: 10.1007/978-3-642-13654-2_34. 8

[103] N. P. Kozievitch, R. da S. Torres, S. H. Park, E. A. Fox, N. Short, A. L. Abbott, S. Misra, and M. Hsiao. Database for fingerprint experiments. *Poster for CESCA (Center for Embedded Systems for Critical Applications) Day, Virginia Tech, Blacksburg, VA, USA*, 5 2010. 15

[104] N. P. Kozievitch, R. da S. Torres, S. H. Park, E. A. Fox, N. Short, A. L. Abbott, S. Misra, and M. Hsiao. Rethinking Fingerprint Evidence Through Integration of Very Large Digital Libraries. *VLDL Workshop at 14th European Conference on Research and Advanced Technology for Digital Libraries (ECDL2010)*, pages 23–30, 07 2010. 14, 17, 25

[105] N. P. Kozievitch, R. da S. Torres, A. Santanchè, D. C. G. Pedronette, R. T. Calumby, and E. A. Fox. An Infrastructure for Searching and Harvesting Complex Image Objects. *Information Interaction Intelligence Journal*, 11(2):39–68, 2011. 2, 11, 13

[106] N. P. Kozievitch, R. da Silva Torres, F. Andrade, U. Murthy, E. A. Fox, and E. Hallerman. A teaching tool for parasitology: Enhancing learning with annotation and image retrieval. In *Proc. ECDL 2010*, pages 466–469, 2010. DOI: 10.1007/978-3-642-15464-5_58. 50

[107] N. P. Kozievitch, E. Fox, and R. da S. Torres. Analyzing Compound Object Technologies from the 5S Perspective. Technical Report IC-11-01, Institute of Computing, University of Campinas, 2011. 4, 38

[108] D. B. Krafft, A. Birkland, and E. J. Cramer. NCore: architecture and implementation of a flexible, collaborative digital library. In *JCDL '08: Proceedings of the 8th ACM/IEEE-CS Joint Conference on Digital Libraries*, pages 313–322, New York, NY, USA, 2008. ACM. http://doi.acm.org/10.1145/1378889.1378943 [last visited July 4, 2012]. DOI: 10.1145/1378889.1378943. 3, 38

[109] S. R. Kruk, T. Woroniecki, A. Gzella, and M. Dabrowski. JeromeDL—a semantic digital library. In J. Golbeck and P. Mika, editors, *Semantic Web Challenge*, volume 295 of *CEUR Workshop Proceedings*. CEUR-WS.org, 2007. DOI: 10.1007/978-3-540-85434-0_10. 73

[110] B. Lagoeiro, M. A. Gonçalves, and E. A. Fox. 5SQual: A quality tool for digital libraries. In *Proceedings of the 7th ACM/IEEE Joint Conference on Digital Libraries*, page (demonstration), New York, NY, USA, 2007. ACM Press. 25

[111] C. Lagoze and H. V. de Sompel. The Open Archives Initiative: building a low-barrier interoperability framework. In *JCDL '01: Proceedings of the 1st ACM/IEEE-CS Joint Conference on Digital Libraries*, pages 54–62, New York, NY, USA, 2001. ACM Press. DOI: 10.1145/379437.379449. 4

[112] C. Lagoze, H. V. de Sompel, P. Johnston, M. Nelson, R. Sanderson, and S. Warner. Open Archives Initiative Object Reuse and Exchange - Abstract Data Model- v.1.0. http://www .openarchives.org/ore/1.0/datamodel, 2008. 7

[113] C. Lagoze, D. B. Krafft, S. Payette, and S. Jesurogai. What is a digital library anyway? beyond search and access in the NSDL. *D-Lib magazine*, 11(11), 2005. DOI: 10.1045/november2005-lagoze. 38

[114] C. Lagoze and H. V. Sompel. Compound Information Objects: the OAI-ORE Perspective. *Open Archives Initiative Object Reuse and Exchange*, White Paper, http://www.openarchives.org/ore/documents, 2007. 1, 3, 7

[115] O. Lassila and R. R. Swick. Resource Description Framework (RDF). Model and Syntax Specification, available at http://www.w3.org/tr/1999/rec-rdf-syntax-19990222. Technical report, W3C. 69

[116] Y. Lei, V. Uren, and E. Motta. SemSearch: A search engine for the semantic web. *Proc. 5th Intern. Conf. on Knowledge Engineering and Knowledge Management Managing Knowledge in a World of Networks, Lect. Notes in Comp. Sci., Springer, Podebrady, Czech Republic (Oct 2006)*, pages 238–245, 2006. DOI: 10.1007/11891451_22. 73

[117] D. B. Lenat and R. V. Guha. *Building large knowledge-based systems. Representation and inference in the Cyc project.* Addison-Wesley, Massachusetts, 1990. 75

[118] X. Li, Y. Wang, and A. Acero. Extracting structured information from user queries with semi-supervised conditional random fields. In *Proceedings of the 32nd international ACM SIGIR*

Conference on Research and Development in Information Retrieval, pages 572–579. ACM, 2009. DOI: 10.1145/1571941.1572039. 110

[119] Library Of Congress. METS—Metadata Encoding and Transmission Standard. http://www.loc .gov/standards/mets/, 2003. 4

[120] L. Liu, C. Wang, M. Wu, and G. He. Research of intelligent information retrieval system ontology-based in digital library. In *IT in Medicine and Education, 2008. ITME 2008. IEEE International Symposium on*, pages 375–379, Dec. 2008. 73

[121] T. Y. Liu, Y. Yang, H. Wan, H. J. Zeng, Z. Chen, and W. Y. Ma. Support vector machines classification with a very large-scale taxonomy. *SIGKDD Explor. Newsl.*, 7(1):36–43, 2005. DOI: 10.1145/1089815.1089821. 95, 96

[122] M. Lopez, A. Gomez-Perez, J. Sierra, and A. Sierra. Building a chemical ontology using methontology and the ontology design environment. *Intelligent Systems and their Applications, IEEE*, 14(1):37–46, Jan 1999. DOI: 10.1109/5254.747904. 68

[123] P. Lopez. Automatic extraction and resolution of bibliographical references in patent documents. *Advances in Multidisciplinary Retrieval*, pages 120–135, 2010. DOI: 10.1007/978-3-642-13084-7_10. 109

[124] C. Lynch, S. Parastatidis, N. Jacobs, H. Van de Sompel, and C. Lagoze. The OAI-ORE effort: progress, challenges, synergies. In *JCDL '07: Proceedings of the 2007 conference on Digital libraries*, page 80. ACM, 2007. DOI: 10.1145/1255175.1255190. 4, 7

[125] D. Maier and L. M. L. Delcambre. Superimposed information for the Internet. In *WebDB (Informal Proceedings)*, pages 1–9, 1999. 31, 32, 33

[126] P. Manghi, M. Mikulicic, L. Candela, D. Castelli, and P. Pagano. Realizing and Maintaining Aggregative Digital Library Systems: D-NET Software Toolkit and OAIster System. *D-Lib Magazine*, available at http://www.dlib.org/dlib/march10/manghi/03manghi.html, 16(3/4), 2010. DOI: 10.1045/march2010-manghi. 10

[127] P. Maniatis, M. Roussopoulos, T. J. Giuli, D. S. H. Rosenthal, and M. Baker. The LOCKSS peer-to-peer digital preservation system. *ACM Trans. Comput. Syst.*, 23(1):2–50, 2005. DOI: 10.1145/1047915.1047917. 140, 144

[128] G. Mann and A. McCallum. Simple, robust, scalable semi-supervised learning via expectation regularization. In *Proceedings of the 24th international conference on Machine learning*, pages 593–600. ACM, 2007. DOI: 10.1145/1273496.1273571. 110

[129] C. D. Manning, P. Raghavan, and H. Schütze. *Introduction to Information Retrieval*. Cambridge University Press, New York, NY, USA, 2008. DOI: 10.1017/CBO9780511809071. 95

[130] C. C. Marshall. Annotation: from Paper Books to the Digital Library. In *DL'97*, pages 233–240, 1997. DOI: 10.1145/263690.263806. 30

[131]   A. Maslov, J. Creel, A. Mikeal, S. Phillips, J. Leggett, and M. McFarland. Adding OAI-ORE Support to Repository Platforms. *Journal of Digital Information (JoDI)*, 11(1), 2010. 11, 18

[132]   J. Melton and A. Eisenberg. SQL multimedia and application packages (SQL/MM). *SIGMOD Rec.*, 30(4):97–102, 2001. DOI: 10.1145/604264.604280. 4

[133]   G. A. Miller. WordNet: a lexical database for English. *Commun. ACM*, 38(11):39–41, November 1995. DOI: 10.1145/219717.219748. 67

[134]   G. A. Miller, R. Beckwith, C. Fellbaum, D. Gross, and K. Miller. WordNet: An on-line lexical database. *International Journal of Lexicography*, 3:235–244, 1990. DOI: 10.1093/ijl/3.4.235. 67

[135]   M. Minsky. A framework for representing knowledge. In J. Haugeland, editor, *Mind Design*. MIT Press, Cambridge, Massachusetts, 1981. DOI: 10.1016/B978-1-4832-1446-7.50018-2. 3

[136]   F. Mintzer, J. Lotspiech, and N. Morimoto. Safeguarding digital library content and users. *D-Lib Magazine*, 3, 1997. http://www.dlib.org/dlib/december97/ibm/12lotspiech.html. DOI: 10.1045/december97-lotspiech. 135

[137]   R. Mizoguchi, M. Ikeda, K. Seta, and J. Vanwelkenhuysen. Ontology for modeling the world from problem solving perspectives. In *IJCAI Workshop on Basic Ontological Issues in Knowledge Sharing*, 1995. 67

[138]   L. Moreau, B. Clifford, J. Freire, Y. Gil, P. Groth, J. Futrelle, N. Kwasnikowska, S. Miles, P. Missier, J. Myers, Y. Simmhan, E. Stephan, and J. V. den Bussche. The Open Provenance Model—core specification (v1.1). In *JCDL '09: Proceedings of the 9th ACM/IEEE-CS Joint Conference on Digital Libraries,* Doctoral Consortium, available at http://www.ieee-tcdl.org/Bulletin/v5n3/Kozievitch/kozievitch.html, last accessed on 05/05/11. Elsevier, 2009. DOI: 10.1016/j.future.2010.07.005. 10

[139]   B. L. Moreira, M. A. Gonçalves, A. H. Laender, and E. A. Fox. 5SQual—a quality assessment tool for digital libraries. In *Proc. WDL 2006, Florianopolis, SC, Brasil*. WDL, 2006. 140

[140]   W. Murray, A. Pease, and M. Sams. Applying formal methods and representations in a natural language tutor to teach tactical reasoning. In *11th International Conference on Artificial Intelligence in Education (AIED)*, pages 349–356, 2003. 79

[141]   S. Murthy, L. Delcambre, and D. Maier. Explicitly representing superimposed information in a conceptual model. In *Conceptual Modeling - ER 2006*, pages 126–139, Berlin, Heidelberg, 2006. Springer-Verlag. DOI: 10.1007/11901181_11. 33, 46

[142]   S. Murthy, D. Maier, and L. Delcambre. Querying bi-level information. In *Proceedings of WebDB workshop*, 2004. DOI: 10.1145/1017074.1017078. 33

[143]   S. Murthy, D. Maier, L. Delcambre, and S. Bowers. Putting integrated information into context: Superimposing conceptual models with SPARCE. In *Proceedings of the First Asia-Pacific Conference of Conceptual Modeling*, pages 71–80, Denedin, New Zealand, 2004. 31, 33

[144] S. Murthy, D. Maier, L. Delcambre, and S. Bowers. Superimposed applications using SPARCE. In *Proceedings of the 20th International Conference on Data Engineering*, Los Alamitos, CA, USA, 2004. IEEE Computer Society. DOI: 10.1109/ICDE.2004.1320089. 33

[145] U. Murthy. A superimposed information-supported digital library, 2007. Presented at the Doctoral Consortium—held in conjunction with JCDL'07. 33

[146] U. Murthy. *Digital Libraries with Superimposed Information: Supporting Scholarly Tasks that Involve Fine Grain Information,* available at http://scholar.lib.vt.edu/theses/available/etd-04142011-175752/. Ph.D. dissertation, Virginia Tech, 2011. 30, 32, 34, 50, 52, 53, 56

[147] U. Murthy, K. Ahuja, S. Murthy, and E. A. Fox. SIMPEL: a superimposed multimedia presentation editor and player. In *JCDL '06: Proceedings of the 6th ACM/IEEE-CS Joint Conference on Digital Libraries*, page 377, 2006. DOI: 10.1145/1141753.1141873. 33, 46

[148] U. Murthy, E. A. Fox, Y. Chen, E. Hallerman, R. da S. Torres, E. Ramos, and T. Falcao. Superimposed image description and retrieval for fish species identification. *13th European Conference on Research and Advanced Technology for Digital Libraries*, 2009. DOI: 10.1007/978-3-642-04346-8_28. 30, 50

[149] U. Murthy, E. A. Fox, Y. Chen, E. Hallerman, R. da S. Torres, E. J. Ramos, and T. R. Falcao. Species identification: fish images with CBIR and annotations. In *JCDL '09: Proceedings of the 9th ACM/IEEE-CS Joint Conference on Digital Libraries*, pages 435–436, New York, NY, USA, 2009. ACM. DOI: 10.1145/1555400.1555500. 30, 50

[150] U. Murthy, R. Richardson, E. A. Fox, and L. Delcambre. Enhancing concept mapping tools below and above to facilitate the use of superimposed information. In A. J. Cañas and J. D. Novak, editors, *The Second International Conference on Concept Mapping*, San Jose, Costa Rica, 2006. 47

[151] A. Nadeem and M. Javed. A performance comparison of data encryption algorithms. In *Information and Communication Technologies, 2005. ICICT 2005. First International Conference on*, pages 84–89, aug. 2005. DOI: 10.1109/ICICT.2005.1598556. 136

[152] S. Nagaraj. Access control in distributed object systems: problems with access control lists. In *Enabling Technologies: Infrastructure for Collaborative Enterprises, 2001. WET ICE 2001. Proceedings. Tenth IEEE International Workshops on*, pages 163–164, 2001. DOI: 10.1109/EN-ABL.2001.953407. 137

[153] R. Neches, R. Fikes, T. Finin, T. Gruber, R. Patil, T. Senator, and W. Swartout. Enabling technology for knowledge sharing. *AI Magazine*, 12(3):36–56, 1991. 69

[154] M. L. Nelson, B. Argue, M. Efron, S. Denn, and M. C. Pattuelli. A survey of complex object technologies for digital libraries. Technical Report TM-2001-211426, NASA, 2001. 1, 3, 4

[155] M. L. Nelson and H. V. de Sompel. IJDL special issue on complex digital objects: Guest editors' introduction. *International Journal of Digital Libraries*, 6(2):113–114, 2006. DOI: 10.1007/s00799-005-0127-y. 1, 4

[156] M. L. Nelson and K. Maly. Buckets: Smart objects for digital libraries. *Communications of the ACM*, 44(5):60–61, 2001. DOI: 10.1145/374308.374342. 6

[157] M. L. Nelson, K. Maly, M. Zubair, and S. N. T. Shen. Buckets: Aggregative, intelligent agents for publishing. *Webnet Journal*, 1(1):58–66, 1998. 6

[158] M. L. Nelson, G. Marchionini, G. Geisler, and M. Yang. A bucket architecture for the Open Video Project. In *Proceedings of the 1st ACM/IEEE-CS Joint Conference on Digital Libraries*, JCDL '01, pages 310–311. ACM, 2001. 6

[159] T. H. Nelson. Xanalogical structure, needed now more than ever: parallel documents, deep links to content, deep versioning, and deep re-use. *ACM Comput. Surv.*, 31(4es), 1999. DOI: 10.1145/345966.346033. 34

[160] NetCDF. Network Common Data Form- v.4.1. http://www.unidata.ucar.edu/software/netcdf/, 2010. 4

[161] B. Neuman and T. Ts'o. Kerberos: an authentication service for computer networks. *Communications Magazine, IEEE*, 32(9):33–38, sep 1994. DOI: 10.1109/35.312841. 136

[162] A. Newell. The knowledge level. *Artif. Intell.*, 18(1):87–127, 1982. DOI: 10.1016/0004-3702(82)90012-1. 75

[163] N. Nguyen and Y. Guo. Comparisons of sequence labeling algorithms and extensions. In *Proceedings of the 24th international conference on Machine learning*, pages 681–688. ACM, 2007. DOI: 10.1145/1273496.1273582. 109

[164] I. Niles and A. Pease. Towards a standard upper ontology. In *FOIS*, pages 2–9, 2001. DOI: 10.1145/505168.505170. 79

[165] N. F. Noy and D. L. McGuinness. Ontology development 101: A guide to creating your first ontology. Technical report, Stanford Knowledge Systems Laboratory and Stanford Medical Informatics, 2001. 71

[166] OAC. Open Annotation Collaboration, available at http://www.openannotation.org/, 2009. 35

[167] OAI. Open Archives Initiative Protocol for Metadata Harvesting—v.2.0. http://www.openarchives.org/OAI/openarchivesprotocol.html, 2001. 4

[168] OCLC. XTCat NDLTD Union Catalog, 2004. 89, 91

[169] U. of Richmond. The Disaster Database Project. http://learning.richmond.edu/disaster/index .cfm, 2011. [Online; accessed 26-September-2011]. 84

[170] C. K. Ogden and I. Richards. *The meaning of meaning*. Trubner & Co, London, 1923. 64

[171] C. OSSO. DesInventar: Inventory system of the effects of disasters. http://www.desinventar.org/, 2011. [Online; accessed 26-September-2011]. 84

[172] S. Park and E. Fox. Enriching the VT ETD-db System with References. In *Proceeding of 14th International Symposium on Electronic Theses and Dissertations*. NDLTD, 2011. 107, 115

[173] S. H. Park. *Discipline-Independent Text Information Extraction from Heterogeneously Styled References Using Knowledge from the Web*. Ph.D. thesis, Virginia Tech, Blacksburg, VA, 2013. 111

[174] S. H. Park, N. Lynberg, J. Racer, P. McElmurray, and E. A. Fox. HTML5 ETDs. *13th International Symposium on Electronic Thesis and Dissertations (ETD 2010), UT Austin Libraries, Austin*, 06 2010. 10, 12, 34

[175] G. Z. Pastorello, Jr, R. D. A. Senra, and C. B. Medeiros. Bridging the gap between geospatial resource providers and model developers. In *GIS '08: Proceedings of the 16th ACM SIGSPATIAL international conference on Advances in geographic information systems*, pages 1–4, New York, NY, USA, 2008. ACM. DOI: dx.doi.org/10.1145/1463434.1463489. 6

[176] A. Pease. *Ontology: A Practical Guide*. Articulate Software Press, Angwin, CA, 2011. 67

[177] A. Pease and I. Niles. IEEE Standard Upper Ontology: a progress report. *The Knowledge Engineering Review*, 17(01):65–70, 2002. DOI: 10.1017/S0269888902000395. 66

[178] F. Peng and A. McCallum. Information extraction from research papers using conditional random fields. *Information Processing & Management*, 42(4):963–979, 2006. DOI: 10.1016/j.ipm.2005.09.002. 109, 110, 111, 112

[179] T. A. Phelps and R. Wilensky. Multivalent documents. *Communications of the ACM*, 43(6):82–90, 2000. DOI: 10.1145/336460.336480. 33, 35

[180] T. A. Phelps and R. Wilensky. Robust Intra-document Locations. *Computer Networks: The International Journal of Computer and TelecommunicationsNetworking. Elsevier North-Holland, Inc., New York, USA*, 33(1-6):105–118, 2000. DOI: 10.1016/S1389-1286(00)00043-8. 33, 35

[181] L. Rabiner and B. Juang. An introduction to hidden Markov models. *ASSP Magazine, IEEE*, 3(1):4–16, 1986. DOI: 10.1109/MASSP.1986.1165342. 109

[182] B. G. Raggad. *Information Security Management*. CRC Press, 2010. 133

[183] N. Rathod and L. N. Cassel. Building a search engine for computer science course syllabi. In *13th ACM/IEEE-CS Joint Conference on Digital Libraries*, pages 77–86, 2013. DOI: 10.1145/2467696.2467723. 65

[184] M. Recker and B. Palmer. Using resources across educational digital libraries. In *JCDL '06: Proceedings of the 6th ACM/IEEE-CS Joint Conference on Digital Libraries*, pages 240–241, New York, NY, USA, 2006. ACM. DOI: 10.1145/1141753.1141805. 30

[185] D. Rehberger, M. Fegan, and M. Kornbluh. Reevaluating access and preservation through secondary repositories: Needs, promises, and challenges. In *Research and Advanced Technology for Digital Libraries, LNCS 4172*, pages 39–50. Springer, 2006. DOI: 10.1007/11863878_4. 10, 35

[186] M. Romanello, F. Boschetti, and G. Crane. Citations in the digital library of classics: extracting canonical references by using conditional random fields. In *Proceedings of the 2009 Workshop on Text and Citation Analysis for Scholarly Digital Libraries*, pages 80–87. Association for Computational Linguistics, 2009. DOI: 10.3115/1699750.1699763. 109

[187] P. Ruijgrok and M. Slabbertje. Requirements for Management & Storage to support complex objects & ORE in DSpace. In *Knowledge Exchange Group - Research paper - Enhanced E-theses Project Deliverable 9.1,* available at http://igitur-archive.library.uu.nl/DARLIN/2010-0526-200239/UUindex.html, last accessed on 05/05/11, 2009. 2

[188] M. E. Ruiz and P. Srinivasan. Hierarchical text categorization using neural networks. *Information Retrieval*, 5(1):87–118, January 2002. DOI: 10.1023/A:1012782908347. 94, 95

[189] S. Rumsey and B. O'Steen. OAI-ORE, PRESERV2 and digital preservation, Ariadne, 6, available at http://www.ariadne.ac.uk/issue57/rumsey-osteen/, 2008. 11

[190] N. Sager. *Natural Language Information Processing: A computer grammar of English and its applications*. Addison-Wesley, 1981. 106

[191] K. Saidis and A. Delis. Integrating Multi-dimensional Information Spaces. *Second Workshop on Very Large Digital Libraries, in conjunction with the 13th European Conference on Research and Advanced Technology for Digital Libraries (ECDL 2009)*, 07 2009. 15

[192] D. Sánchez and A. Moreno. Automatic generation of taxonomies from the Web. In *Practical Aspects of Knowledge Management, 5th International Conference*, pages 208–219, 2004. 72

[193] R. Sandhu and P. Samarati. Access control: principle and practice. *Communications Magazine, IEEE*, 32(9):40–48, sep 1994. DOI: 10.1109/35.312842. 138

[194] A. Santanchè and C. B. Medeiros. Fluid web and digital content components: from a document-centric perspective to a content-centric perspective. In *Proceedings of the XX Brazilian Symposium on Databases*, pages 10–24, 2005. 6, 11

[195] A. Santanchè and C. B. Medeiros. A Component Model and Infrastructure for a Fluid Web. *IEEE Transactions on Knowledge and Data Engineering*, 19(2):324–341, February 2007. DOI: 0.1109/TKDE.2007.16. 3, 6

[196] A. Santanchè, C. B. Medeiros, and G. Z. Pastorello Jr. User-author centered multimedia building blocks. *Multimedia Systems*, 12(4):403–421, March 2007. DOI: 10.1007/s00530-006-0050-0. 3, 6

[197] R. L. T. Santos, P. A. Roberto, M. A. Gonçalves, and A. H. F. Laender. A Web services-based framework for building componentized digital libraries. *Journal of Systems and Software*, 81(5):809–822, May 2008. DOI: 10.1016/j.jss.2007.07.029. 12

[198] R. C. Schank. *Tell Me a Story: Narrative and Intelligence*. Northwestern University Press, 1995. Introduction-Morson, Gary Saul. 3

[199] D. Schonberg and D. Kirovski. Fingerprinting and forensic analysis of multimedia. In *Proceedings of the 12th annual ACM international conference on Multimedia*, MULTIMEDIA '04, pages 788–795, New York, NY, USA, 2004. ACM. DOI: 10.1145/1027527.1027712. 135

[200] F. Sebastiani. Machine learning in automated text categorization. *ACM Computing Surveys (CSUR)*, 34(1):1–47, 2002. DOI: 10.1145/505282.505283. 93

[201] U. Shah, T. Finin, A. Joshi, R. S. Cost, and J. Matfield. Information retrieval on the Semantic Web. In *Proceedings of the eleventh international conference on Information and knowledge management*, CIKM '02, pages 461–468, New York, NY, USA, 2002. ACM. DOI: 10.1145/584865.584868. 73

[202] R. Shen, N. S. Vemuri, W. Fan, and E. A. Fox. Integration of complex archeology digital libraries: An ETANA-DL experience. *Information Systems*, 33(7-8):699–723, 2008. http://dx.doi.org/10.1016/j.is.2008.02.006 [last visited July 4, 2012]. DOI: 10.1016/j.is.2008.02.006. 12, 18

[203] S. B. Shum, E. Motta, and J. Domingue. ScholOnto: An ontology-based digital library server for research documents and discourse. *International Journal on Digital Libraries*, 3(3):237–248, 2000. Sept. 73

[204] C. Smythe and A. Jackl. Reusable Asset Specification (RAS) - version 2.2, available at http://www.imsglobal.org, 2002. 4

[205] C. Smythe and A. Jackl. IMS Content Packaging Information Model, specification, IMS Global Learning Consortium, Inc., 2009. 4

[206] V. Srinivasan, M. Magdy, and E. Fox. Enhanced Browsing System for Electronic Theses and Dissertations. In *Proceeding of 14th International Symposium on Electronic Theses and Dissertations*. NDLTD, 2011. 115

[207] W. Stallings. *Cryptography and Network Security*. Pearson Prentice Hall, 4 edition, 2006. 132, 135, 143, 146

[208] V. C. Storey, R. H. L. Chiang, and G. L. Chen. Ontology creation: Extraction of domain knowledge from web documents. In *24th International Conference on Conceptual Modeling*, pages 256–269, 2005. DOI: 10.1007/11568322_17. 72

[209] R. Studer, R. R. Benjamins, and D. Fensel. Knowledge Engineering: Principles and Methods. *Data Knowledge Engineering*, 25(1-2):161–197, 1998. DOI: 10.1016/S0169-023X(97)00056-6. 64

[210] G. Stumme and A. Maedche. FCA-MERGE: Bottom-up merging of ontologies. In *Seventeenth International Joint Conference on Artificial Intelligence*, pages 225–234, 2001. 84

[211] G. Stumme and A. Maedche. Ontology merging for federated ontologies for the Semantic Web. In *Proc. Intl. Workshop on Foundations of Models for Information Integration, Viterbo, Italy, Sept. 16-18, 2001*. LNAI, Springer 2001, Sept. 2001. DOI: 10.1.1.21.3387. 72

[212] H. Suleman and E. A. Fox. Designing protocols in support of digital library componentization. In *Proceedings of the 6th European Conference on Research and Advanced Technology for Digital Libraries (ECDL2002), LNCS 2458*, pages 75–84. Springer, Rome, Italy, 2002. DOI: 10.1007/3-540-45747-X_43. 4

[213] H. Suleman, E. A. Fox, and M. Abrams. Building quality into a digital library. In *Proceedings of the Fifth ACM Conference on Digital Libraries: DL '00, June 2–7, 2000, San Antonio, TX*. ACM Press, New York, 2000. June 4-7, 2000. DOI: 10.1145/336597.336669. 140

[214] SURF. The SURF Foundation. http://www.surf.nl/en, 2010. 12

[215] SURF - ESCAPE. Enhanced Scientific Communication by Aggregated Publication Environments. http://code.google.com/p/surf-escape/, 2009. 11

[216] TEI. Text Encoding Initiative: TEI: Yesterday's information tomorrow, 2005. 34

[217] H. S. Thompson and D. Connolly. W3C XML Pointer, XML Base and XML Linking, 1997-2003. Description of work done by the W3C XML Linking Working Group. 34

[218] W. Tolone, G.-J. Ahn, T. Pai, and S.-P. Hong. Access control in collaborative systems. *ACM Comput. Surv.*, 37(1):29–41, March 2005. DOI: 10.1145/1057977.1057979. 136, 137, 138

[219] R. S. Torres, C. Medeiros, M. Gonçalves, and E. Fox. A digital library framework for biodiversity information systems. *International Journal on Digital Libraries*, 6(1):3–17, 2006. DOI: 10.1007/s00799-005-0124-1. 2, 51

[220] P. Tyrvainen. Concepts and a design for fair use and privacy in DRM. *D-Lib Magazine*, 11, 2005. http://www.dlib.org/dlib/february05/tyrvainen/02tyrvainen.html. 134

[221] Ubuntu. Ubuntu Manpage: pnmtojpeg. http://manpages.ubuntu.com/manpages/lucid/man1/pnmtojpeg.1.html, 2013. [Online; accessed 30-December-2013]. 117

[222] University Corporation for Atmospheric Research. jOAI Software. http://www.dlese.org/dds/services/joai_software.jsp, 2002. 25

[223] M. Uschold and M. Grüninger. Ontologies and semantics for seamless connectivity. *SIGMOD Record*, 33(4):58–64, 2004. DOI: 10.1145/1041410.1041420. 70, 71

[224] w3schools. Semantic Web Tutorial. http://www.w3schools.com/semweb/default.asp/, 2011. [Online; accessed 26-September-2011]. 80

[225] S. L. Weibel and T. Koch. The Dublin Core Metadata Initiative: Mission, Current Activities, and Future Directions, available at http://www.dlib.org/dlib/december00/weibel/12weibel.html. *D-Lib Magazine*, 6(12), December 2000. 91

[226] K. Williams and H. Suleman. A Survey of Digital Library Aggregation Services. In *Scholarship at Penn Libraries*, available at: http://works.bepress.com/martha_brogan/10, 2003. 3

[227] M. Winslett, N. Ching, V. Jones, and I. Slepchin. Assuring security and privacy for digital library transactions on the web: client and server security policies. In *Research and Technology Advances in Digital Libraries, 1997. ADL '97. Proceedings., IEEE International Forum on*, pages 140–151, may 1997. DOI: 10.1109/ADL.1997.601210. 137

[228] X. Xu, F. Zhang, and Z. Niu. An ontology-based query system for digital libraries. In *PACIIA (1)*, pages 222–226. IEEE Computer Society, 2008. DOI: 10.1109/PACIIA.2008.360. 73

[229] G. R. Xue, D. Xing, Q. Yang, and Y. Yu. Deep classification in large-scale text hierarchies. In *SIGIR '08: Proceedings of the 31st annual international ACM SIGIR Conference on Research and Development in Information Retrieval*, pages 619–626, New York, NY, USA, 2008. ACM. DOI: 10.1145/1390334.1390440. 95

[230] Y. Yang, J. Zhang, and B. Kisiel. A scalability analysis of classifiers in text categorization. In *Proceedings of the 26th annual international ACM SIGIR conference on Research and development in informaion retrieval*, SIGIR '03, pages 96–103, New York, NY, USA, 2003. ACM. DOI: 10.1145/860454.860455. 96

[231] J. Yu and X. Fan. Metadata Extraction from Chinese Research Papers Based on Conditional Random Fields. In *Fuzzy Systems and Knowledge Discovery, 2007. FSKD 2007. Fourth International Conference on*, volume 1, pages 497–501. IEEE, 2007. DOI: 10.1109/FSKD.2007.394. 107, 110, 111, 112

[232] Q. Zhu. 5SGraph: A Modeling Tool for Digital Libraries. Masters thesis, Virginia Tech Dept. of Computer Science, 2002. http://scholar.lib.vt.edu/theses/available/etd-11272002-210531/ [last visited July 4, 2012]. 25

[233] Q. Zhu, M. A. Gonçalves, R. Shen, L. Cassel, and E. A. Fox. Visual semantic modeling of digital libraries. In *Proc. 7th European Conference on Digital Libraries (ECDL 2003), 17-22 August, Trondheim, Norway, Springer LNCS 2769*, pages 325–337. Springer, 2004. DOI: 10.1007/978-3-540-45175-4_30. 12

[234] J. Zou, D. Le, and G. Thoma. Locating and parsing bibliographic references in HTML medical articles. *International journal on document analysis and recognition*, 13(2):107–119, 2010. DOI: 10.1007/s10032-009-0105-9. 110, 111, 112

Editors' Biographies

EDWARD A. FOX

 **Edward A. Fox** grew up on Long Island, New York. He attended the Massachusetts Institute of Technology (MIT), receiving a B.S. in 1972 in Electrical Engineering, through the Computer Science option. His undergraduate adviser was J.C.R. Licklider. His thesis adviser was Michael Kessler. At MIT he founded the ACM Student Chapter and the Student Information Processing Board, receiving the William Stewart Award.

From 1971–1972 he worked as Data Processing Instructor at the Florence Darlington Technical College. From 1972–1978 he was Data Processing Manager at Vulcraft, a Division of NUCOR Corporation, also in Florence, SC. In the fall of 1978 he began his graduate studies at Cornell University in Ithaca, NY. His adviser was Gerard Salton. He received an M.S. in Computer Science in 1981 and a Ph.D. in 1983. From the summer of 1982 through the spring of 1983 he served as Manager of Information Systems at the International Institute of Tropical Agriculture, Ibadan, Nigeria. From the fall of 1983 through the present he has been on the faculty of the Department of Computer Science at Virginia Tech (also called VPI&SU or Virginia Polytechnic Institute and State University). In 1988 he was given tenure and promoted to the rank of Associate Professor. In 1995 he was promoted to Professor.

Dr. Fox has been an IEEE Senior Member since 2004, an IEEE Member since 2002, an IEEE-CS Member since 2001, and a member of ACM since 1967. He was vice chairman of ACM SIGIR 1987–1991. Then he was chair 1991–1995. During that period, he helped launch the new ACM SIG on Multimedia. He served as a member of the ACM Publications Board 1988-1992 and as Editor-in-chief of ACM Press Database and Electronic Products 1988–1991, during which time he helped conceive and launch the ACM Digital Library. He served 2000–2006 as a founder and Co-editor-in-chief of the ACM Journal of Education Resources In Computing (JERIC), which led to the ACM Transactions on Education. Since 2013 he has been editor for Information Retrieval and Digital Libraries for the ACM Book Series. Over the period 2004–2008 he served as Chairman of the IEEE-CS Technical Committee on Digital Libraries, and continues to serve on its Executive Committee. Dr. Fox served 1995–2008 as Editor of the Morgan Kaufmann Publishers, Inc. Series on Multimedia Information and Systems. Dr. Fox has been a member of Sigma Xi since the 1970s and a member of Upsilon Pi Epsilon since 1998.

In 1987 Dr. Fox began to explore the idea of all students shifting to electronic theses and dissertations (ETDs), and has worked in this area ever since. He led the establishment of the Networked Digital Library of Theses and Dissertations (operating informally starting in 1995, incorporated in May 2003). He serves as founder and Executive Director of NDLTD. He won its 1st Annual NDLTD Leadership Award in May 2004.

Dr. Fox has been involved in a wide variety of professional service activities. He has chaired scores of conferences or workshops, and served on hundreds of program or conference committees. At present he serves on ten editorial boards. From 2010 to 2013 he was a member of the board of directors of the Computing Research Association (CRA; he was co-chair of its membership committee, as well as a member of CRA-E, its education committee). He chairs the steering committee of the ACM/IEEE-CS Joint Conference on Digital Libraries.

Dr. Fox has been (co)PI on over 115 research and development projects. In addition to his courses at Virginia Tech, Dr. Fox has taught over 78 tutorials in more than 28 countries. His publications and presentations include: 17 books, 107 journal/magazine articles, 49 book chapters, 184 refereed (+40 other) conference/workshop papers, 61 posters, 66 keynote/banquet/international invited/distinguished speaker presentations, 38 demonstrations, and over 300 additional presentations. His research and teaching has been on digital libraries, information storage and retrieval, hypertext/hypermedia/multimedia, computing education, computational linguistics, and sub-areas of artificial intelligence.

RICARDO DA SILVA TORRES

Ricardo da Silva Torres received a B.Sc. in Computer Engineering from the University of Campinas, Brazil, in 2000. He earned his doctorate in Computer Science at the same university in 2004. Dr. Torres has been Director of the Institute of Computing, University of Campinas since 2013. He is co-founder and member of the RECOD lab. He is the author/co-author of more than 100 articles in refereed journals and conferences and serves as PC member for several international and national conferences. Dr. Torres has supervised 24 master and 5 Ph.D. projects. His research interests include image analysis, content-based image retrieval, databases, digital libraries, and geographic information systems.

Printed in the United States
by Baker & Taylor Publisher Services